MACHIAVELLI'S
SHADOW

MACHIAVELLI'S SHADOW

The
Rise and Fall
of
Karl Rove

PAUL ALEXANDER

MODERN TIMES

© 2008 by Paul Alexander

Modern Times is an imprint of Rodale Inc.

Rodale books may be purchased for business or promotional use or for special sales.
For information, please write to:
Special Markets Department, Rodale Inc., 733 Third Avenue, New York, NY 10017

Printed in the United States of America

Rodale Inc. makes every effort to use acid-free ⊗, recycled paper ⊙.

Book design by Susan P. Eugster

Library of Congress Cataloging-in-Publication Data

Alexander, Paul, date
    Machiavelli's shadow : the rise and fall of Karl Rove / Paul Alexander.
        p.   cm.
    Includes index.
    ISBN-13 978-1-59486-825-2 hardcover
    ISBN-10 1-59486-825-5 hardcover
    1. Rove, Karl.   2. Rove, Karl—Influence.   3. Rove, Karl—Political and social
views.   4. Political consultants—United States—Biography.   5. United States—Politics
and government—date   6. United States—Politics and government—1993-2001.
7. Republican Party (U.S. : date)   I. Title.
E840.8.R68A44   2008
973.931092—dc22
    [B]   2008018480

Distributed to the trade by Macmillan

2   4   6   8   10   9   7   5   3   1   hardcover

For Lauren

CONTENTS

CHAPTER ONE

BEING KARL ROVE

In the winter of 2008, the weather in this part of Iowa had been so inclement that the night's event had been postponed from February until March 9. It was a Sunday evening, and all around Iowa City the cornfields lay barren, spotted here and there with snow. Since 1972, Iowa has been the home of the first presidential caucus in the nation, in January, when the weather is not much better. Many presidential careers have been launched in the cold fields of Iowa on caucus night. That was the case a little more than seven years ago, when a young and inexperienced governor from Texas, George W. Bush, known at the time mostly for being the son of a former president, won the Iowa caucus by a relatively modest margin and solidified his status as front-runner for the Republican nomination. He won that nomination, despite suffering a devastating upset in the New Hampshire primary, on his way to claiming the presidency. The political mastermind who had charted Bush's course on his path to victory was a soft-spoken, nebbishy, yet ruthlessly calculating political strategist named Karl Rove, who on this night was returning to the state where his candidate had first taken his place on the national political stage seven years ago. Only now, with most of two terms of a Bush presidency behind him, Rove was viewed much differently than he had been at the beginning of Bush's presidential career.

The evening's event had been announced well in advance. Immediately after the first press releases went out, the event became contentious. As part of the University of Iowa Lecture Series, Rove would make an appearance at an evening entitled "Reflections from the Architect"—a reference to the title Bush had given Rove following Bush's successful reelection in 2004. But even in the early announcements, odd details emerged. "In accordance with the contract with Rove and his speaker's agency," read one media alert, "television and radio journalists and news videographers and photographers may shoot and tape the event for the first five minutes of Rove's remarks and time preceding the speech. They can then move to a designated media area in the northeast corner of the room, take a seat with the audience, or leave the room. Reporters may take notes, but no recording devices may be used." It was the type of star-treatment security arrangement normally afforded an A-list celebrity or international dignitary, not a political consultant. At the moment, in fact, this particular political consultant didn't even have a client, since he had left his position at the White House a little more than six months before and was not looking to consult for a campaign during this election cycle. Besides making the rounds of the lecture circuit, he was a news analyst for the Fox News Network and occasional columnist for *Newsweek*.

Then again, maybe Rove knew what he was doing by trying to control the media. An antiwar group, the University of Iowa Antiwar Committee, had announced in February that it intended to protest Rove's appearance. "Our issue isn't that he is a conservative or an analyst," said organization member David Goodner, who described Rove as "a traitor and an accomplice to war crimes." Instead, Goodner and other critics were offended that the university was paying Rove $40,000 for the single appearance. Since July 2005, the University of Iowa Lecture Committee had brought 33 speakers to campus, paying Janet Reno $21,000 and

Joseph Wilson $12,500. Rove's fee represented the largest amount paid by the committee to a speaker since July 2005. So it should not have been surprising that on the night of the event, as the audience headed to the Iowa Memorial Union, where the lecture was to take place in the Main Lounge, there were protesters such as Tim Gauger, a university employee who, disguised as Rove, stood in the cold outside the building attempting to get people to sign a poster-size mock check made out to Rove in the amount of $40,000.

Undeterred by the protesters, at 7:30 p.m. Rove took his place on the stage alongside Frank Durham, the University of Iowa journalism professor who had been chosen to moderate the event. Wearing a light brown suit and a gold tie, Rove sat in a tan wingback chair and looked out into the audience of 1,200 packed into the auditorium. The crowd was restless, animated. Shouts of "Liar!" rang out as Rove looked over at Durham, who sat in a matching chair.

"Liar! Liar!"

Even though Iowa is an agricultural state in the middle of the nation's heartland, Iowa City, home to a university with a number of departments nationally recognized for their excellence, has a decidedly liberal population, mostly because so many residents are connected with the university. A number of those people with liberal leanings had shown up on this night. They were not silent.

"Liar! Liar!"

Durham began the program by posing a question to Rove. He had recently received a telephone call from a woman in western Iowa, he said, and she was angry with him for the role he was playing in bringing Rove to the university. "That man is responsible for the deaths of our soldiers," Durham recalled the woman saying, "and we just buried another one today." The audience waited as Durham continued, saying, "And I realized she had just been to a funeral of a soldier." He then put the question to Rove, "If you had been with me, how would you have answered her?"

"Shameful! Shameful!"

Rove turned in his chair to face the audience. He had been able to control the message of the Bush White House for seven years, in part by carefully dictating the rules the media had to follow. The Bush operation even did what it could to control the composition of an audience, usually by distributing tickets beforehand to people who they knew would be friendly to Bush. But on the lecture circuit, though he could still try to manipulate the media, Rove was unable to control the makeup of the audience.

"Liar!"

"First of all," Rove forged ahead, "the president met with a lot of families . . . "

Then there was a burst of noise. The crowd, clearly not handpicked, did not want to hear a canned answer.

"I have had to staff those meetings," Rove continued.

"War criminal!" a voice from the audience rang out. "Here in Iowa!" There was a long eruption of applause.

"MC Rove!" another voice shouted, referring to the strange, rap-inspired dance Rove performed at the White House Correspondents Dinner in 2007.

"I've had to staff these meetings," Rove plodded ahead, recalling his job of dealing with death benefit checks that didn't make it to families, grave markers he had had to order.

Another voice from the audience: "Have you shed a single tear?"

Rove seemed knocked off his guard. He had appeared before hostile audiences before, but none quite as volatile as this one.

"I've shed a lot of tears," he said and without pause began to relate a trip he had gone on with Bush to see a family in northern Nevada. Just as he was reaching the emotional part of his story, another voice rang out, challenging him.

"You've got a chance to ask your question later and make your stupid statements," Rove blurted out. "Let me make mine!"

Now there was applause from his supporters in the room. Rove proceeded to tell the story about the family Bush had met with. They had lost one son in the war in Iraq and another son who was in the military would soon be deployed to Iraq, and the mother shared her feelings about the war with the president. "She was powerful," Rove said. Then, Rove described the father—brooding, emotional. When Bush addressed him, the father explained why he was upset. Because he was 61, he was too old to volunteer for the Army Reserve, where he wanted to use his medical skills as an orthopedic surgeon on the battlefield. He wanted Bush to grant him a waiver.

"Talk to Rove," Rove said Bush had told the doctor.

Next Rove recalled the measures he went through to get the man a waiver, which he had been able to do.

"I know it's a controversial war," Rove said, "and I will defend it." He would do so, he said, because the war had been able "to liberate 50 million people."

"It's not true!" someone shouted. *"It's not true!"*

It was then that the room erupted into shouts of protest. The evening continued in this way, more or less, until both the interview and the question-and-answer session ended. There were a number of highlights. One occurred when an audience member asked Rove about his refusal to cooperate with legal proceedings involving Valerie Plame Wilson, the covert CIA agent whose identity Rove had helped reveal to the public after her husband, Ambassador Joseph Wilson, wrote an op-ed piece highly critical of the Bush administration's reasons for invading Iraq.

"I haven't been indicted yet," Rove said, "but I fully expect to be by the end of the year."

About Wilson, who had gone on a fact-finding mission to Niger during the buildup to the war, Rove added, "With all due respect, Joe Wilson lied about his [intelligence-gathering] trip to Africa."

A chorus of boos.

When another audience member asked what the "true" body count was in Iraq, Rove went on the offensive, charging the person with "perpetrating libel on the military of the United States by accusing them of killing innocent Iraqis."

More boos.

When Rove defended the Bush legacy by saying "he will be seen as a consequential president in controversial times," the boos were mixed with cheers.

Finally, someone yelled, "Can we have our $40,000 back?"

"No, you can't," Rove snapped.

Then, almost as a way to sum up the evening, an audience member told Rove that Keith Olbermann, host of a nightly political television program, had named him the "worst person ever."

Rove seemed undaunted. "Ever?" he asked. "Yeah," he answered himself, "worse than Hitler, worse than Stalin, worse than Mao, and worse than the person who introduced aluminum baseball bats."

How had Karl Rove ended up here? What had happened over the course of his career to engender such vitriol in an audience? Much about Rove still remains below the surface, but what is clear is that the story line of his life took him from troubled youth in Utah to a role as a central player in the administration of a two-term president. It had been a singular journey.

Political strategists have engineered the careers of presidents in the past. Tex McCrary saw the potential national appeal of General Dwight D. Eisenhower, approached him about running for president, and guided his path to the presidency in 1952; some historians believe there never would have been a President Eisenhower if not for Tex McCrary. Robert Kennedy was an undeniable force behind his brother John F. Kennedy, advising him on his congressional races and serving as the manager of his presidential campaign in 1960; as attorney general, he held a pivotal position in his brother's administration. James Carville and Paul Begala's combined talents played a significant role in the election of Bill Clinton as president in 1992; their guidance helped steady Clinton through a turbulent primary season, brought on mostly by revelations concerning Clinton's private life.

There are other examples. Ronald Reagan had Michael Deaver, Richard Nixon had H. R. Haldeman, and Jimmy Carter had Jody Powell and Hamilton Jordan, politicos so newsworthy they ended up on the cover of *Rolling Stone*. These strategists worked largely behind the scenes to get their candidates elected, and some even served the candidate once he entered office. But never before in our history has there been a political operative—and a nonfamily member, at that—who achieved the level of access and influence that Karl Rove did with George W. Bush. Indeed, no political strategist ever followed his candidate into the White House to play a role so vital in the daily governing of the country that many observers believe that for years he influenced large parts of domestic and even foreign policy. "We have never had a political consultant with as much power in the White House as Karl Rove had," says Ed Rollins, who ran national campaigns, including Ronald Reagan's reelection bid in 1984. "It's absolutely historic."[1]

The marriage of Bush and Rove had a kind of logic behind it. Before they teamed up in early 1990, each man had achieved only marginal success. Bush was a failed businessman and self-proclaimed reformed alcoholic who had been able to live an elitist, privileged life thanks to the wealth and legacy of the Bush family, which had reached its high point when Bush's father served first as vice president and then as president. While his father had been at the very epicenter of power in the United States from 1981 until 1993, when he left the White House, George W., whose repeated attempts to make it in the oil business had gone bust, could point to no accomplishment other than being the front man for the Texas Rangers Major League Baseball team—a job the sports organization legitimized by calling him an owner even though his ownership position was so small at 1.8 percent as to be negligible.

In a family of overachievers, Bush was seen as the black sheep, a relative failure. So he set his sights on making a name for himself in government, despite his one previous attempt to win elected office—he ran for Congress from Midland, Texas, in 1978—having ended in failure. Rarely has someone with presidential ambitions had such modest credentials as George W. Bush aspired to the presidency—an ambition that, considering his family connections, would have seemed reasonable had he not proven to be such a disappointment in his professional life up to that point.

In January 1993, when George H. W. Bush's exit from politics freed up his sons to run for offices of their own, Rove was nowhere near where he wanted to be in *his* life either. He had moved to Texas in 1977, and in a decade and a half he had built a direct-mail business based originally in Houston and then in Austin. He had run a number of successful campaigns in Texas. However, for someone who had the unbridled drive to become a player on the national political stage, Rove was far from achieving that vaunted status. He might have been highly regarded in certain circles in Texas, but outside of the state, except as a result of a few races where friends had brought him in to consult, no one had ever heard of Karl Rove. In one early article in the *Washington Post* that referenced him, the reporter actually misspelled his name, using a C instead of a K.[2]

Even in Texas, during much of the 1980s and into the 1990s Rove found himself in a protracted struggle with John Weaver, a fellow political consultant with whom he conducted a much-discussed feud, probably engendered by the fact that Weaver had more political clout at the time than Rove did. As for national politics, Rove played a minor role in the 1988 Bush presidential campaign, and his standing in the 1992 Bush effort was so insignificant that, when he leaked to syndicated columnist Robert Novak an untrue and unflattering item about the son of one of Bush's best friends who was also working on the campaign, the senior Bush fired Rove on the spot.

George W. Bush had been competing with his father for years—perhaps going all the way back to the younger Bush's boyhood—and it's possible that his father's firing of Rove elevated the consultant in his eyes. Whatever the reason, oedipal or not, once Rove teamed up with the younger Bush the spotlight began to focus on them both. Separately, they had lived ordinary, nondescript lives defined by frustration and unfulfilled potential; certainly, neither man seemed headed for the history books. But together, they created a synergy that catapulted them to a level they had never individually achieved.

For years, Rove had embraced the legacy of Lee Atwater, the political guru who was the driving force behind the election of George H. W. Bush in 1988. After Atwater died from a brain tumor in 1991, Rove was even more shameless about claiming to be a disciple of Atwater, who all but perfected the use of negative campaigning. To hear Rove talk, he and Atwater had enjoyed a mentor–protégé relationship, with Rove learning the technique of the dirty trick from the master himself. This story became a part of the myth that grew up around Rove, the implication being that Atwater had passed on to him the mantle of being the best in hard-knuckle politics. There was only one problem: It wasn't true. Not only was Atwater not a mentor to Rove, he didn't even particularly like him and, as a result, had had little to do with him over the years—no doubt one of the reasons Rove had achieved so little standing at the national level prior to Atwater's death. "Atwater was supposed to have worked closely with Rove in the College Republicans," says Roger Stone, a one-time colleague of Atwater in a political consulting firm. "In all honesty, I think that was a fiction. Atwater put up with Rove because he was there, but he never really liked him. Most of the time, we just rolled our eyes at Karl."[3]

Then, in 1994, with Rove running his campaign, Bush defeated the colorful and popular incumbent Ann Richards to become the governor of Texas and, in large part because of the type of campaign he orchestrated, one in which Richards was regularly the target of character assassination, the myth of Rove as the inheritor of the Atwater mantle was solidified, whether legitimate or not. Rove had run dirty campaigns in Texas before, some of them noteworthy in the 1980s, but knocking off Richards was different. She had been the hit of the Democratic National Convention in 1988 for her stirring call-to-arms keynote address that invoked a new populism. The speech also contained the soon-to-be-famous dig at Bush Senior, "Poor George. He can't help it— he was born with a silver foot in his mouth." Defeating a figure with as high a profile as Richards focused national attention on Rove—finally. Indeed, it was the first race Rove had won that brought him major attention outside of Texas, and it was a position that he no doubt loved.

Almost from the moment he was elected governor of Texas, Bush was a player on the national stage. As a consequence, more attention was focused on Rove, who, in the wake of Bush's victory, found himself part of a privileged inner circle. When it became evident that Rove could run Bush for president, Rove went about reinventing Bush as a national figure and in the process reinvented himself as well.

In his search for models, Rove found a candidate–consultant combination that deeply appealed to his ego. It didn't matter that they had lived almost a century before. Bush would be cast in the role of William McKinley, who was elected president in 1896 and reelected in 1900, and Rove would assume the part of Mark Hanna, a rich, politically sophisticated industrialist from Cleveland who had taken McKinley at the lowest point in his career—after he had been voted out of Congress and had returned home to Canton, Ohio, in 1891—and orchestrated and financed two winning bids for Ohio governor followed by a successful run for the presidency. That Rove was neither rich nor an industrialist was beside the point; Rove hoped to evoke Hanna's political genius.

"[Rove] got hooked two years ago during a class at the University of Texas," the *Washington Post* reported in July 1999. "Rove dug deeply into the story of a canny, soothing heartland governor whose party was riven by tactical and religious squabbles. Raising money on a scale previously unimagined, while scarcely leaving his front porch, McKinley remade the party in his own charming image . . . . Republicans dominated Washington for the next 35 years."[4] Of McKinley, Rove himself said at the time, "He understood the new economy. It was a period of rapid industrialization. He also understood the changing demographic. Immigrants were now providing the manpower."

As for Hanna, the man behind the candidate, he was viewed not just as a political genius but as someone who had taken a failed congressman from a small town in Ohio and carefully steered him into the White House. Just as impressive was the fact that that election ushered in an era of Republican domination of government that lasted for a generation. Democrats in McKinley's time, according to the *Washington Post*, "would complain that McKinley was a mere puppet of moneybags Hanna . . . but historians generally believe they were a well-matched team of two strong men." *Well-matched team, two strong men.* Rove found those descriptions deeply appealing.

Heading into the presidential campaign of 2000, Rove would assume the status of king maker, although he would be careful in the way he depicted this role publicly. Bush was sensitive about people whom he considered his subordinates stepping into the limelight, which he believed should belong to him alone. With some work, Rove recast Bush in the McKinley mold. The Texas governor would be folksy, affable, down-home, the master of the common touch, even if in reality he was not. In the early part of 1999, Bush even conducted his own version of a "front porch" campaign, reminiscent of the one McKinley had run in 1896 when, instead of traveling around the country to go to the voters, McKinley had taken to his front porch in Canton and spoken to voters who had traveled there to hear what he had to say. Rove's "front porch" campaign had delegations of Republicans from a number of states descending upon the governor's mansion in Austin to meet Bush and urge him to run for president. The process may have been phony, since it was thoroughly choreographed by Rove and had little to do with whether or not Bush was going to run (that decision had already been made), but Rove relished it.

Stories about McKinley swirled through Republican circles, although most Republicans did not necessarily remember when McKinley had actually governed, much less that eventually, on September 6, 1901, not long into his second term, he was assassinated in Buffalo, New York, by one of those immigrants he had reached out to in his campaign, a crazed anarchist who shot him in the belly with a pistol. Still, like McKinley, Bush was seen as the likable governor of a major state who could pass himself off as a populist, despite the fact that massive amounts of corporate money would be used to get him elected. Simply put, Bush would be beholden to corporate America while appearing to the public to be an ordinary guy who talked and acted like one of them, just as McKinley had been.

During the Texas governor years, Bush took to referring to Rove as Turd Blossom, a Texas term used to describe a flower growing from a pile of cow manure. Apparently, this was Bush's way of declaring that Rove had the innate ability to turn something from bad to good. While in some way a laudatory comparison, the nickname had more than a slight edge to it, for no matter how you looked at it, cow manure was involved. As the years passed and the moniker Turd Blossom lost its charm, Bush—always one for nicknames—began to call Rove Boy Genius, a much more suitable description for the myth Rove was creating about himself.

Finally, there was the book. For years, Rove had told people the book he read regularly, perhaps as often as once a year, was *The Prince* by Niccolò Machiavelli, the 16th-century Italian political thinker whose devious theories lurked behind the elegant prose of *The Prince*: *The end justifies the means. One must win at all costs. It is better to be feared than loved.* "Rove's political bible is *The Prince* by Machiavelli," according to Tom Pauken, the chairman of the Republican Party in Texas in the 1990s, "and [Rove's] 'scorched earth' approach to political campaigns is simply a reflection of his willingness to say or do whatever it takes to win elections for candidates or defeat those opposed to his interests."[5] There were other books favored by Rove, such as *The Dream and the Nightmare* by Myron Magnet, but Machiavelli's treatise remained his bible. It didn't hurt, in creating the Rove myth, that he was said to have gotten the practice of reading the book yearly from Lee Atwater.

With his role models—Atwater, Hanna—his nicknames—Turd Blossom, Boy Genius—and his bible—*The Prince*—in place, Rove was on his way to creating a mythology about himself. He was ready to assume what for years he had believed would be his rightful spot on history's political stage. He first achieved that position when he got George W.

Bush elected president in 2000—and then lost it one hot August day in 2007 on the lawn of the White House when Bush accepted what would be spun as his resignation and Rove accompanied Bush on one last trip down to Texas on Air Force One.

What would come of their legacy? How would Bush and, by extension, Rove be viewed by history, on the stage of which Rove wanted so desperately to stand? By Bush's second term, Rove had begun talking a lot about securing "a permanent Republican majority." McKinley had achieved a majority that was, if not permanent, at least in place for 35 years. But would Bush's two terms lead to such a majority? For 35 years? Longer? Maybe even one that was permanent, as Rove hoped?

"Instead of having a permanent majority," Pauken says, "Rove has potentially put in place a situation that will lead to the destruction of the Republican Party as we've known it in the Barry Goldwater–Ronald Reagan tradition. Rove has taken what people have worked 30 years to achieve in the Goldwater–Reagan years and squandered it all away. He's participated in the potential destruction of the conservative moment in the long term." Others agree. "Every Republican I know looks at the Bush administration as a total failure," says Matt Towery, chairman of Newt Gingrich's political organization. "I felt like the political operation was running things, so they never created policy goals. Political consultants are paranoid by nature. That's the thing about the Bush White House—no one knew who was in charge and yet everyone knew: Karl Rove."[6]

"The Rove legacy will be a fractured party and I hope that the same word can't be applied to the country, but I'm not sure," Congressman Tom Tancredo of Colorado says. "I don't know what damage has been done to the country, but I can guarantee that the party has been crippled dramatically. For a guy who believed himself to be the most brilliant political guru on the planet, to do what he did politically to us is unforgivable. It will take generations to recover. I don't know how long; maybe never."[7]

Was that why Rove was forced to resign his job at the White House, the real story of why he stepped down? Did his failure to achieve a permanent Republican majority leave him vulnerable to being purged after the administration's pivotal mishandling of the aftermath of Hurricane Katrina, its mismanagement of US attorneys, the corruption connected with Jack Abramoff, the repeated misuse of government facilities for political purposes—all of which involved Rove—threatened to bring down not just him but the Bush administration as a whole?

"I think the legacy," Ed Rollins says, "is that Karl Rove will be a name that'll be used for a long, long time as an example of how not to do it, as opposed to an example of how to do it. Rove could have broadened the base of the party. He had an opportunity to strengthen state parties. But, I think, at the end of this, the party will be weaker in numbers in the Congress, numbers of governors, numbers of state legislatures, and numbers of Republicans. He did little to attract young people to become Republicans. Anybody who's a Republican today became a Republican during the Reagan era. Nobody who's come of age during the Bush era will stand up and say, 'I'm a Bush Republican. I'm going to spend the rest of my life being a Bush Republican.'"[8]

Rove will also be remembered for his willingness to perform ruthless, often unethical acts in order to make sure his candidate won. Once he reached the White House, as part of his effort to achieve a permanent Republican majority, he would put into place a plan that included a corruption of the state and federal governing systems that bordered on the diabolical, a scheme that went so far as to create a sort of government within a government to carry out his actions. But in order to achieve what he wanted he had to win elections, and to win those elections, in true Machiavellian style, he would do or say whatever he had to, no matter who got damaged in the process, no matter how badly. Nixon's political hit men had perfected the dirty-tricks playbook and Atwater had practiced it, but Rove took the art of the Nixonian approach to campaigning—destroy the opponent at all costs while relentlessly motivating your own base to vote—to a whole new level. The trail of destroyed lives Rove left in his wake was unimportant to him, and there were many such lives. "Collateral damage," he once called them.

CHAPTER TWO

A YOUNG REPUBLICAN

"Nothing special about the Roves," Karl Rove would one day say about his family. Maybe that's what he wanted people to believe, but the reality was quite different. Born in 1950 in Denver, on Christmas Day, Karl Christian Rove was the second of the five children of Louis C. Rove Jr. and Reba Louise Wood Rove, a mineral geologist and a gift shop manager. (Karl's siblings were Olaf, Reba, Eric, and Alma.) Because of the transient nature of Louis's job locating minerals underground and working for whatever mining company needed his services, most frequently Getty Oil, the family relocated from Denver to Sparks, Nevada, and then to Salt Lake City. Rove's father hunted for, as one report would describe it, "zinc, lead, uranium, copper, and molybdenum—the raw materials of atomic bombs, battery electrodes, metal alloys, spark plugs, even drugs."[1] If mobility defined Rove's early life, poverty was part of the family background, too. During the Great Depression, Rove's grandfather had supported his wife and children by working on a highway road crew, a job produced by the public works programs championed by Democrats to help pull the country out of its catastrophic economic abyss. Even so, Rove's mother grew up in a falling-down shack with walls of tarpaper.

In Salt Lake City, in 1965, Rove entered Olympus High School as a sophomore. Slender and sporting eyeglasses like Mr. Magoo's, he often arrived for class wearing a coat and tie and carrying a briefcase—an ensemble, complete with ink pens stuck in a plastic pocket protector, that only reinforced his fellow students' opinion that he was a nerd. It was not a description Rove would have argued with; he knew he was a geek. With that as a given, he entered student government in 1968 at Olympus High, only to be elected student council president, perhaps because of another trait he possessed—an insatiable gift of gab. No matter what the circumstances and whether or not it was appropriate, as a teenager, Rove just could not shut up. He would not stop talking. One topic he often held forth on was government.

"Already showing a great interest in history and politics," the *Salt Lake Tribune* later noted, "Rove was first spurred to participate in politics by the late Eldon Tolman, the legendary Olympus High civics teacher. . . . [Rove was also] fond of packing box after box after box of notes to debate tournaments to intimidate opponents."[2] The boxes of notes resulted from the countless hours he spent in the library exhaustively researching for each debate, although occasionally, just to psych out opponents by making them think he had out-prepared them, Rove was not above bringing boxes full of blank cards as decoys. When he was not holed up in the library doing research or making the moves necessary to advance in debating or student government, Rove waited tables to earn spending money.

As for politics, it was as if Rove had been born a true-blue Republican. At age nine, he supported Richard Nixon over John Kennedy for president, and, according to Rove, a young girl punched him out because his political views were different from hers. "The little girl across the street I can remember beating the hell out of me in 1960 because I was for Nixon and she was for Kennedy," Rove said about the incident. "She had a couple of years and a few pounds on me, and I can remember being on the pavement."[3] In his youth, in place of the sports-themed posters that more commonly adorned his contemporaries' bedroom walls, he slept with a "Wake Up America" poster—a relic from Barry Goldwater's failed 1964 presidential campaign—plastered above his bed. The first book he could remember reading, he would claim, was *Great Moments in History*. It's hard to tell how many of these details are true and how many Rove made up later to flesh out the myth he created about himself, but some facts are clear. One involved his parents.

In the spring of 1969, his father began traveling back and forth to Los Angeles, presumably on business trips, but Karl could also sense a divide growing between his parents. As it happened, the Roves were not a family devoted to religion. A childhood friend, Mark Dangerfield, would recall that Rove "was raised in a completely nonreligious home."[4] In time, Rove himself would observe: "I'm not sure I've ever found faith. Others . . . I know how much their faith sustains them. . . . I haven't been good enough yet."[5]

In the fall of 1969, Rove, now 18, matriculated to the University of Utah, where he received a $1,000 scholarship from the William Randolph Hearst Foundation and chose political science as his major.[6] That Christmastime, right around Karl's 19th birthday, the fractures in the Rove marriage worsened when Louis, after years of living in denial, announced that he was gay and left his wife and family. "I had to start to fend for myself," Rove said years later.[7] A divorce followed, but in the meantime Karl discovered, from offhand comments made by an aunt and uncle at the dinner table, that the man he believed to be his father was not his biological father, but rather his adoptive stepfather. Rove had never known his real father—he would not encounter him for another 20 years, and when he did the man wanted nothing to do with him—and until the age of 19 he had had no reason to doubt that his father was who he had said he was.

Young Karl had to deal with a series of shocks: realizing that the man he had thought was his father was his stepfather, that he knew nothing about his real father, and that, as it turned out, his stepfather left his mother not for the ordinary reasons people divorce but because he was gay. Even more troubling, members of Rove's own family had known Louis Rove was not Karl's real father, so they were parties to his mother's deceit.

It must have been disturbing for Karl, having just turned 19, to discover that his life had been based on a complex network of lies, secrets, and denials. The emotional damage caused by the very underpinnings of his life being cut out from under him must have been extensive.

To make matters worse, Rove had to watch as his mother, whom he loved even though she had lied to him, had her world destroyed by the desertion of her husband. The reason for his leaving may have been understandable, but that didn't lessen the loss.

≋

Despite the upheaval in his family, Rove continued to attend the University of Utah. To make money—now a requirement since money was tight after his parents' divorce—he took a job at a convenience store. At the university, he joined the College Republicans. It was in that organization that Rove explored more deeply his true calling: politics. "By 1970," one report would state, "19-year-old Karl Rove was hungry for the political life and eager to experience it at its gritty ground level. He found himself in Illinois, where Everett Dirksen, the folksy and legendary Republican senator, had just died. Rove was hired to organize a youth campaign for Dirksen's appointed but forgettable successor, Ralph Tyler Smith. It was a difficult task, but Rove took it on."[8]

While in Illinois, Rove perpetrated an event that would become a notorious part of the myth that later emerged around him. Rove decided to exercise his emerging love of the dirty trick by posing as a volunteer for the campaign of Alan J. Dixon, the Democrat running in the state treasurer race, and infiltrating Dixon's headquarters so he could steal campaign stationery. Then he made up 1,000 fake invitations to the headquarters' official opening event, promising "free beer, free food, girls, and a good time for nothing," and distributed them around Chicago, hitting skid row, homeless shelters, a rock concert, and a hippie commune. On the announced day, Dixon headquarters was overrun by hippies, fringe characters, and the homeless. The episode later became identified with Rove so completely that when he was ascending the ranks of the Republican political machine in Texas, a journalist asked him about what had happened in Illinois. "I was 19 and I got involved in a political prank," Rove explained.[9] As it turned out, the prank didn't work. Dixon won the race for state treasurer and later became a United States senator.

At the time, Rove was beginning to catch the attention of people besides Illinois state politicians. "I first met Karl out in Utah when he was living with his mother," Joe Abate says. "I was really impressed with him." In 1971, Abate was the chairman of the College Republicans; an auxiliary organization of the Republican National Committee, its formal name was the College Republican National Committee. Through the spring and early summer, Abate was so pleased with Rove that he asked him to become executive director, essentially the second-in-command job at the College Republicans. Rove accepted the position, even though it required him to drop out of the University of Utah and move to Washington, DC. The position meant, in essence, that Rove was now working for the RNC. "I recognized early on that Karl was one of the most creative technicians I had ever met," Abate says. "I could see how later he got into the direct-mail business because he put together some great brochure and campaign material. He was a dynamo with a lot of energy. He worked 24-7. He was very contentious and very brilliant at a young age."[10]

In the coming years, Rove attended the University of Maryland (in 1971) and George Mason University (between 1973 and 1975), both in the Washington area. Presumably, he needed to attend college because he was the executive director of the College Republicans, but as he became more involved in politics he appeared less interested in college. However, his enrollment did have one undeniable additional benefit. As the Vietnam War ground on and the mandatory draft reached its peak, Rove was able to maintain his college deferment at least part of the time, ensuring he would not have to serve in the military.

According to published reports, Rove had registered with the Selective Service System during his senior year at Olympus High and was given an identification number of 42-24-50-1691. His classification was 1S-H, indicating that he was not eligible for the draft because he was a high school student. After graduating in the spring of 1969, Rove was reclassified in June as 1-A, meaning that he was eligible for the draft. In the lottery then being used to draft young men according to their birthdays, Rove's number was 84 out of 365. Young men with numbers up to 195 were drafted that year, so Rove probably would have been drafted. That likelihood was increased on January 19, 1970, when he passed the Armed Forces Physical Examination. However, Rove was not drafted because his enrollment at the University of Utah resulted in his reclassification on February 17 to 2-S, signifying deferment due to college enrollment. During the 1969–1970 academic year, Rove was a full-time student. Then, in 1970–1971, he became a part-time student, which should have made him available for the draft, although apparently his part-time status escaped notice. He was not drafted.[11]

At the end of the spring term in 1971, Rove moved to Washington to work for the College Republicans but still maintained his deferment.

Rove enrolled at the University of Maryland in the fall of 1971, but he dropped out after only a few weeks, failing to complete his first semester. Finally, on December 14, 1971, Rove was reclassified again, this time as 1-A, denoting that he was available for the draft. For some reason, though, he was still not drafted, and on April 27, 1972, he was reclassified as a 1-H, meaning that he was no longer subject to the draft. He was part of a large group of young men—4.4 million—who had been placed so low on the list they were never going to be drafted. This was done as a first step in what would be the elimination of the draft altogether.

In future years, those close to Rove would contend that the best way to make him furious was to repeat the contention made by some that, by handling his college enrollment the way he did, he was dodging the draft. He would argue that he was merely attending college. At the peak of the Vietnam War, he enrolled in colleges that earned him deferments from the draft. He may not have liked being called a draft dodger, but, by taking the actions he did, he *did* avoid the draft—a development underscored by the fact that, even as he attended one institution of higher learning after another, he never graduated from any of them.

Rove clearly had other interests besides serving in the military, such as running the College Republicans. As Abate neared the end of his term as chairman, he encouraged Rove to run for the position because he had been so successful as executive director. He would not be unopposed; it was shaping up to be a three-way race between Rove, Robert Edgeworth, and John T. "Terry" Dolan (who later founded the National Conservative Political Action Committee). Dolan was running at the suggestion of Morton Blackwell, a legendary figure in the conservative movement who had gotten his start in the College Republicans. Rove had the support of the more moderate wing of the Republican Party, especially the Northeast liberals. For his part, Edgeworth appeared to be the spoiler.

Described by one colleague at the time as being "thin, bespectacled, lively, friendly, and a joker who loved graphics and technology," Rove did not have the race for chairman locked up. Later, Rove recalled that his campaign had been helped considerably by budding Republican consultant and strategist Lee Atwater, whose long car trip with Rove in Atwater's brown Pinto would become a part of the Rove myth, but some contend that Atwater's involvement in Rove's campaign was overstated by him. In time, Rove would try to glom onto the Atwater mystique by playing up his claim that they were close friends. "I guess I'm more cerebral and lack his great people skills," Rove would say. "And I'm more of a nerd. Lee was a nerd in high school, but then he learned to play the guitar and talk to girls, and I never did. That's serious."[12]

In any event, the election for the chairmanship of the College Republicans in 1973 occurred at their convention, held in June at a resort at Lake of the Ozarks in Missouri. "The idea was to make it the hardest place to get to in the country—to discourage delegations from coming," says Roger Stone, who attended the convention. "All of these college kids ended up driving there from Wisconsin, New York, Florida, everywhere. The convention turned into a shouting match. There was a dispute over rules. Eventually, Dolan dropped out to support Edgeworth, and the election ended up disputed. Karl was declared the winner in one room, and the other guy was declared the winner in the next room. I was supporting Dolan and when Dolan said, 'I'm going to support Edgeworth,' I said, 'I'm heading to the airport.' I left. I was on the other side of Karl. I was more conservative—then."[13]

Joe Abate attended the convention, too. "It was a hotly contested race," he says. "We were all conservatives, but it was the far right that opposed first me as chairman and then Karl. We were viewed as moderates, but we felt strongly the College Republicans should be open to anyone. The election for chairman was disputed. All of the so-called liberal states of the Northeast supported Karl."[14] Years later, Rove would say Atwater had fixed the election in his favor by convincing a number of women to vote for Rove. Again, it's hard to tell how much of the information is true and how much was invented by Rove after the fact—and after Atwater's death—to align himself with Atwater.

As it happened, Rove was lucky, because the contested election was referred to the chairman of the Republican National Committee, who himself had been raised in the tradition of the Northeast liberal Republicans—George H. W. Bush. A former oilman from Texas and a congressman from Texas's Seventh District from 1967 until 1971, Bush had just arrived at the RNC at the request of President Nixon after serving for two years as the United States ambassador to the United Nations. "The dispute," Stone says, "went to RNC chairman George H. W. Bush to decide. He said, 'I've got better things to do than adjudicate a fight among a bunch of college kids,' so he threw the ball to Anne Armstrong."[15]

A business woman and respected member of the Republican party, Armstrong could not have been a more perfect person to bring into the controversy, at least for Rove. Only months earlier, on February 15, 1973, as if he had known that one day he might need her good graces, Rove had written Armstrong an effusive note, to which he had attached a plan for something he called "New Federalism Advocates"—a concept he believed might be helpful to the Republicans in the midterm elections of 1974. "Just a short note to thank-you for taking time out of your busy schedule yesterday afternoon to talk with me," Rove had written. "Appreciate anything you might be able to do for me." What she "might be able to do" for Rove was now obvious: She could help him become the College Republicans' chairman.[16] "Bush used to have a dwarf, like Mini-Me," Stone says. "His dwarf's name was Tom Lias. Tom attached himself to Bush at the United Nations and followed him to the RNC. It was Tom and Anne Armstrong who began studying the matter."[17] The outgoing chairman also weighed in on whom his successor should be. "When the election was brought to Chairman Bush," Abate says, "they had hearings on it and it was my recommendation that Karl had been elected legitimately."[18]

Before a chairman could be selected, a story broke in the *Washington Post* that could have proved damaging to Rove. "Republican National Chairman George Bush has opened an investigation into allegations that a paid official of the GOP taught political espionage and 'dirty tricks' during weekend seminars for college Republicans during 1971 and 1972," the newspaper reported. "Some of the 1972 seminars were held after the Watergate break-in. . . . Bush said he will urge a GOP investigating committee to 'get to the bottom' of charges against Karl C. Rove, 22, who was executive director of the College Republican National Committee, an affiliate of the GOP, from June 1971, to February, 1972."[19] The charges stemmed from seminars Rove and Bernie Robinson, another College Republican, had given for members in which they related dirty tricks such as "dumpster diving" (digging through an opponent's garbage in search of material that could be used against him in a campaign) and espionage (such as Rove's infiltration during the Illinois state treasurer race that netted him an opponent's stationery). The *Post* ran with the story about Rove after receiving a copy of a tape of Rove and Robinson giving one of their dirty-tricks training sessions.

While Bush protested to the *Post* that he would "get to the bottom" of whatever Rove was up to, whatever he ultimately did or did not discover about Rove and his activities apparently didn't bother him in the least. The investigation into Rove and Robinson as well as the hearings held by Armstrong had no impact on who the next chairman of the College Republicans would be. "After a hearing and testimony," Abate says,

"Bush recommended Karl, who was installed as chairman."[21] Bush sent out the letter naming Rove chairman in early September 1973. With the job came assignment as special assistant to the chairman of the Republican Party; as executive director Rove had also been a member of the RNC executive committee, and he retained that position in his new capacity.

So Rove had won the first election in which he was directly involved, in this case as the candidate himself, and it was a contested election decided by a third party amid a swirl of allegations concerning unethical campaign practices and maybe even illegal behavior. It would not be the last time Rove was involved in an election that ended in a dispute so contentious that a third party had to step in to declare a winner, nor would it be the only time Rove's motives and actions would be called into question.

⇌

Once installed as chairman, Rove now had to appoint a new executive director. "I was the one who got Karl his first Washington job," Abate says, "and I was the one who got Lee Atwater his first Washington job, too, because one of the things I asked Karl to consider when he was chairman was to hire Lee as his executive director. Karl agreed, and Lee was Karl's executive director for about one year."[21] Stories about ego clashes between Rove and Atwater would circulate in Republican gossip channels for years.

One person about whom Rove had no qualms, of course, was George H. W. Bush, the man who had given him his chairmanship. Years later, Rove would recall with great affection his association with Bush during this time. "[He] was incredibly gentle," Rove would say. "Great character. Very thoughtful. Really generous in his openness and attitude. Clearly pained by Watergate as it unrolled."[22]

It would be during this same period that Rove met Bush's oldest son for the first time. The encounter would leave a lasting impression on Rove. "It was the day before Thanksgiving, 1973," Rove would recall. "Chairman Bush's chief-of-staff called me and said, 'I've got to be at a meeting on the Hill, the chairman's got to be at a meeting at the White House, the other people in the office have already gone, and the eldest son's going to be coming down from Harvard. He's going to arrive at the train station, early afternoon. He'll call over here when he gets to the train station. Meet him down in the lobby and give him the keys to the family car.' I can literally remember what he was wearing: an Air National Guard flight jacket, cowboy boots, blue jeans, complete with the—in Texas you see it a lot—one of the back pockets will have a circle worn in the pocket from where you carry your tin of snuff, your tin of tobacco. He was exuding more charisma than any one individual should be allowed to have."[23] The son about whom Rove would gush in such emotional tones, the first glimpse of whom would stay with him for years, was George W. Bush.

For the next two years, Rove worked as chairman of the College Republicans. In 1976, he served as finance director of the state Republican Party in Virginia and through a direct-mail campaign only, he brought in $400,000 without holding any fund-raising events—a testament to Rove's ability to churn contributions through direct mail. Then, in 1977, Rove decided to make a move. Between 1974 and 1976, George H. W. Bush had served as the chief of the United States Liaison Office in the People's Republic of China, after which he held the post of director of the Central Intelligence Agency from 1976 until 1977. That year, he headed back to Texas, to Houston, where, in anticipation of a run for the presidency in 1980, he established a political action committee named the Fund for Limited Government. Headed by his friend James A. Baker III, the committee needed a number of operatives who knew their way around Republican circles, strategists who could help position Bush for his run for national office. One of those employees would be someone who had been educated in the use of Nixonian dirty tricks and who was seasoned from having served in the College Republicans. George H. W. Bush liked what he saw in Karl Christian Rove, so much so that he sent him to Houston to help Baker run his political action committee. At 27, Rove may still have been young, but with the experience he had acquired while working for the College Republicans, even if he had not earned a college degree, he was ready for the next phase of his life.

CHAPTER THREE

DEEP IN THE HEART OF TEXAS

1.

When Rove moved to Houston in 1977, he was venturing into a state that had historically been controlled by the Democrats. First as a member of the Senate and then from the White House, Lyndon Johnson had loomed over the state for years. A towering presence on the American political landscape, Johnson had controlled the very inner workings of the political system in Texas. He had left the White House less than a decade before Rove arrived in Texas and had died just a few years before, in 1973. Of the 30 statewide offices, only one was held by a Republican, US senator John Tower. George H. W. Bush had used Texas as a base from which to launch his political career, with qualified success. In 1964, he ran for the US Senate and lost to Democrat Ralph Yarborough. He won a seat in the House of Representatives in 1966, but Richard Nixon convinced him to give that up to run again for the Senate in 1970. The second time, he lost to Lloyd Bentsen, a surprise winner over Yarborough in the primary. As a consolation, in 1971 Nixon named Bush US ambassador to the United Nations, which began a string of appointments much more impressive for his political résumé than any elected position in Texas. Bush then returned to Texas to prepare for a run for the White House in 1980, and he brought with him his protégé from the College Republicans—Karl Rove.

Located in a modest office in a bank building, the Fund for Limited Government, the political action committee Rove worked for, was little more than a front operation for Bush's nascent presidential effort. Besides politics, Rove had been eager to move to Houston because, in Washington, through the Republican National Committee, he had met an attractive, socially connected young woman named Valerie Wainright, whose family, also from Houston, was friends with the Bushes. Rove had married Wainright on July 10, 1976, in a wedding that was rather surprising to some since Rove was anything but social. It made sense, then, for the couple to be living in her hometown. Rove's lack of social graces and status could be overlooked since he was on the make on the political front, now in the employ of one of the state's most famous Republicans, a man who was planning to run for president. There was, however, no doubt about it: Rove may have had a lot of fine qualities, but fitting into Houston's social set was not one of them.

The Democratic lock on Texas began to break in 1978, when Bill Clements was elected governor. He was the first Republican to hold the office in the state since Reconstruction. That same year, at Bush's suggestion, Rove served as an informal adviser to the congressional campaign of Bush's son, George W., whom he had met in 1973. The younger Bush lost the race for a House seat representing the 19th Congressional District, which included the town of Midland, but the campaign marked the first time Bush and Rove teamed up as candidate and adviser.

The following January, Rove resigned from Bush's political action committee to work as deputy director of the Governor William P. Clements Committee, concentrating on the governor's direct-mail efforts. Around this time, Rove's marriage to Wainright collapsed; it ended in divorce in January 1980. His marriage behind him, Rove moved to Austin, the state capital, to become special assistant for administration and deputy assistant to the governor of Texas.

In 1981, Rove was appointed as a regent for the Texas Woman's University in Denton and as the treasurer for the Texas Women's Employment and Education program in Austin. He held each post for two years. Also in 1981, Rove went into business for himself. His first client was Clements, which no doubt helped him line up other clients for the 1982 campaign—the Republican candidates for lieutenant governor, agriculture commissioner, and attorney general. That same year, in a surprise move, Rove also worked for Phil Gramm, a Democratic member of the US House. Gramm would later change parties in order to run for the US Senate in 1984, an election he won. But in 1982, Clements was Rove's main client. Clements's campaign was so lackluster that he shocked the Texas political establishment by losing the general election to Mark White, the attorney general. The state was in an economic slump that was being blamed on the governor, but neither Rove nor Clements saw White's victory coming. Then again, in 1982, every one of Rove's clients lost as Democrats won all major state races. The winners included Jim Mattox as attorney general, Ann Richards as treasurer, Jim Hightower as agriculture commissioner, and Garry Mauro as land commissioner.

While these events were unfolding in Rove's professional life, developments occurred in his private life that would have a profound effect on him. Still reeling from the breakup of his marriage in early 1980, he found himself also having to deal with the emotional baggage created by his stepfather's lifestyle. It is unclear whether Rove ever effectively dealt with the trauma he undoubtedly experienced when the man he had known as his father announced he was gay and left the family, although according to friends, Rove *did* put his father's coming out behind him. Then Louis Rove took up another activity in such a public way that it was impossible for his family not to know about it. During the late 1970s and early 1980s, Rove's father began to engage in the sexual fetish of body piercing. In fact, he had so many piercings on his genitalia that some might consider it self-mutilation. With his friends, Louis Rove was open about his fetish and the parts of his body he had had pierced; he even held piercing parties at his home in Los Angeles, complete with nurses to oversee the activities. In time, he let himself be photographed by piercing fetish magazines such as *Piercing Fans International Quarterly*, even appearing on magazine covers.

It's hard to imagine that Rove's mother did not know about her ex-husband's activities. For years after the collapse of her marriage, Reba Rove suffered emotional damage from which she never fully healed. Living by herself in Reno in 1981, caught up in a depression from which she could not emerge, Reba Rove committed suicide.

"In 1997," a magazine later reported, "Rove told the journalist Thomas Edsall that his mother, [after the divorce] largely withdrew from family life. When Rove was in his mid-20s, she would sometimes ask to borrow money, and from time to time would send him packages with old magazines or broken toys. 'It was like she was trying desperately to sort of keep this connection,' Rove told Edsall, until finally, in 1981, she 'drove out to the desert north of Reno and filled the car with carbon monoxide, and then left all of her children a letter saying, don't blame yourselves for this.' It was, Rove thought, 'the classic fuck-you gesture.' "[1]

As he had in the past and as he would in the future, Rove dealt with his crisis by throwing himself into his work. However, 1982 was disastrous in professional terms, with all of his candidates losing, including his prize client, Bill Clements. So, emerging from 1982, Rove started on a comeback. Never again did he want to have another barrage of losses. Moving into the remainder of the 1980s, Rove would do whatever it took to win—no matter what. As it happened, for part of the decade, he would have considerable help from someone many Texas observers believed to be an overzealous agent assigned to the Austin office of the Federal Bureau of Investigation. For years, his name—Greg Rampton—would be linked with Rove's. Rampton had served in Atlanta; Albuquerque, New Mexico; and Washington, DC, before arriving in

Austin. Even though they would both deny it, members of the Texas political community would believe that for many of the 12 years Rampton was based in Austin, he and Rove worked in tandem to take down Democrats, each advancing his own career by collaborating with the other.

⇌

The first known Democratic victim of Greg Rampton was Vic Feazell. The strange episode involving Feazell began with the case of Henry Lee Lucas, a convicted murderer who, in 1983, after serving his time in Michigan for killing his mother, was arrested by the Texas Rangers on a firearms violation. However, once in the custody of the Rangers, he was charged with the murders of an elderly woman and an acquaintance of his. Subjected to brutal treatment by the Rangers, Lucas confessed to the murders to improve his living conditions in jail, or so he later claimed. Once he was incarcerated, the confessions kept coming, supposedly because, again according to Lucas, the more murder cases he confessed to, the better his living conditions became.

Before long, the Henry Lee Lucas Task Force was set up by the Texas Rangers just to process what was turning into a steady string of confessions to unsolved murders committed across the country. Tens of murders soon became hundreds. The number of confessions Lucas ultimately made is generally believed to total 350, although some crime experts contend that Texas authorities processed his confessions to as many as 3,000 unsolved cases. Lucas was being flown around the country to crime scenes to confess to murders he claimed to have committed years before. If he had committed even a fraction of the murders he confessed to, he would have been the worst serial killer in history. There was only one problem. He had confessed to murders he could not possibly have committed, such as a 1979 murder in Oklahoma he claimed he carried out despite irrefutable medical records indicating that at the time of the crime he had been confined to a hospital in West Virginia, almost 1,000 miles away. Finally, local officials in Texas became dubious. There were just too many murders, and too much of the evidence didn't add up. The first official to take action was Vic Feazell, the district attorney of Waco, Texas.

Feazell had received information from reliable sources calling into question Lucas's confessions to three murders in Feazell's jurisdiction, McLennan County. Apparently, Lucas had not even been in McLennan County when the murders occurred. After a government employee tipped off the Texas Rangers that Feazell might air his doubts about the validity of some of Lucas's confessions—a move that would be embarrassing to the Texas Rangers—the Rangers initiated a widespread investigation of Feazell, complete with help from FBI agent Greg Rampton.[2]

Feazell called Lucas, who was in jail near Austin, to Waco to appear before a grand jury in an effort to prove that he might not have committed all of the murders. Feazell used the same grand jury to begin examining the actions of the Texas Rangers' Henry Lee Lucas Task Force. In April 1985, the story of Lucas's hoaxes broke, tarnishing the reputation of the Texas Rangers and reflecting negatively on several other government agencies. At the same time, Feazell came under attack, becoming the subject of a vicious, all-out assault on him, his private life, and his office. His phones were tapped, his bank records were subpoenaed by federal officials, his mail was opened illegally. The investigation of Feazell combined the efforts of the FBI, local law enforcement, and the US Attorney's Office. A grand jury handed down a multiple-count indictment charging him with bribery, and Feazell was arrested on the morning of September 17, 1985, when he showed up for work at the courthouse. The local news media had even been alerted so they could broadcast his "perp walk" on live television.

"When the feds arrested me at the courthouse," Feazell says, "another group descended on a restaurant where my wife and four-year-old son were eating breakfast. Rampton was there and appeared to be in charge of the group. They took them out of the restaurant and made them ride back to our house in the back seat of one of the FBI cars. Rampton was in charge of the search of my house. There were at least 12 agents there, my wife later told me. They unwrapped everything in the freezer, emptied all the drawers, went through our son's toys, dug up our flower garden, and raked the insulation in the attic. They took a toy syringe from a play doctor's kit in my son's room and listed it on the search warrant return as 'drug paraphernalia.'

"Rampton made my wife and son sit on the couch in the living room. My wife turned on the TV to take my son's mind off of what was going on. As she did, regular programming was interrupted to show live coverage of me being arrested. My four-year-old son suffered emotional trauma as a result of this. To him, the bad men with guns had come to get him and they had taken his daddy to jail."[3]

While the Texas political establishment—of which Rove was a member—watched this drama play out not just in Waco but across the state, any interested observer could see how effectively a politician can be destroyed by the combined forces of the government, especially if an FBI agent and a US attorney are willing to collaborate in the takedown. In Feazell's case, the efforts of government officials were aided considerably by the local media outlets. Channel 8 in Dallas, WFAA, carried the perp walk live and then aired 11 reports on Feazell as he was being investigated.

The charges against Feazell centered on a claim that, as district attorney, he had taken cash bribes from attorneys for not prosecuting their clients who had been arrested for drunk driving. There was only one hitch: None of the claims was true. In June 1987, following a five-week trial that saw the government call 65 witnesses, it took the jury just six hours to find Feazell innocent. Then, in an effort to clear his name,

Feazell sued WFAA, the television station that had broadcast the news stories about him being investigated by the FBI and other government agencies. Feazell argued that the indictments brought against him had been bolstered by the television stories, which, he claimed, contained libelous material—the charge that Feazell and one of his associates were "strong-arming" lawyers and their clients for bribes in exchange for dropping drunk-driving charges. "I had to prove everything they were saying about me was a lie," Feazell says, "and not only a lie but, because I was a public figure, I had to prove it was said with malice" to meet the legal definition of libel.[4] A jury agreed with Feazell and awarded him $58 million—the largest jury award in a libel case in American history. Eventually, Feazell settled for a smaller amount—rumored to be about $20 million.

"Vic Feazell was indicted because he was a high-powered Democratic district attorney in Waco," says Garry Mauro, the state's land commissioner from 1983 until 1999. "Feazell was a Christian Coalition Democrat, which was scaring the shit out of Rove. He was even a preacher. So Rampton and a Channel 8 reporter teamed up and ran the most salacious TV and *Dallas Morning News* stories. He had two lawyers in Waco who gave him a $1,000 contribution each and they tried to prove that one of their clients got off [on a charge of] DWI because Feazell was given a contribution. They indicted Feazell and in the trial the two lawyers said, 'Yes, we gave money but we didn't get any special treatment.' He was found not guilty."[5]

This much was true: During 1985 and 1986, when Greg Rampton was attempting to ruin Feazell, Rampton had caught the attention of Karl Rove. "Rampton had been a lead investigator out of the Austin FBI office in a legislative sting operation called BriLab," James Moore, journalist and co-author of *Bush's Brain*, would say. "Since Democrats held almost every office at that time, they were his targets. . . . Rove knew Rampton by reputation."[6] No doubt Rove had realized he could use Rampton's services, for it was more than obvious that Rampton knew how to take out a political enemy and felt little pity as he did it.

Rove needed all the help he could get. During the first half of the 1980s, he had worked on the campaigns of various Texas candidates and had made some headway in establishing a name for himself, but not much. Outside Texas, he was unknown. "When I first met him around this time," Ed Rollins says, "Karl was in Texas, a direct-mail guy, but he was not thought of as a significant player. Maybe he was [considered significant] in Texas, with Bill Clements and others, but not on a national level. He was always on the fringe. He was not a significant player."[7] Others agree. "During this time, I had heard his name maybe one time," says Matt Towery, who was chairman of Newt Gingrich's political organization when Gingrich later took over the House. "Karl Rove was not someone we would have paid any attention to. Nobody knew who the guy was."[8]

2.

In 1986, Rove worked on the campaign of Bill Clements, who was trying to win back the Texas governorship from Democrat Mark White. The campaign was not easy for Clements, who had never possessed the raw political skills White had. Heading into the homestretch, the race was still either man's to win, but the polls indicated that White, trailing Clements in September, was closing the gap by early October.

For the entire race, there was only one scheduled debate, to be held on the evening of Monday, October 6, in Houston, and broadcast state-wide to a prime-time audience. As a debater, Clements was no match for White, who was bright, articulate, and in command of the facts on almost any relevant subject. If White performed well and Clements struggled, as many political experts believed would be the case, the polls

would get even closer. The best way to take the focus off the debate—
and distract the public from the fact that Clements was the inferior candidate—was to create a sideshow. What unfolded next was pure political
drama. It was also vintage Rove.

On the day of the debate, Rove called a press conference in his office,
though he refused to tell the reporters the subject, or even the nature, of
the announcement; he would only say it was newsworthy. In Rove's
playbook, if he could not improve his candidate, he would tear down the
opponent and change the coverage of the campaign. This time, he had
to do it fast, since the debate was that evening.

"The Clements office was down the street from the capitol in Austin," says one of the reporters Rove phoned. "I remember walking down
Congress Avenue to the Bill Clements campaign office. Me and all of
the other reporters got in the elevator and we went up and we were
directed into Karl's office where he was sitting behind his desk." With
the reporters jammed into Rove's modest office—a dozen or so print
journalists as well as a cluster of television reporters accompanied by
their camera crews—the assembled media was ready for the big revelation, the urgent news Rove had summoned them for.

"Then," the reporter says, "Karl announced that they had found an
electronic bugging device in his office on Sunday night and that the
Clements campaign believed it had been planted by the White campaign."
As for who might have planted the bug, Rove parsed his words. "Obviously, I don't know who did this," Rove said. "But there is no doubt in my
mind that the only ones who would benefit from this detailed, sensitive
information would be the political opposition." That's why Rove had suspected his office had been bugged—because the White campaign seemed
to possess "detailed, sensitive" information discussed only in Rove's
office, such as the idea of bringing in Lee Atwater to work for Clements in
the last month of the campaign. Private investigators, Rove said, had

searched the Clements headquarters on Sunday night and found the device, a small, black instrument the size of a matchbox, behind a red, white, and blue needlepoint picture of an elephant that hung on the office wall. The device was turned over to the FBI. The investigation was headed by Greg Rampton, who had conducted a total sweep of the Clements campaign offices. "So," according to the reporter in attendance, "we were all sitting there and Karl finished his statement and we all just looked at one another and suddenly everyone broke out laughing."[9]

Undeterred by the guffaws of disbelief, Rove sat behind his desk, keeping a straight face. He had his moment. In all of the political work he had done so far, this was the first time the spotlight had been focused squarely on him. He was ready for the attention, too. He played his moment to the hilt, even if the reaction of the Austin press corps indicated that they did not believe what he was saying.

Downstairs, on Congress Avenue after the press conference, the reporters were demonstrably doubtful about the truth of Rove's announcement. "Do you believe any of this?" one reporter asked the clique of journalists gathered to discuss what they had just heard.

"Nope," another said, "but it's going to be on the front page of my paper tomorrow."

It didn't matter if Rove was telling the truth. It was a good story, so the reporters were going to run with it. As a consultant for the campaign of the former governor, now running to win a second term by beating the man who had defeated him, the media would be obliged to report Rove's story about an electronic bugging device, regardless of their doubts. The mere fact that he was making the accusation was news itself. In the world of politics, it is almost impossible to prove a negative. How could it be proved that the bug had *not* been planted by the White campaign? Conversely, how could it be proved that Rove *had* planted it himself? That was the trick: Put the press in a position where they had to prove a negative and they would run the story every time. They would ignore the opposition's denial, as they did when Mark McKinnon of the White campaign issued a statement that said the "whole thing stinks and the wind is blowing from the Clements campaign."[10] Calling Rove's charges "ludicrous and bizarre," McKinnon added, "If the Clements campaign found a bug, that is a serious matter. But if they are blaming us, that is a bunch of bull. We think it's terribly curious that this should come up on the day of the debate."[11]

All over Texas that night, the story of the White campaign bugging the Clements headquarters led the evening news on television, and the next day it got major play in the two papers in Dallas, the two papers in San Antonio, the two papers in Houston, and other, smaller newspapers. The *Houston Post* even ran it under a banner headline. The coverage of the debate in Houston, in which White outperformed Clements as expected, was buried by the sensational story of political espionage. If Rove had wanted to obliterate the story of Clements's failings as a debater—and, by implication, as a candidate—he had succeeded. The validity of Rove's accusation was lost to the better story of one candidate bugging the headquarters of another. The ploy worked. While Clements never improved as a candidate, a cloud of suspicion hung over White until election day, when he lost the race to a clearly inferior candidate.

As for the bugging itself, nothing further ever happened. By Tuesday, October 28, 1986, according to a published report, it had been decided that neither staff in the race for governor would be held accountable for the bugging of Rove's office. US attorney Helen Eversberg said, "At this time, there is no reason to believe that anyone on White's or Clements' staff was involved in the bugging." She did say that the FBI would continue its investigation, which was looking into the activities of Knight Diversified Services, a Fort Worth-based security firm brought in by Rove to look into the planting of the bugging device.[12]

For Rove, the year 1986 was eventful not only in terms of his career, but also as far as his personal life was concerned. After dating Darby Tara Hickson, a graphic artist who worked at Rove's direct-mail company, for some time, the couple married on January 25, 1986. Their son, Andrew, would be born three years later. Rove was so competitive that he could not relax even in his private life. "[E]ven in croquet he'd be hitting my ball so far I was crying on vacation," Darby would later tell a reporter, adding, "I told Karl the other day, 'You see things in black and white. I see lots of gray.'"[13]

That intensity seemed to spill over from his professional life. "He's smart, quick, funny, good company, if he's so inclined," says Bill Miller, a consultant who worked both for and against Rove in Texas and came to consider him a friend. "He's an interesting character. I always got along with him. I didn't like the bad Karl. He didn't scream at me, but he screamed at others. He's got a temper and a loud voice and he used it. He's got an aggressive personality. He's known for getting hot. There are buttons people know about. Losing and getting screwed with will piss him off in a hurry."[14]

3.

"I was also one of the people Rampton investigated," Garry Mauro says about events that transpired in 1988. "They brought 16 FBI agents into my office. I was running the Texas Veterans Land Board, which is a [low-interest real estate] loan program for Texas veterans. I had heard Rampton was looking into my stuff because he was interviewing people, and I had my general counsel call the US Attorney's Office to say, 'Look, we understand you have some questions. We'll gladly provide any information we've got.' The day of the Democratic state convention in 1988, Rampton brought a subpoena to our office and leaked it to the press. So

I got on an airplane to go to Houston to the convention and when I landed I had 100 cameras wanting to talk to me about my subpoena.

"With Vic Feazell, Rampton tried to prove if you gave a political contribution you got favored treatment. That's what they were trying to prove with me too. They subpoenaed all my documents because they were going to prove if you gave Garry Mauro a political contribution your loan would be approved and you'd be closed faster. They put all my information on a computer and did a retrograde analysis and all they proved was you didn't get special treatment. I gave *everyone* special treatment. They proved that and they never issued a statement."[15]

While Rampton was continuing his investigations, Rove was engaging in his own fights. "In 1984," says Tom Pauken, a player in Texas Republican politics in the 1980s, "I had broken with George H. W. Bush. I had been a fan of his both in terms of Reagan's selection of him as vice president and in terms of knowing him since the mid-1960s, when I was national chairman of the College Republicans. I stayed in touch all through the 1970s. I had a good relationship [with him] during the first term of the Reagan administration. But I finally broke with Bush and James Baker in 1984 when I was dispatched by the White House to the Rio Grande Valley to deal with some problems down there. It was a sensitive assignment and we were having some success and Baker tried to pull the trigger on me. I didn't like the way these guys did business. So I broke with the Bush family.

"Then, in 1988, I supported Bob Dole and that's when Karl took some shots at me. At that time George W. got all upset and yelled at me at the state convention. 'How dare you do this after all my father has done for you!' It was that Bush loyalty thing. It's a one-way street, sort of like loyalty to the king. You're expected to be loyal. And, no, Bush hadn't really done that much for me except to be friendly. I wasn't in the club and I didn't want to be in it. But I did what I did and that was the burning of the bridge, if you will."[16]

If Rove had taken shots at Pauken, they were nothing compared to what he would do to John Weaver. Once described as "a tall, terse Texan" with a "constant brooding presence,"[17] Weaver, born in 1959, had established himself during the 1980s as an important Republican political strategist in the state. In fact, in some ways, he was in the process of becoming what Rove wanted to be: Texas's preeminent Republican consultant. For a time, Rove and Weaver, along with another consultant named Reggie Bashur, had discussed forming a consulting firm together. In retrospect, the odds of such a company being formed were small, given the fact that Rove seemed to prefer being a solo act. But had there been any chance of Rove, Weaver, and Bashur launching a firm, the possibility was dashed on election night in 1988. What transpired that night would fracture the relationship between Rove and Weaver so severely that it would never be totally restored.

$\equiv$

In the summer of 1988, after the Democrats had concluded their national convention in Atlanta, George H. W. Bush was 17 points behind Michael Dukakis in the national polls. At the time, Bush was facing intense scrutiny by the press over whether he was even a Texas resident. He had lived with the charge of being a carpetbagger ever since he had moved down from Connecticut after graduating from Yale University in 1948 to go into the oil business, but from 1981 on, while living in Washington as vice president under President Reagan, he had used as his official residence a hotel in Texas named the Houstonian. So the charge resurfaced that he was not a real Texan, but rather a Connecticut-Yankee-come-South in search of his fortune, which was now in the form of a presidential bid.

As a result, Bush made up his mind about one thing going into the fall election: No matter what, he was *not* going to lose Texas. So, he decided to set up a special committee in the state called Victory '88, a precursor to the 527 political action committees that would later become prevalent. After the Democrats held their convention but before the Republicans gathered in New Orleans for theirs, Bush called a meeting at his residence at the Houstonian to talk about Victory '88, whose executive director, he had decided, would be John Weaver.

In that meeting Bush could not have been more clear. "I don't know if I'm going to win this election or not," he told the assembled group, Weaver among them, "but I am not going to lose Texas. I want you to put together a team."[18]

Bush's order was directed to Weaver, who was the head of the Republican Party in Texas. Having gotten his marching orders from Bush himself, Weaver left the meeting, resigned from the state party, and assembled Victory '88, taking members of his state party staff with him. Soon after the committee was formed, there was a conference call between the committee members in Texas—six altogether—and Lee Atwater, the chief strategist, and James Baker, Bush's best friend who oversaw the campaign, at the national campaign headquarters in Washington.

"Here is how you are going to do this," Atwater said on the call. "Whatever you want, you get."

"I'm going to need an unlimited budget and no oversight," Weaver said. "We get to do things here that do not have to be run through the national campaign."

Baker and Atwater agreed. In the end, Victory '88 had a $15 million budget—and no oversight from Washington.

At this pivotal moment in the history of the Bush family, it was Weaver—not Rove—whom Bush had put in charge of the state that mattered most to him. While Weaver was running Victory '88, Rove was given minor consulting contracts that were being farmed out to run-of-the-mill consultants in Texas. "He was just another vendor," as one

Victory '88 staffer puts it.[19] In short, Rove was not a player, although he desperately wanted to be. According to sources familiar with the campaign, Rove was unhappy about being left out of the inner circle and jealous of Weaver, who was solidifying his base of support in the Republican Party not only in Texas, but now, with the blessing of the Bush family, on the national level.

In a brilliant campaign move, Atwater destroyed the candidacy of Democratic nominee Michael Dukakis with a television ad about Willie Horton. Horton, an African American serving time in Massachusetts for murder, was mistakenly given a weekend furlough from the prison. He didn't return. Months later, he broke into a Maryland couple's home, raped the woman twice; beat, knifed, and bound the man; and stole their car. The ad placed the blame for Horton's crime spree on Dukakis, the state's governor at the time and a supporter of the furlough program for inmates who were eligible for parole, which Horton was not. Atwater fulfilled his promise to "strip the bark off the little bastard [Dukakis]" and "make Willie Horton his running mate."[20] It worked. Bush won. Even better, Bush won Texas by a comfortable margin, thanks to the efforts of Weaver and Victory '88. On the night of the election, Republicans nationwide celebrated, but not Rove. He remained an observer on the sidelines, while his colleague from his College Republican days, Atwater, had just become the most celebrated political consultant in the country, and Weaver, his old friend who was threatening to eclipse him in Texas political circles, was enjoying the unequivocal gratitude of the Bush family. Rove had to do something.

On election night, once it was apparent that Bush had won, the celebration began in earnest in Houston, where Bush and his family had traveled to watch the election returns and where the national—and international—press had gathered to cover the evening's events. Never before had Rove had such access to such a large and influential assemblage of reporters. Rove used the opportunity to do what he had so often enjoyed doing in the past. He wandered through the press corps spreading a rumor. He told selected reporters that John Weaver had made a pass at a male staffer during the course of the campaign. There was no truth to the rumor, and when a reporter tried to confirm the story with a member of the staff of Victory '88, Rove's efforts were derailed.[21]

"A reporter said to me, 'Karl is repeating a rumor about John,'" the staffer says. "'Is there anything to it?'" The staffer assured the reporter there was not.[22] The denials may have succeeded in killing the story, but the rumor—or the fact that Rove had started it—would not die. It remained alive in gossip channels in political circles for years.

There was an undeniable irony. On the night Rove should have been rejoicing about the election of a Republican president, he was intent upon starting a damaging rumor about a man whom he had once viewed as a potential business partner, but now considered an archrival. Rove may have been a minor player in Texas in 1988 as his contemporaries were becoming major players on a national scale, but he still was driven by a desire to be a national player himself. He was not above using the techniques he employed to take out his opponents to discredit members of his own party who had achieved more than he had. "In 1988, Texas was Weaver's show," one Republican says. "That's why Rove started to take Weaver out."[23]

&

To indicate just how marginal Rove was to the Bushes in 1988, an observer had only to look at his dealings with George W.—the man he had gushed over when he met him in 1973 and helped in his congressional race in 1978. Ten years later, Bush, a Texas businessman who still had political aspirations, was a man on the make.

According to the myth he created about himself in later years, Rove had seen the potential of George W. Bush from that first meeting. Yet in 1988, Rove was nowhere to be found around Bush. It was a Victory '88 staffer who escorted Bush around Texas as he campaigned for his father, and it was a Victory '88 staffer who accompanied him to the Republican National Convention, held that year in New Orleans at the Superdome, from where Bush did television interviews with stations back in Texas. He was doing the media rounds not only for his father but also for himself, since even then, in the summer of 1988, George W. Bush was planning to run for governor of Texas as early as 1990. He wanted to have his face splashed across television screens back in Texas in anticipation of that run.

Bush was not shy about his political aspirations. He openly described a potential run. But Rove was so unimportant that Bush did not even seem to be aware of Rove's place in his father's campaign. Indeed, by no means did Rove appear to be an inevitable part of any future run Bush might undertake, in 1990 or beyond. "I was with Bush every day at the convention in New Orleans," a Republican staffer says, "and Rove was not in the picture. He was nowhere to be found."[24] Ultimately, Bush did not run for governor in 1990, because his father, who was the sitting president, decided it would be inappropriate for his son to run for governor in his home state while he was in the White House. That was just fine with Laura Bush, who did not want her husband to run for office again anyway. So Bush put his aspirations on hold until his father left the presidency.

As for Rove, in 1988, he had been relegated to the down-ballot races. That year, he worked for Tom Phillips, a candidate for the Supreme Court. When Phillips won, he became the first Republican on the Supreme Court in Texas.

"Rove was in a jam in 1990," Tom Pauken says, "when he backed Kent Hance [to be the Republican nominee for governor], and Clayton Williams, an entrepreneur businessman from West Texas, overwhelmed him and won without a runoff. Karl didn't see that coming. He is a formula guy in his campaigns and he has other people do his dirty tricks. But his approach is dependent on having control of the money and being dominant on the money. When he didn't have dominance on the money—as with Clayton Williams—someone can come out of the blue and win. So Karl was in trouble politically."[25]

Fortunately for Rove, in 1990, he had another race to run that would help him redeem himself for missing the opportunity to back Williams. At some point in 1989, Rove had decided he wanted to run a candidate for commissioner of agriculture. In Texas, the post was more important than it sounds. A statewide elected office, the agriculture commissioner is responsible not just for farming and ranching issues, but also for consumer-protection measures, such as the accuracy of pumps at gasoline stations and produce scales at grocery stores. The right politician can use the office as a launching pad to a position such as governor or United States senator. So Rove went searching for a candidate he could run, and when he found him—a young, attractive member of the Texas House of Representatives named Rick Perry—he didn't let the fact that he was a Democrat stop him.

Although Perry was the state chairman for Al Gore for President in 1988, conversations with Rove convinced him to switch parties. Rove's pitch was simple. As of 1989, the future of the Democratic Party in Texas was waning. If Perry wanted to rise through the ranks of Texas politics, he needed to be a Republican. So, in 1989, Perry changed parties, with the intention of running for agriculture commissioner—a campaign that Rove would manage. Perry's opponent was the incumbent Jim Hightower, a folksy, down-home Democrat who was almost as popular as Ann Richards, the state's Democratic rising star. Hightower would be hard to beat, and Rove knew it.

Since he was again working with a marginally talented candidate—Perry's lame delivery of stump speeches and the perception that he was an intellectual lightweight were not helped by his pretty-boy good looks—Rove had to do what he was becoming expert at: raising his opponent's negatives. In Hightower, Rove saw a candidate who was out of step with the direction in which the state was evolving politically. In short, Hightower was a liberal, so much so that in the 1988 presidential race he had endorsed and campaigned for Jesse Jackson. But Hightower's liberalism was not enough to guarantee his reelection. So, during 1989, six years into his tenure as commissioner, word began to spread through Austin that the office of Jim Hightower was being investigated by—here was that name again!—Greg Rampton. Around the same time, Perry formally left the Democratic Party and entrusted his political future to Rove.

"We found out about the investigation probably at some point in 1989," says Mike Moeller, the chief deputy commissioner at the Department of Agriculture in Texas from 1985 until 1990. "We learned about the investigation and then subpoenas showed up, I think, in early January 1990."[26]

The investigation was conducted by the US Attorney's Office. The US attorney at that time, Ron Ederer, had been appointed at the recommendation of US Senator Phil Gramm, a close ally of Rove's. Ederer sent in Rampton, who had a history of working with Rove dating back to the bugging of the Clements headquarters. Whether Rove was involved in the Rampton investigation would *not* be left open to debate, as most smear campaigns involving Rove would be. The master of the third-party smear, Rove would never admit to his involvement in an attack. Someone else was always to blame, and he knew nothing. Except with Hightower. "This summer," Rove wrote on a federal questionnaire in 1989, "I met with agent Greg Rampton of the Austin FBI office at his request regarding a probe of political corruption in the office of Texas Agriculture Commissioner Jim Hightower."[27] Then, in 1991, appearing before a Texas state Senate committee, Rove was asked if, "during the Rick Perry campaign [run against Jim Hightower, Rove had engaged in] any conversations with FBI agent Rampton about the course and conduct of that campaign." Rove admitted, "Yes, I did, two or three times."

Rarely in the future would Rove put himself in a position where he would have to answer to a government agency. The federal questionnaire had been issued by the Senate Foreign Relations Committee in response to Rove's nomination for an appointment to the Board for International Broadcasting; he would serve on that board in 1991. The appearance before the Texas state Senate committee resulted from his nomination for a position on the East Texas State University Board of Regents—an unexpected nomination since Rove himself did not hold so much as a bachelor's degree. He would serve as a regent during the 1990–1991 academic year. On these two occasions, Rove learned his lesson about creating an official government paper trail, and he rarely supplied information about himself in the future.

Starting in early 1990, after word was released to the press that Hightower was under investigation, there was a steady stream of leaks as the campaign proceeded. At the center of the investigation were two men, Bob Boyd and Russell Koontz, who had previously served as deputy commissioners. Each had a small consulting contract with the Agriculture Department to advise Hightower on legislative matters and earned modest monthly stipends for doing so. But because the two men together had raised $6,000 for the Hightower campaign, the government was investigating Hightower's office for violation of a federal code that prohibits consultants on government payrolls from raising money for political campaigns. The amount of money raised was beside the point; it was the act of raising the money that was illegal—or so it may have seemed. In truth, however, even under the federal law, a consultant can raise money for a political candidate as long as the fund-raising does not take place on government time. During the campaign, no charges were filed; there was only the never-ending drip of negative publicity generated by leaks about the investigation.

In June 1990, the Perry campaign, under Rove's supervision, mailed out a fund-raising letter charging that Hightower ran a corrupt office that was under investigation by the FBI even though that information had not been made public and no indictments had been issued. Despite attacks such as this one, Rove still had not been able to take out Hightower. As of late September, less than six weeks before the election, Hightower remained up in the opinion polls, 55 to 35 percent. The Hightower campaign still felt it had a good chance of winning, especially since the mandatory quarterly fund-raising disclosures did not indicate that Perry was raising more money than they were. However, what the Hightower campaign did not know was that Rove had been holding off on reporting significant campaign contributions.

"A month before the election," *Texas Monthly* later reported, "Perry alleged the FBI was investigating Hightower and his department. In the last days of the race, Perry claimed, in TV spots designed by Rove and [a second consultant], that 'there will be people in the Department of Agriculture, going up to possibly its highest levels, who will be indicted.' Not only did the negative ads work . . . but the information turned out to be eerily accurate."[28] According to a subsequent published report, "Rove . . . often leaked things to reporters, such as whose names were on subpoenas before they were issued."[29]

The undisclosed contributions made to the Perry campaign, in excess of $1 million, would not be revealed until the last quarter—after the election—and that allowed Perry to make a massive media buy during the month of October. This bombarding of the Texas airwaves caught the Hightower campaign off guard. "In the last two weeks of the campaign," Moeller says, "they carpet-bombed Houston, the Dallas–Fort Worth metroplex, and East Texas with a series of television ads that were just absolutely appalling. One had a photo of [Jesse] Jackson and Hightower with their arms around each other's shoulders. They ran that in East Texas—just a blatantly racist ad. Another ad featured a flag burning, with the implication that Hightower was for flag burning. As the flag burned, words came up on the screen about Hightower being a liberal—as if he was in favor of flag burning. As these ads were running, the polls completely turned around. And because they waited until so late in the campaign, we didn't have an opportunity to answer. We couldn't have if we wanted to, because we hadn't raised the money. Because we didn't know about the money they had been waiting to report, we didn't know we had to. I'm guessing they did a million dollars' worth of TV ads in targeted markets."[30]

On election day, in a three-way race, both Hightower and Perry came in with 48 percent of the vote. By the end of the night, Perry had won in a squeaker election, with a margin of less than 15,000 votes.

Because Hightower had made rumblings in the past about running for the US Senate, Rove was delighted with his defeat. But, if Hightower continued to harbor political aspirations, they were dampened by indictments that were handed down in January 1991, the month Perry was sworn in as the new agriculture commissioner. Hightower was not indicted, but three members of his staff—Mike Moeller, Peter McRae, and Billie Quicksall—were charged with not trying to stop the fund-raising efforts of Boyd and Koontz, who were also charged. The prosecution was built on the notion that Boyd and Koontz had improperly raised money for Hightower by spending an inordinate amount of time on the fund-raising and by using threatening tactics, and that the Hightower aides had allowed it to happen. Moeller was charged simply because he, not Hightower, was the signatory on the government contract for one of the men.

"The case was built on very thin air," Moeller says about the indictments, which were handed down by an Austin grand jury convened by a US attorney. Ultimately, assistant US attorney Dan Mills prosecuted the case. "They wanted Hightower, obviously," Moeller says. "But his name never appeared on any of the documents. So they went to each of us, through our attorneys, and said, 'If you can give us Hightower, we'll let you go.' The truth is, we didn't think we had broken any laws, and we didn't know of any laws Hightower had broken. So we said, 'No. We'll have a trial.'"[31]

There almost *wasn't* a trial, when a judge dismissed most of the case in the spring of 1992. But the US Attorney's Office appealed the ruling and won in 1993, causing the charges to be reinstated. At the ensuing trial, which took place in September and October of 1993, the judge ruled Boyd and Koontz were incapable of standing trial due to their failing health, so the charges against them were dismissed. This left only the Hightower aides, who were found guilty, in part because the judge would not permit their defense to argue that the case was motivated by politics and because the evidence accumulated against Boyd and Koontz was allowed to be used against them, even though the two older men were not on trial. In late November, Moeller and McRae were given sentences of 27 months in federal prison; because he was older, Quicksall was given a slightly more lenient sentence—12 months. All three men ended up serving time, with reductions of their sentences for good behavior.

In Moeller's case, he spent almost two years in prison because he had been the state's signatory on a $10,000 contract with Boyd; that was his only connection to the case. The ordeal destroyed him financially, costing him $100,000 in legal fees, and tore apart his marriage, which ended in divorce. "Personally, it was devastating," he says. "It was a nightmare to go through. And it all happened because I signed a contract for an agency I worked for. By the same token, I understand why Rove is so successful. He's a take-no-prisoners kind of guy. In an interview once, he described Pete, Bill, and me as collateral damage—and that's just the way it goes."[32] Rove's plan worked, too: Hightower never again ran for public office.

In the end Moeller could see that investigations being carried out by Rampton usually involved high-profile Democrats. Besides Mark White, Rampton had investigated Hightower, Garry Mauro, and Bob Bullock, the lieutenant governor elected in 1990. (He would serve until 1998, just months before his death in June 1999.) Moeller learned that Rampton was pursuing Bullock from Bullock himself. "Bullock sent word he wanted to talk to me," Moeller says. "He had just become lieutenant governor. When I got to his office, he closed the door, sat down, and wrote something on a piece of paper. He said, 'I don't want you to say anything out loud. I haven't been in office long enough to know whether this place is bugged. I just want you to look at this name and let me know if it means anything to you.'"[33]

Bullock handed Moeller a piece of paper. On it, he had written "Greg Rampton."

Moeller told Bullock the name meant a great deal to him.

"Well, he's been after me, too," Bullock said.

4.

While Rove's candidate ended up winning the agriculture commissioner race in 1990, setting him up for higher offices in Texas (Perry would later become lieutenant governor and then governor), Rove still had not broken through to become what he wanted to be: the dominant political consultant in the state, the first move in making himself a player on the national scene. An episode that indicated just how unimportant Rove remained in national Republican politics, not to mention how petty and vindictive he could be in his business dealings, unfolded in 1992 as George H. W. Bush was running for reelection against Bill Clinton.

Because Ross Perot was running as a third-party candidate, the race was going to be unpredictable. So the decision was made to replicate the Victory committees established in select states in 1988, a concept that had worked so well for Bush the first time around. Once again, the flagship Victory committee would be in Texas, and to head it up Bush chose Rob Mosbacher Jr., the son of Robert Mosbacher, who was not only one of Bush's closest friends but also had been his secretary of commerce. Like any political operation, Victory '92 in Texas had a number of contracts with various consultants, but two were lucrative. One was the direct-mail contract; the other was for fund-raising mailings. The direct-mail contract was the preferred one, since the fee was large and did not depend on recipient response. The fund-raising contract was less desirable, because the fee was determined by the amount of money raised from the mailing. That sum could be larger or smaller than expected, depending on a number of factors often not under the control of the campaign.

Victory '92 in Texas awarded the more appealing direct-mail contract to Campaign Services Group, a company owned by John Weaver—who arguably was still the most influential political consultant in the state despite Rove's attempt to slander him on election night in 1988. Weaver and Rove had not been on good terms since then. The less desirable fund-raising contract was given to Rove + Company, which, according to sources familiar with the campaign, infuriated Rove.

Rove decided he was going to get even for not being awarded the better contract. His move would foreshadow similar ones in the future. He called syndicated columnist Robert Novak and told him Mosbacher was going to be fired from Victory '92 in Texas and replaced by Phil Gramm. There was no truth to the story, but Rove didn't care. To verify the story, Novak called Mark Sanders, the director of communications for Victory '92 in Texas. When Novak told him what Rove had said, Sanders denied it emphatically.[34]

"Well, Mr. Novak, you are wrong," Sanders said.

"Nope, I'm right, and I'm going with it."

When Sanders asked Novak for the name of his source, Novak did not hesitate to tell him who it was: Karl Rove.

Despite the campaign's repeated denials, Novak ran the story in his syndicated column. "A secret meeting of worried Republican power brokers in Dallas last Sunday reflected the reality that George Bush is in serious trouble in trying to carry his adopted state," the column stated before it called the campaign a "bust" and said Phil Gramm had taken away Mosbacher's authority to run the committee. Novak added that the meeting was attended by "political consultant Karl Rove, who had been shoved aside by Mosbacher."[35]

Most of the Texas papers that carried Novak's column refused to print this particular one since the campaign had issued denials before the story appeared. When Mosbacher learned the source of the story, which *did* run in papers outside of Texas, he fired Rove. For all intents and purposes, Rove's involvement with the 1992 Bush campaign came to an end.

Rove's fortunes began to change in 1993. In the wake of George H. W. Bush's loss in 1992, his oldest son began making plans to do what he had wanted to do in 1990: run for governor of Texas. Starting in August 1993, George W. Bush put together the team he hoped would take him to victory. His campaign manager would be Joe Allbaugh, an old and trusted friend. His director of communications would be Karen Hughes, a local television news broadcaster who had ventured into politics, becoming the Texas press coordinator for the Reagan–Bush campaign in 1984. Finally, as his political strategist, Bush chose Rove. These three aides—Allbaugh, Hughes, and Rove—would make up what became known as Bush's Iron Triangle.

It's not clear why Bush chose Rove to be his political point person. It may have boiled down to the fact that, because Rove had had conflicts with his father's campaigns in the past, Bush felt that, if given the opportunity, Rove would be loyal to him. Bush often brought into his inner circle people who had had disagreements with his father while distancing himself from those who had been close to his father in the past. There had been, and always would be, an unspoken competition between the father and son. More than likely, Rove was aware of that conflict and knew how to play the wedge in his favor.

As Bush headed into 1994, running against the popular incumbent, Ann Richards, Rove was not only orchestrating the Bush gubernatorial campaign, he was also trying to solidify Bush's base of support within the Republican Party in Texas. Here, Rove encountered more than his share of problems, since Tom Pauken, one of the pivotal Republicans in the state, did not endorse Bush or his politics and did not intend to allow Rove to maneuver Bush into a party takeover without resistance. That summer, Pauken ran for chairman of the Republican Party in Texas, much to Rove's dismay.

"They put Congressman Joe Barton in the race against me," Pauken says. "Karl was doing a lot of the negative stuff on me—as usual from afar. He's got his favorite reporters. It's the old story. But the race for the chairmanship occurs at the convention. Money doesn't matter. We were heavily outspent. But all of the convention delegates are there and you are able to work the grass roots. Karl had some reporter put out that I was fired from the Reagan administration, which could not be further from the truth. He had a person working for the Fort Worth paper who wrote that piece. It was absolutely untrue, but that never stopped Karl. Even so, I beat them two to one at the convention.

"When I became chairman of the Texas Republican Party that summer, the first thing I did was fire Karl Rove. Karl was the chief political consultant to the party, handling all of the direct mail, and Karen Hughes was the executive director. I fired her next. But I knew what Karl was up to. One of the reasons I ran was because the political consultants were running the party. We've got to get back to talking about ideas and standing for principles. These people are too much in the driver's seat. It's not a new phenomenon, but it's gotten worse with the Karl Roves of the world.

"So Karl quickly moved to cut off our money at the state party. I was viewed as the last independent holdout to Bush and Rove's control of Texas. I wasn't a loyal Bushie. I wasn't a crazy either. They tried to tag me as a religious nut, but I'm actually a Reagan–Goldwater conservative. I came out of the Goldwater tradition."[36]

Bush may not have had the support of the leadership of the Republican Party in Texas, but Rove did not let that stop him from strategizing a formidable campaign for governor. In that race, Bush ran on four issues: welfare reform, public school reform, juvenile justice reform, and tort reform. For much of the campaign, experts gave him no chance. After all, he was running against a woman who had become a folk hero not only in Texas but around the country—a grandmother who had used her keynote address at the 1988 Democratic National Convention to catapult herself into the Texas governorship. But Rove kept Bush on message, never allowing him to stray off the point. Bush rarely, if ever, talked about anything other than the four issues on which he was running.

"Bush ran one of the most disciplined races I've ever seen," says Earl Black, a professor of political science at Rice University and an expert on the politics of the South. "He had experience from his father's presidential campaigns. He spent time organizing in the suburban areas— Republican strongholds. He then went out to the small towns, particularly in West Texas. Most important, he didn't attack Ann Richards, even though there was a history of her attacking his father, until the last 10 days. And then he didn't attack her but linked her to Bill Clinton, who was unpopular in Texas."[37]

Bush himself may not have attacked Richards, but, in a move Rove had all but perfected and would use frequently in the future, Bush surrogates went out and attacked Richards for him. On one occasion, Bill Ratliff, a Bush supporter and a Rove client who was a state senator, called a press conference in Mount Pleasant, located in the heart of conservative East Texas, at which he announced his concern over the number of lesbians Richards had working for her. Before long, an organized whisper campaign was underway suggesting that Richards herself was a lesbian. One push call asked voters if they would be "more or less likely to vote for Governor Richards if [they] knew her staff is dominated by lesbians."[38] Divorced for years, Richards had never remarried; this, her appointment of gay people to government jobs, and her close friendships with strong-willed, independent-thinking women seemed to leave her open to accusations that she herself might be gay. That she was *not* was beside the point. Rove had learned long ago that it is impossible to prove a negative, so the whisper campaign about Richards went into high gear. How could Richards prove she was not a lesbian? "We thought [Rove] was behind [the whisper campaign]," Richards spokesperson Chuck McDonald later told *Texas Monthly*. "A concerted, ongoing drumbeat of criticism that Ann Richards is gay or likes gays or hangs out with gays— there is only one source ultimately to generate and contribute to feed that beast."[39] A Richards staffer says, "The whisper campaign about Ann being a lesbian, totally untrue, was harmful to us. None of us knew at the time that Karl's father was gay, but if we *had* known I'm not sure how we could have used it. Karl made sure his smears were always carried out by a third party, never himself, and certainly never his candidate."[40]

Maybe it was Bush's disciplined campaign, maybe it was the whisper campaign, maybe it was a combination of Bush running an almost flawless campaign and Richards sometimes appearing as if she were so exhausted by the ugliness of the race that she just wanted it to be over—whatever the reason, on election day in November 1994, even as Richards enjoyed an approval rating in the low 60s, she lost to Bush with 46 percent versus 54 percent. It was a stunning victory for Bush, and an even more stunning loss for Richards. The only race more shocking on that night was Jeb Bush's loss in his race for governor of Florida. Immediately, the pundits began to try to figure out how Jeb's brother—the one who was supposed to lose to the folk hero—had won in Texas.

"I didn't think W. would win in 1994," one Republican insider says. "I thought Jeb would win and W. would lose. Jeb was a better candidate. He was a real conservative. He seemed to be running a better campaign and George was Curious George. Jeb ran a real hard-right campaign, and maybe he overshot the runway a little. But the Republican tide was rising there then. It was rising around the country, and Bush the candidate exceeded expectations. Richards had branded him "Shrub," and everybody thought he was an idiot and when they saw him he wasn't an idiot. In fact, he was a pretty likeable guy. He proved that likeability still matters in politics. People would meet him and say, 'He's not a shrub, and you're pretty shrill, lady.' Plus, Richards had appointed all of these lesbians to all these positions. She went out of her way to put women in positions, which was way over the top to your average Texan. Richards did it to herself."[41]

A second person emerged from the victory a winner: Karl Rove. Finally, after toiling in the party for two decades, after living in the shadows of colleagues like Atwater and Weaver who had become more successful, after enduring his share of defeats, Rove had done it. He had run a campaign that ended in a win that meant something not only in Texas, but also on the national level. For no sooner had Bush won than he became a national figure, the focus of presidential speculation. Rove was a victor, too, even if it had taken a former president's son running in the former president's home state to pull off the win. "Rove lost a lot more races than he won," Garry Mauro says. "He was a failure long before he was a success. The advantage he had was that he had unlimited resources with Bush. I don't think he would have beat Richards if he didn't have a former president's son running. What would he have done with a normal candidate? He did have normal candidates and he'd [gotten] his ass kicked."[42]

The win went to Rove's head. Before long, he was doing what most angered Bush: trying to insinuate himself into the spotlight that Bush believed belonged solely to him. While Rove never left Rove + Company to join the governor's staff, he had complete access to him and often attended planning sessions and staff meetings as if he were on the state payroll. He wasn't, but he remained a consultant. Bush's political action committee paid Rove + Company $6,000 per month. Another Rove client was Philip Morris USA, which paid him $3,000 per month—an arrangement that would later cause controversy when the state became embroiled in a lawsuit involving the tobacco industry. But early in Bush's first term as governor, it was not Rove's client list that got him in trouble, it was his love of publicity. Rove made himself available to the press one time too many and felt Bush's wrath as a result.

"George Bush told me that he fired Karl Rove but that he hired him back two or three days later," says Mickey Herskowitz, a longtime friend of the Bush family. "The reason Bush fired him was because Rove took credit for something publicly that Bush had done. Rove couldn't resist telling a story to a writer and making himself into the hero of the story, which he had done on [an occasion] involving a piece of legislation. That's why Bush fired him, at least for a few days. This was early on, after Bush was elected governor in 1994. They weren't close yet. It took a while for them to become reliant on each other, dependent on each other. Maybe he just didn't talk to Rove for a while and then took him back after he apologized, but the way he related it to me was he fired him."[43]

Bush may have been elected governor, but he still didn't have a lock on the Republican Party in Texas, which annoyed Rove and the rest of Bush's inner circle. Pauken was defiant of Bush, whom he did not consider to be a true conservative in the tradition of Goldwater and Reagan. He also disliked Rove. Frustrating Rove even more, Pauken ran again for chairman of the Republican Party in Texas in 1996—and won.

"I was reelected by a wide margin," Pauken says, "but there was more drama at the convention. Rove had it wired for Bush to be the chairman of the delegation to the Republican National Convention"—where the party would nominate Robert Dole as its presidential candidate—"and Dick Weinhold, the head of the Texas Christian Coalition, to be the vice chairman. Normally, it would have been the chairman of the party who would be the chairman of the delegation and the governor would be the honorary chairman. They were trying to control the convention in 1996 because they had in mind 2000 and running for president. They wanted to showcase Bush.

"So they nominated Bush and Weinhold at the state party convention. Then someone nominated me to be chairman of the delegation and all hell broke loose. We took a recess and all these Bush advisers came up and said, 'You can't stand against the governor. You've got to step down.' Others said, 'You are supposed to be the chairman of the delegation. You can't let the Bush people control this.' So I finally decided, 'I'll leave the room but I'll stand for election.' I won overwhelmingly. All the Bush people were on their phones like you wouldn't believe!"[44]

So Bush did not serve as chairman of the Texas delegation to the national convention. Pauken officially cast the votes from Texas for Dole. But there was additional drama concerning the Dole nomination. Though it was not known at the time, the Dole campaign had approached Bush to see if he would be willing to subject himself to a background check, which was necessary for his name to be put on the short list of people Dole was considering for his running mate.

"Early on, I dealt with Karl some during the 1996 race as we were putting the campaign together," says Scott Reed, Dole's campaign manager. "I sought advice on what to do in Texas, but Texas wasn't high on the priority list. He recommended the way to structure the campaign—where to go, the order to do things, basic information you get from governors on how to win a state. Then I called Rove in the late spring or early summer after we had won the nomination to see if W. would be interested in being considered to be on the ticket as vice president. Dole and I decided that I should reach out to Karl to see if W. wanted to be vetted. We ended up vetting five or six guys, and they have to cooperate to be vetted by filling out papers and things. Karl's reaction was to take a pass because W. wasn't really ready for national politics. Now, they may have concluded we were going to lose and they didn't want to be included in it, but most first-term governors are not ready. Fast-forward to 1999 and W. made his first move into national politics when he traveled outside of Texas to give a major speech, and it was a disaster. Now *that* was four years later. Rove was right."[45]

⇌

In 1998, Rove finally got rid of a political enemy in Texas—Tom Pauken. "In 1998, I ran for attorney general," Pauken says, "and Rove got Barry

Williamson in the race and John Cornyn in the race, but Cornyn was his man. Cornyn is a wholly owned subsidiary of Karl Rove. Rove worked for Cornyn. They got Williamson to do the negative third-party stuff on me. Before you knew it, I was in third place behind Cornyn and Williamson. They attacked me for being anti-Bush. They got Dave McNeeley to do a nasty column and circulated that in other papers and the mail. TV and radio attacked me for being anti-Bush. It was trashy stuff, personal stuff. Williamson spent more money attacking me than I spent in my entire campaign. They were very concerned I might end up being attorney general. They succeeded. Cornyn won. Rove beat me in the race, not Cornyn. I would be in political exile after that."[46]

The Cornyn race was not the only one Rove won in 1998. In running for reelection, Bush had as his opponent Garry Mauro, perhaps the one Democrat with statewide name appeal who was willing to put himself up as a sacrificial lamb against Bush, who had turned out to be one of the most popular governors Texas had ever had. With an approval rating hovering consistently around 70 percent, Bush did not even need a platform to run on. He was running merely on being who he was. His topics were limited to slogans. He spent many stump speeches imploring teenagers to wait until marriage before they had sex, even though he himself was known for his wild partying and womanizing during what could only be described as a wayward youth.

Whatever Bush did, under Rove's watchful eye, it worked beyond expectations. Bush had become so popular that even Democrats were endorsing him. George Christian, press secretary for none other than Lyndon Johnson, supported Bush, as did Bob Bullock, the Democrat who had worried that his office was bugged. Bullock endorsed Bush—and he was godfather to one of Mauro's daughters! Only diehards like Liz Carpenter, the press secretary for Lady Bird Johnson, were holdouts. "G.W. is extremely likable," Carpenter said. "The Bushes all have good manners and great civility. But they don't have a lot of vision. Anyway, I'm a Bible-thumping, foot-washing, full-immersion Democrat who can never bring myself to vote for a Republican."[47] The election was not close. Bush defeated Mauro 69 percent to 31 percent.

At age 48, Rove was on the brink. After his lopsided reelection win, George W. Bush became a viable candidate for president. Since his childhood, Rove had longed for the day when he could step onto the national political stage and take his place as a player. Now he was on the verge of doing just that. All of the failures and disappointments would be behind him. At present, he had to focus on how he was going to transform a governor who had extraordinary skills as a retail politician but virtually no experience as a statesman, a scholar, or an expert on world affairs into a candidate the Republican Party could endorse. On this issue, Rove would have some help. After the scandals of the Clinton administration, the American public seemed eager for a candidate who embraced moral values and personal integrity. Somehow—and it would be mostly Rove's doing—the public would lose sight of the fact that on both of these defining issues Bush had no more credibility than Clinton. With Rove's handling, Bush would be packaged in such a way that voters bought the myth. Before Rove was done, Bush would look like the superior choice to Clinton's vice president, Al Gore, even though on almost every vital trait—intelligence, verbal skills, knowledge of world events, diplomacy, character, integrity, truthfulness—Bush was considered by most to be inferior.

CHAPTER FOUR

THE SOON-TO-BE PRESIDENT
OF THE UNITED STATES

1.

Years after the fact, Karl Rove would contend that it was at sometime in 1995, once Bush had begun to go about his duties as governor of Texas, that Rove realized Bush might truly be presidential material. Specifically, Rove was impressed with Bush's ability to work with the Democrats who controlled much of the state government. If Bush could get along with Bob Bullock, one of the state's legendary Democratic figures, he would be able to play well on the national level. Rove began to have Bush read books like *The Dream and the Nightmare,* Myron Magnet's attack on the freewheeling attitudes of the 1960s and the legacy of the counterculture, in an effort to broaden his understanding of policy and politics. Rove also introduced Bush to the writings of Marvin Olasky, an opponent of the welfare system who felt the private sector could take care of the nation's less fortunate better than the federal government. It was Olasky who inspired the Bush brain trust, headed by Rove, to develop the concept of "compassionate conservatism"—an idea that Bush, with the religious beliefs he said he acquired after giving up alcohol in 1986 at the age of 40, could endorse.

For his part, since his father had been president, it is hard to imagine that Bush had not considered running for president himself long before he started working well with Democrats as governor of Texas, especially as he had become one of his father's closest advisers. However, to hear Rove talk, it was Rove who deemed that Bush possessed what in the business is referred to as "presidential timber" and also Rove who began grooming him to become a national candidate. The logic went that George W. Bush would not have existed as a presidential candidate without Karl Rove.

Regardless of who decided that Bush had what it took to be president, there was no question that Rove did orchestrate the lengthy buildup to the actual run. In 1998, as a way to ensure Bush won reelection as Texas governor by impressive numbers, Rove determined that Bush should focus on that race exclusively, rather than beginning to set the stage for a national candidacy. So when a national journalist came to Texas to write about Bush as a possible presidential candidate in 2000, he was told Bush would conduct no interviews with national reporters, only those representing Texas publications.

Then, after pulling off his expected landslide victory, Rove spent the early weeks of 1999 organizing Bush's version of President William McKinley's "front porch" campaign strategy by having an endless stream of Republican operatives and elected officials trek to Austin to meet with Bush and offer their support for a presidential bid. "I believe it was beef," one dreamy-eyed Republican from North Carolina told a reporter after leaving a meet-and-greet luncheon at the governor's mansion, "but I was so excited by seeing the kind of candidate that we haven't had in a long time, I didn't pay much attention to what I was eating."[1] Another Republican, this one from Iowa, gushed, "After meeting George Bush, you know that if he runs, he will be the next president of the United States."[2]

Bush would stay in Texas until May, the national press was told, because he would not leave the state, not even to stump in Iowa or New Hampshire, while the Texas legislature was in session. At the same time, Rove also continued to block access to Bush by the national press. In early

March 1999, all national reporters were held at bay—a CNN camera crew was halted at the gate to the grounds of the governor's mansion—while Bush and his wife Laura informally met with local reporters to tell them that within the week, he would announce the formation of a presidential exploratory committee. Bush held his press gaggle in order to keep his promise to Texas voters that if he decided to run for president, he would tell them first. "I began to feel more comfortable inside," Bush told the Texas media that day as he and Laura sat on patio chairs behind the governor's mansion, a warm Texas breeze whipping through downtown Austin. "I began to get a sense of peace inside my soul and my heart." Even in informal chats, even at this early stage of what was not yet a campaign, Bush projected an air of the religious about what he was doing.

As it turned out, Rove was able to keep Bush away from the national media for much of 1998 and the first part of 1999—a brilliant strategy since, on one of Bush's first forays outside Texas to give a speech in Indiana, his performance was hesitant and amateurish. By shielding Bush from the national press, Rove kept well guarded the secret that Bush was not ready for coverage beyond Texas, where reporters had rarely been critical of him since he had started running for governor in 1993. But a Rove blunder probably forced the Bush team to announce earlier than planned that an exploratory committee was being formed. On February 26, Rove told a reporter from the *New York Times* on the telephone that "there's no doubt he's going to file the exploratory committee," adding, "we haven't been Mario-ized"—an apparent reference to New York governor Mario Cuomo's inability to make a decision about entering the presidential race in 1992.[3] Rove's premature revelation irritated Bush so badly that he told the Texas press corps on the day the *Times* story broke that the formal announcement would be made when *he* wanted to make it—not when *Rove* wanted him to. "There was a tension between Rove and Bush from the start," says George Shipley, a Democratic strategist in Texas.

"Rove always felt he was more important than he was; in his mind the race was all about him. Bush had to remind him on occasion that, while he did need him and need him badly, *he* was the candidate, not Rove."[4]

With the formation of the Bush exploratory committee in early March 1999, the campaign started to follow Rove's master plan: Keep Bush out of the glare of the national media spotlight, secure an endless string of endorsements, and unleash the most effective fund-raising machine in political history—a cash-generating operation so efficient it would make Mark Hanna's financing of the McKinley campaign a century before look like a small-time operation. It worked, too. In the first four months, the fund-raisers brought in $36.3 million—more than any other presidential candidate had ever amassed in a time period four times as long. Between early March and late June, contributors sent Bush some $2.3 million a week. The sheer number of contributors—nearly 80,000— stunned even seasoned fund-raisers. Moreover, the Bush fund-raisers had not followed a traditional model. Instead of setting up headquarters in each state, they had run the entire operation out of Austin. "They just started faxing out letters asking for money," one prominent Republican says. "I didn't think they had enough fax machines in Austin to send out the number of letters they'd need. But apparently they did."[5]

There would be people to pay back, of course: those in Big Oil, Little Oil, Big Insurance, the tort reform movement, the corporate world in general. "There will be bunk beds in the Lincoln Bedroom if Bush is elected president," Craig McDonald, director of Texans for Public Justice, a group that monitors campaign contributions and corporate influence in Texas politics, said at the time. "There'll be folks there from oil and gas, the utilities industry, the insurance business, and the tort reform movement. People don't know it yet, but Bush is not a moderate when it comes to business versus the consumer. He's a radical, pro-corporate Republican."[6]

The success of the fund-raising effort should not have been surprising. After all, in the past Bush had proved he could raise money. In 1994, in his race against Ann Richards, he had amassed $16 million—an enormous sum considering how popular Richards was. Then, in 1998, Bush had brought in an even more impressive $25 million, despite the fact that he needed nowhere near that amount to defeat his opponent, Garry Mauro, who was consistently nearly 40 percentage points down in the opinion polls, the margin by which he lost the election. Over two campaigns Bush had raised $41 million—the most money ever accumulated by a candidate running for governor.

With the kind of cash he had flowing into his presidential campaign, there was an air of inevitability about Bush winning the nomination. Since all of the money in the Republican coffers was going to Bush, he *had* to be the nominee.

"You know, a lot of that early success was inheriting the father's fund-raising apparatus," Republican strategist Ed Rollins says. "Rove knew the game well. And, I think, he was blessed by [there being] no serious challengers to Bush. There were a lot of governors who thought of themselves as more significant than Bush was in 2000, but Karl—and, certainly, through Bush—sort of bluffed everybody out of the game by saying, 'You know, we're going to raise $35 million; we're going to raise $50 million.' And they went on to do it. People like George Pataki and Frank Keating and others, who were seriously thinking about running for president, realized they could not match the money. Finally, Rove took the fact that national polls were showing Bush [had] great name identification, which turned out, much of it, to be his father's. Rove staked out their position: We're the inevitable nominee and we'll crush anybody who challenges us."[7]

As the money came in, Rove had the luxury of keeping Bush off the national political stage, and when Bush did emerge as a presidential candidate, he could control the circumstances in a way few candidates are allowed. Officially, Bush surfaced from his long period of guarded silence in June 1999, when on a beautiful sunny day in Iowa, he announced he was running for president.

$$\equiv$$

The day had all the trappings of a perfectly planned media moment. Flying in that morning on a campaign plane named Great Expectations, Bush arrived in Cedar Rapids to appear, as one paper noted, "on a stage piled with bales of hay, a shiny red forklift positioned at his back . . . at a barbecue set amid cornfields"[8]—a made-for-television tableaux that had been carefully vetted by Rove, as was Bush's speech. "I'm coming here today to tell you this: I'm running for President of the United States. There is no turning back. And I intend to be the next President of the United States."[9]

Bush then addressed what would be two dominant themes in his campaign. "My first goal is to usher in the responsibility era," Bush said, "an era that stands in stark contrast to the last few decades, when the culture has clearly said: If it feels good, do it. If you've got a problem, blame someone else. Each of us must understand we are responsible for the choices we make in life. We're responsible for the children we bring into the world. We're responsible to love our neighbor as we want to be loved ourselves." Then Bush hit his big note: compassionate conservatism. "You've heard me talk about compassionate conservatism," he told the crowd that day in Iowa. "I know this approach has been criticized. But why? Is compassion beneath us? Is mercy below us? Should our party be led by someone who boasts of a hard heart? I know Republicans across the country are generous of heart. I am confident the American people view compassion as a noble calling. The calling of a nation where the strong are just and the weak are valued."

Rove had expertly directed the early phase of the Bush campaign, and throughout the summer and into the fall he continued to run it with ironclad control. Bush was rarely allowed to go off script. Voters were hard-pressed to find moments when they could have one-on-one exchanges with him. His campaign appearances were carefully handled and he made as few of them as possible. Meanwhile, the endorsements and the cash piled up, and the campaign enjoyed its front-runner status. It seemed inevitable that Bush would win the nomination. There was only one flaw with this approach: It did not necessarily fly with voters, especially those in New Hampshire. Trouble was looming for Bush—trouble created by the very way that Rove was running the campaign. Keeping Bush as guarded and scripted as he was ended up making voters suspicious about why Bush was being so carefully handled. This could have proven fatal for Bush in New Hampshire.

It was not the first problem the campaign would encounter. To understand the mind-set Rove and the others in charge of the campaign had, all that was necessary was to examine the way they had dealt with a book that would be Bush's official campaign document—a book written for Bush by a close friend of his family's, someone Bush's father trusted so much that he would later recruit him to write *his* father's biography.

2.

The ordeal had begun in the spring of 1999, when it was becoming apparent that George W. Bush was going to run for president. The problem was created by Bush himself, acting on his own, and in the end it was solved by Rove and Karen Hughes. It started when Bush was approached by Mickey Herskowitz, a fixture of the writing scene in Texas who had written a sports column for upward of four decades and had coauthored numerous books with well-known Texans, among them Dan Rather and John Connally. Herskowitz had become close friends with Bush's father because of their mutual interest in baseball, and he had known George W. since Bush was a teenager. No doubt that was why Bill Adler, a literary agent working with the blessing of New York publisher William Morrow and Company, had approached Herskowitz. Morrow wanted to publish Bush's autobiography but did not have access to Bush or his inner circle. Would Herskowitz be interested in co-authoring the book, and, if so, could he get to Bush?

As it happened, Herskowitz *was* interested, and he did have access to Bush. He called the governor's office in Austin, explained to a staffer why he needed to talk to Bush and was told that Bush would get in touch with him. Before long, Herskowitz got a call from Bush's secretary explaining that Bush could not guarantee seeing him but that Herskowitz was welcome to fly to Austin and try to fit a meeting into the governor's schedule. So Herskowitz traveled to Austin and checked into the Capitol Marriott, where he waited for Bush to call. Finally, at eight o'clock at night on the day he had flown in, the phone rang. "Mickey, this is the governor," Bush said. "Tell me more about your idea." Herskowitz described the idea to Bush—Bush's autobiography would be written by Bush with Herskowitz—and Bush didn't hesitate. "Let's do it," he said, without discussing the project with anyone on his staff. It was Bush's decision, made on the spot. Bush didn't hesitate because he felt the book might counterbalance some of the negative books he knew would be published in conjunction with his run for the presidency.

The next day, Herskowitz met with Bush in the governor's office. Together, they spoke with an editor at Morrow. Within hours, they had a deal. The advance for the book was said to have been $500,000; Bush and Herskowitz agreed to split all proceeds fifty-fifty.[10] Bush assured Herskowitz that, should anything happen, Bush would make sure Herskowitz was paid. "Mickey," Bush said flatly, "no matter what happens, you are going to get your money."

It took three months for the publisher and Bush's lawyers to work out a contract, but when they did both sides agreed to an August 1, 1999, deadline for fall publication. It stipulated that the book would be made up of 30 percent biographical material and 70 percent political material, meaning that the book would not be the revelatory autobiography Herskowitz had wanted, but instead more of a traditional campaign compendium. Still, in May 1999, as soon as the contract was signed, Herskowitz began to interview Bush in Austin, usually at the governor's mansion but occasionally at the governor's office in the statehouse. In all, there were at least a dozen in-depth interviews, probably as many as Bush would ever conduct with any print journalist.

In the interviews Herskowitz found that Bush was surprisingly candid, perhaps because there were no handlers present while they were talking. Bush explained in detail the complicated saga of his service in the National Guard, revealing that once he had moved to Alabama to work on a political campaign there, he had never reported for Guard duty because he had been "excused." Bush chronicled his frustrating efforts as an oilman in Texas and even went so far as to tell Herskowitz that he had "floundered" as a businessman. Bush discussed a number of subjects that were not going to be addressed in the book, and he spoke in an honest and unguarded way. Since Bush had control over the final edit of the book, Herskowitz knew that some of the better material might end up being left out. If Bush himself didn't edit it, his handlers, principal among them Rove, certainly would. Still, Herskowitz tried to get Bush to be as open as possible in the interviews, and Bush was.

On the topic of his father, Bush drew sharp distinctions, going so far as to say that if he had been in his father's position in 1991, after driving the Iraqi army out of Kuwait in the Gulf War, he would not have hesitated to push on to Baghdad and overthrow Saddam Hussein—a move his father had decided at the time was too risky. "In 1999," Herskowitz says, "Bush told me, 'If I had had the capital my father had in 1991, I guarantee you I would have gone into Baghdad. I would have taken care of Saddam Hussein.' He was contrasting his temperament to that of his father, whose temperament was more cautious. He was going out of his way to be critical of his dad, but he was saying he thought one of the mistakes his father made in terms of his reelection was his failure to use his political capital. He felt if his father had taken out Saddam Hussein, he would have been a hero forever."[11]

There was one subject that didn't come up often with Bush: his staff. Generally speaking, Bush didn't like to talk about the people who were advising him, including Rove. In fact, Rove was discussed only when Herskowitz brought up anything related to politics. While he would supply information about his life, Bush was vague about politics. Every time Herskowitz approached a political topic, Bush referred him to Rove. "In his own words," Herskowitz says, "Bush said he hadn't settled on his positions yet—choice versus abortion, welfare, free trade, the economy. He hadn't been primed and prepped on these things yet. He said, 'These things are still evolving and you can get this from Karl, when we've got them ready for you.'"

But once Herskowitz had finished interviewing Bush for the biographical portion of the book, he had a problem getting Rove to sit down and discuss the book's political chapters, which were key since the contract called for them to make up 70 percent of the book. While he was waiting for Rove, Herskowitz wrote chapters based on his interviews with Bush as well as information gleaned from published sources about Bush's political beliefs. Finally, the deadline was creeping up on Herskowitz, so he again asked for time with Rove to discuss Bush's political thinking. "Instead," Herskowitz says, "I got a box that I guess Karen Hughes asked one of the staff people to send me that was supposed to be loaded with political material I would find useful. What it turned out to be was a box of 200 speeches, but basically it was 5 core speeches Bush had given 40 times each—for Mother's Day, for the Battle of San Jacinto Day, for Texas Independence Day. So I called up and said the speeches were really useless to me. There was nothing in the speeches that illuminated the political beliefs of the governor or how he arrived at his political convictions. The speeches were stereotypes. He was for motherhood, apple pie, and Chevrolet. So I was told that Rove would fill in the blanks."

Herskowitz finally arranged to speak with Rove by telephone—an in-person meeting was impossible because Rove was heading off for a two-week vacation—and on the agreed-upon day Herskowitz called Rove's office at 10 o'clock in the morning and was told that Rove was in a meeting. He called an hour or so later—same answer. So he called at two, at four, at six—in total, eight times in one day. Rove was always in a meeting. Finally, at 10 o'clock that night, Rove's secretary said, "Oh, I'm sorry. You just missed him. He just drove off and left for his vacation."

"What happened to my interview?" Herskowitz asked.

"I'm so sorry," the secretary said. "He was just tied up all day getting things cleared off his desk before his vacation."

Because it was now nearing the end of June and Herskowitz had just over a month to meet the deadline to finish the book, he was frustrated. When he asked if Rove could call him from his vacation for an hour-long conversation, the secretary said he could not, because he was going to be unreachable by phone for two weeks.

It was never clear to Herskowitz why Rove had made himself unavailable for interviews for a book that had been endorsed by Bush himself. How could it be that Herskowitz had had such unencumbered access to the governor but could not get a single interview—not even on the telephone—with the governor's political consultant? Who was in charge here? Something about the process didn't make sense. After all, Herskowitz was under the assumption that a good book would serve Bush's best interests. It was Bush who had more to gain from the publication of the book than Herskowitz did.

Herskowitz had drafted 10 chapters and submitted them to the campaign. Apparently, some members of the staff—Herskowitz felt that Rove was one of them—were unhappy with the content, even though the information had come from Bush himself and often used Bush's exact wording. Bush could be charmingly honest about his shortcomings, and nowhere was he more candid than in his discussions about his failed businesses. Bush may have used the word *floundered* to describe his tenure as an oilman in Midland, but that word disturbed Bush's handlers. "I got a call from one of the campaign's lawyers," Herskowitz says, "stating emphatically, 'We do not consider the governor as having floundered in the oil business. We take the position that he built two oil companies and created equity for the shareholders before he sold them.'"[12]

The fact that the word *floundered* had been used not by Herskowitz but by Bush himself seemed lost on the campaign lawyer, who also did not seem to understand that, by the terms of the contract, the campaign had the right to do the final edit of the book. The lawyer appeared angry, and from what Herskowitz could tell, for some reason he was angry *with him*.

With Rove on vacation, Herskowitz concluded that the book could not be completed on time, at least not by him. Herskowitz decided that Rove and other handlers had become worried when they realized how freely Bush had talked with him about subjects they considered to be potentially harmful, such as Bush's National Guard service and his business career.

So when Herskowitz got a call from a campaign lawyer telling him to take a break from the book for a few days, he did, particularly since he had determined he could never meet his deadline without Rove's help. Finally, after he had not heard anything from the campaign for longer than he expected, Herskowitz called the publisher to find out the status of the project. The editor was surprised the campaign had not been in touch with Herskowitz and told him someone from the campaign would call him at once.

When the call came, it was from a lawyer telling Herskowitz that he was no longer working on the project and that he should destroy anything in his possession concerning the book. He was also told he was not to be in touch with the publisher again, even though it had been Herskowitz, not the Bush campaign, who had dealt with the publisher to begin with. Needless to say, Herskowitz was stunned.

Then he got yet another call, this one from a member of Bush's inner circle whom Herskowitz knew well. "Mickey," his friend said, "I shouldn't be making this call, but we had a meeting about you yesterday."

"Why on earth would you have a meeting about me?" Herskowitz asked his friend.

"They want to know how they were going to deal with the Mickey Herskowitz problem."

The Mickey Herskowitz problem? What *Mickey Herskowitz problem*? Herskowitz had had no idea he had *become* a problem. He had coauthored books with numerous public figures and had never had problems with any of them. Apparently, according to his friend, part of the "Mickey Herskowitz problem" would be solved by taking the book away from him and having Karen Hughes finish it. But that was not all they were up to. "Watch your back," the friend said to Herskowitz ominously.

Later that day, Herskowitz began to understand his friend's final comment when he heard the cover story the campaign was putting out to explain why Herskowitz had not finished the book. According to Herskowitz, the campaign told the national press corps that Hughes had replaced Herskowitz because Herskowitz had a drinking problem and had been unable to deliver the manuscript on deadline. That Herskowitz did not drink was unimportant, as was the truth that Herskowitz had not been able to finish the manuscript because Rove would not give him information on Bush's political beliefs and the process by which he had reached them.

Then, at seven o'clock on a Monday morning, as all of this was still unfolding, someone from the Bush campaign knocked on the front door of Herskowitz's home and, when Herskowitz answered, informed him that he had come to pick up all of his tapes, transcripts, and notes. The staffer retrieved the material from Herskowitz's study and left.

Hughes finished the manuscript, which was entitled *A Charge to Keep*. For her part, she did what was expected of her. Hughes wrote the book the campaign wanted, telling the "approved" version of Bush's life. In the end, perhaps it was Hughes, not Herskowitz, who had to write the book. She had served as a reliable mouthpiece for Bush in the past and would again in the future. To some, her devotion to Bush was unnerving. "I've obviously been lied to a lot by campaign operatives," conservative commentator Tucker Carlson would later say about Hughes, "but the striking thing about the way she lied was she knew I knew she was lying, and she did it anyway. There is no word in English that captures that. It almost crosses over from bravado into mental illness."[13]

When *A Charge to Keep* was published in November 1999, it sold extremely poorly, racking up fewer than 20,000 copies in sales, in part because the book offered no new insight into Bush or his political thinking. Hughes had rewritten many of Herskowitz's passages, and what was left could not be termed exciting prose. The campaign also chose that moment to collect a selection of Bush's speeches in a book, with a 50,000-copy print run, and to give the book for free to Bush supporters. Many months later, after the election, Bush let it be known what he thought of *A Charge to Keep*: "For those of you who haven't read the novel," he said, "some of it fiction, some of it nonfiction [sic]."[14]

As for Herskowitz, despite Bush's promise to make sure he was taken care of no matter what happened with his involvement in the project, he was never paid the full amount he was owed for his work. It was the first time he had ever been treated in such a way by a coauthor. When the book came out, Herskowitz did get a bread-and-butter note from Bush thanking him for getting the book started. Herskowitz would also carry with him the memories of his interviews with Bush and the informal time they had spent together. He recalled an incident that in retrospect was particularly illuminating, although it was just one of many that gave rare glimpses into the kind of person Bush really was.

⇌

One day Bush wanted Herskowitz to sit in on an interview he was to give to a local newspaper reporter. For the interview, Bush sat behind his desk in the governor's office. Herskowitz positioned himself in a corner, trying to be inconspicuous. From where he sat, Bush could look past the reporter to a wall of bookshelves filled with row upon row of books, but Bush tried to focus his attention on the reporter. As is the case with many local media people, the reporter, made nervous by her close proximity to the governor, wasn't exactly grilling Bush with hard-ball questions. Most of her questions were innocuous enough that Bush had no trouble answering them off the top of his head. He was dealing with her in the friendly, down-home style for which he had become famous. Finally, no doubt because Laura Bush had made literacy her main topic of interest as First Lady of Texas, the reporter turned to the topic of literature.

"So, Governor," the reporter said, "who is your favorite writer?"

For a moment, Bush looked stumped. A puzzled, deer-in-the-headlights look came over his face. Slowly, Bush looked around the room. Then he saw his answer.

THE SOON-TO-BE PRESIDENT OF THE UNITED STATES

"Mickey Herskowitz," Bush said suddenly.

There was nervous laughter in the room, followed by dead silence. That, apparently, was his answer.

"Well, Governor, what was the last book you read?"

Again, Bush appeared confused. At a loss for words, he gradually cocked his head slightly to one side so he could look at the spines of the books on the shelves behind the reporter—an odd angling of his head that Herskowitz could not help but notice. His head still tilted to one side, Bush answered the reporter.

"*Six Feet Six.*"

Herskowitz could see that that was the title of one of the books immediately behind the reporter.

"*Six Feet Six*," the reporter repeated.

"Yes."

"And what's the book about?"

Bush angled his head a bit more, as if he were having trouble making out what he needed to say next.

"The story of Sam Houston."

Sam Houston. Father of Texas. Legendary figure. It was just the sort of answer the reporter had hoped for.

"That's great," the reporter said. "So what did you take away from that book? What did you learn about Sam Houston?"

There was a long pause, a buildup. Then Bush said one word: "Big!"

The reporter waited—for anything else. A phrase, a thought, even a few more words. But that was it. That was all Bush had to say about one of the seminal figures in Texas history. Yes, that, believe it or not, was his answer. *Big!*

It was also the end of the interview.

Herskowitz knew this as well: What he had just witnessed was precisely what Rove did not want him to know about George W. Bush. It was the reason Rove had handled Bush the way he had until now and would for as long as he could in the future.

$$\rightleftharpoons$$

As it turned out, during the 2000 presidential race, there would be another controversy involving George W. Bush and a book about his life. Because of the nature of the Herskowitz book—a ghostwritten auto-biography—it was clear from the start that Bush and his aides, Rove among them, were involved in the project. The situation around the second book—a biography with which Bush was not going to cooperate—was murkier. Rove and other members of Bush's inner circle quietly participated in the project; their involvement would become part of an ensuing controversy. Over time, the episode would produce a headline-grabbing political scandal as well as its share of collateral damage—a discredited book, a destroyed life.

3.

In the fall of 1998, Richard Curtis, a Manhattan literary agent, placed a telephone call to one of his clients, J. H. Hatfield, an ambitious, highly productive writer who lived in Bentonville, Arkansas. Hatfield had been a good client for Curtis—not a blockbuster author with a string of best-sellers to his credit, but a conscientious worker who in a timely fashion could grind out entertainment books with titles like *Lost in Space: The Ultimate Unauthorized Trivia Challenge for the Classic TV Series* and *The Ultimate Unauthorized Star Wars Trilogy Trivia Challenge* or unau-thorized celebrity biographies such as those he had written about actors Patrick Stewart and Ewan McGregor.

By no means was Hatfield on the A list—or even the B or C lists—of respected journalists, but if he had to—and for the right amount of money, which didn't even have to be that much—he could knock out a publishable book on deadline. In the competitive world of New York publishing, Hatfield was a marketable commodity. So, when an editor at Thomas Dunne Books, an imprint of St. Martin's Press, concurred with Curtis that a quickie paperback campaign-style biography about the Republican Party's rising star, George W. Bush, might be lucrative, Curtis knew whom to call.

Hatfield, a balding, plump-cheeked, slightly built man of 40 who had a well-worn quality to him, was happy to get the chance to write a political biography, even one that would be a quickie paperback. Until now, he had produced books that were not taken seriously by the critics; a book about the Republicans' newest phenomenon was something else entirely. So Hatfield gladly agreed to write a proposal for the book. When Curtis submitted it, St. Martin's offered Hatfield a $25,000 advance with a deadline of May 1999. If the book sold well, Hatfield could collect royalties. Regardless, Hatfield needed the advance money; he and his wife Nancy, who came from a well-to-do Houston family, had recently married and decided to start a family.

Just as important, the book could elevate Hatfield into the league of writers who made a living from their writing. Few people outside of Bentonville knew it, but Hatfield had a regular day job for Wal-Mart as a security analyst, which involved investigating personnel and other situations that could threaten the retail chain. Hatfield was secretive about this part of his life. Then again, he was secretive in general, almost obsessively so. There were whole segments of his life—and one especially dark period—that he had not even told his wife about.

As soon as the book deal was set, Hatfield began interviewing people. Even though Bush was governor of Texas and his father had been president, Hatfield uncovered new information about Bush's early career in the oil business, which had been financed at first by a member of the bin

Laden family of Saudi Arabia (an uncle of Osama's) through an American investment banker; Bush's connection to the Bank of Credit and Commerce International (BCCI) scandal; the enormous profit he'd made from his modest ownership position in the Texas Rangers; and his wayward youth, defined by heavy drinking, rumored drug use, and conflicts with his father. Many of Hatfield's sources talked on the record, but some spoke only on background or off the record—a practice that is common in journalism. As Hatfield had hoped, the writing went smoothly, and in about eight months he completed a manuscript. He submitted it to St. Martin's in May 1999, on schedule.

Then, one day, Hatfield was sitting at the desk in his studio—a converted barn behind his main house—when he received a telephone call, the number for which was unlisted. Normally, when a journalist is doing research, he approaches many sources, but it is rare for a source to call a reporter unsolicited. That, however, was what happened. Listening intently, Hatfield heard a male voice say he was a close associate of Bush's and offer to meet with him, although he would not reveal his name. "I just want to get together with you and set you straight on some things," he said. "I don't want to push you on what to write, but I can make sure you are on the right track."[15]

Hatfield was game, so the two men decided to meet between Bentonville, situated in northwestern Arkansas, and the source's location in Texas. The place of their meeting would be Eufaula, Oklahoma, a town about 160 miles from Bentonville. Eufaula was known for its beautiful lake—their conversations would take place in a boat on the lake, it was decided—and for its criminal history. The home base of Frank and Jesse James, the town proudly announced in its advertising that legendary outlaw Belle Starr was buried nearby.

On the day of the first meeting, Hatfield woke up early. His wife, now pregnant, joked that he should carry a gun. Instead, Hatfield drove straight through to Eufaula. "To be honest," Hatfield later wrote, "I was more than a little timorous about going out in the middle of a lake on a boat with someone who obviously had his own agenda regarding my biography of Bush. . . . Although it now seems and proved to be ludicrous, one of the final scenes in *The Godfather: Part II*, in which Fredo Corleone is shot to death on a boat in Lake Tahoe, kept replaying over and over in my mind.

"At his request, I agreed never to identify [my source] or his actual position in the Bush campaign to anyone. Our discussions while fishing for bass for three days on Lake Eufaula would be only to confirm information that had been previously obtained elsewhere and to add some perspective to the manuscript I had already delivered to my publisher. . . . More importantly, he never told me anything that was incorrect, nor did he try to inflate his knowledge or show off his importance in the Bush circle of advisers. In addition to having access to the Texas governor's office and the presidential exploratory committee, my source had known Bush since the years he lived in Midland. He seemed genuinely committed to helping me 'fill in the blanks' in Bush's life and in establishing the truth where other journalists had erred in their reporting."[16]

As it happened, Hatfield knew who the source was the moment he saw him. He recognized him from photographs. Therefore, Hatfield knew whom he was talking to and the source *knew* he knew. The source, whom Hatfield would call his "Eufaula connection," was Karl Rove.

≈

Over the course of three days, Hatfield covered a number of subjects with Rove, among them Bush's connection to the BCCI scandal; his association with the bin Laden family; and Bush's various debacles in business, to name a few. But a second transaction was also taking place, whether or not Hatfield knew it. Rove was learning the content of Hatfield's book, which was entitled *Fortunate Son: George W. Bush and the Making of an American President.*

Soon, St. Martin's had decided to elevate the book from a paperback to a hardcover, Hatfield's first. Hatfield was elated, especially after St. Martin's started reporting to Richard Curtis the number of advance orders they had received. When St. Martin's wanted to move up the publication date of *Fortunate Son* to compete with another Bush biography, Hatfield was all for it. Advance orders had hit 70,000 copies.

Then, in August, the online news magazine *Salon* ran a gossip column item by Amy Reiter about the buzz in political circles over an anonymous e-mail that said that "back in the late '60s or early '70s, George W. [Bush] 'was ordered by a Texas judge to perform community service in exchange for expunging his record showing illicit drug use' and that this service was performed at the Martin Luther King Jr. Community Center in Houston." The story had Bush arrested in Harris County, Texas, for cocaine possession and Bush's father using his political connections to get a judge to alter his son's record in exchange for performing community service. If true, the story could severely damage Bush's campaign.

The e-mail, the source of which was never identified, only intensified rumors about Bush's past. Bush had admitted to making mistakes in his youth ("when I was young and irresponsible, I was young and irresponsible"), but rumors that he had engaged in much more than heavy drinking—which he acknowledged—were fueled by his repeated failure to state that he could pass an FBI background check prior to 1974. On August 18, Bush stated that he had not used drugs in the past seven years, saying of the timetable: "As I understand it, the current form asks the question, did somebody use drugs within the last seven years? And I will be glad to answer that. And the answer is no."[17] But when the time period was extended to beyond 25 years, Bush refused to answer.

The charges of drug use had dogged Bush, and the anonymous e-mail egged reporters on. The *Salon* gossip item gave the story new intensity. Even though *Fortunate Son* was on the fast track, St. Martin's wanted Hatfield to address the drug allegations. So it was determined that Hatfield would do so in an afterword. In researching the claims of Bush's cocaine use, Hatfield pieced together what he believed was a plausible scenario. In 1972, Bush had performed community service in one of the lower-income wards of Houston at an organization called Project PULL— *Salon* had gotten the venue for the community service wrong—so it would make sense that he had performed the service in exchange for having a drug arrest dismissed. To confirm the story, Hatfield called one of his background-only sources, a friend of Bush's from his undergraduate days at Yale University. The friend verified the story.

After talking to a second background-only source, an informal adviser to Bush who also confirmed the story, Hatfield tried to speak to members of Bush's presidential campaign—traveling press secretary Scott McClellan, media travel coordinator Megan Moran, press secretary Mindy Tucker, and Karen Hughes—none of whom would talk. Finally, Hatfield said, he called the Eufaula connection. Hatfield didn't make the move lightly, for at the end of their three days together in Oklahoma Hatfield had agreed that, unless there was an emergency, he would not be in touch again.

"I wish you hadn't called me," Hatfield later reported Rove as saying when he answered the phone.[18]

"You told me never to contact you again unless it was important," Hatfield said he told Rove, "and I think you would agree that this qualifies as important."

According to Hatfield, Rove said he would call him back in 30 minutes and hung up. When he did call back—precisely on time—he was livid. "On the boat," Hatfield contended Rove said, "you arrogantly told me you had already finished the book, but if I wanted to provide the missing pieces of truth, you would ask all the questions and I would do all the answering. Isn't that correct?"

Hatfield reported that he offered a "lame" acknowledgment that Rove was right.

"Then how the fuck did you let the Project PULL part of his life slip past you? If you were half-ass as good a biographer as you think you are, you would have caught that flagrant inconsistency, asked me about it, and in the process I would have confirmed the truth three months ago."

After berating him, again according to Hatfield, Rove confirmed the story.

With the story now substantiated—at least in his mind—Hatfield polished off the afterword, sent it to St. Martin's, and awaited the publication of his book, scheduled for October 19, 1999. By the time Hatfield flew to New York to start the publicity campaign, the first printing had grown to 90,000 copies—a number big enough for the book to hit the *New York Times* bestseller list.

⇌

On Wednesday, October 20, Hatfield happened to be at St. Martin's offices in the Fuller Flatiron building when a telephone call came in from Pete Slover of the *Dallas Morning News*. Slover had gotten the publisher on the phone and asked an odd question, so the call was forwarded to Hatfield. Now Slover asked him the question: Was he the same James Howard Hatfield who had hired a hit man in Dallas in the late 1980s to kill the manager of a business he had once worked for—a crime for which he had served 5 years of a 15-year prison sentence?

Hatfield was so stunned he did something he said he later regretted: He lied. No, he said, feigning shock, he was not that J. H. Hatfield; it must be a case of mistaken identity. Then, he settled on an aggressive defense—he would blame the Bush campaign for trying to smear him. "Doesn't it sound a little bit weird to you," Hatfield told Solver, "that all of a sudden, the guy that's accusing potentially the next president of the United States of having his record expunged, all of a sudden miraculously has a record himself in the state of Texas? This is all just a little bizarre."[19]

Hatfield hung up. As he was leaving St. Martin's, he was confronted by his publisher, who asked about the call. Hatfield again insisted it was a case of mistaken identity. Then he went to his hotel, checked out, and flew back to Arkansas. He got "the hell out of Dodge," as he later described it, because Slover's information was accurate and Hatfield had never told his wife about the crime—solicitation of capital murder—or the five years he had spent in prison for it. He could only imagine how Nancy and her family would react, now that they were parents to a newborn daughter, Haley.

On Thursday, the *Dallas Morning News* ran a story stating that the author Hatfield and the felon Hatfield both had the same birthday, had lived in Dallas at the same time, and presently lived in Arkansas—proof that the two Hatfields were the same. The next day the newspaper ran a follow-up article detailing how in 1992 Hatfield had pleaded guilty to a second felony, falsifying signatures on checks from a government agency so he could cash them. After Hatfield was released from prison in Texas for solicitation of capital murder, he had then served time in Arkansas for embezzlement and was on parole for that conviction until 2003.

With the credibility of its author now in tatters, St. Martin's recalled *Fortunate Son* on Friday. All 70,000 copies that had been shipped would be pulped once they were returned. (A spokesman for St. Martin's erroneously claimed the book would become "furnace fodder.") Another 20,000 copies in storage would not be shipped. Despite the flood of negative publicity, *Fortunate Son* still shot into the top 50 best-selling titles on Amazon.com, peaking at number 8. Eventually, it would land in the number 30 slot on the *New York Times* hardback bestseller list. Obviously, retailers had ignored the requests of the publisher and sold the book anyway.

Media interest in Hatfield was intense, complete with television satellite trucks parked outside his house in Bentonville. As the story of the discredited Bush biographer made national news, all discussion of Bush's drug use essentially became a moot point. Whether or not Bush had used cocaine in the past was a question that was rarely, if ever, brought up by the media again. Hatfield's criminal past would serve not only to destroy the credibility of *Fortunate Son,* it would also kill the issue of Bush's past drug use once and for all.

≋

In November 1999, Hatfield got a reprieve for *Fortunate Son* when Richard Curtis was approached by a punk rock singer and one-time Kinko's store manager named Sander Hicks who owned Soft Skull Press, an alternative publishing company housed in a basement of an apartment building on Manhattan's Lower East Side. Hicks wanted to capitalize on the book's infamy and rerelease it as soon as possible. Hatfield jumped at the opportunity. Curtis asked Hicks for a $15,000 advance against royalties and, scrapping together money from family and friends, Hicks came up with the advance. There was a caveat Hatfield had to agree to before Hicks would enter a contract: Hatfield had to reveal to Hicks the identities of the three unnamed sources. Hatfield complied.

The rerelease of *Fortunate Son* was set for February 2000—in time for the presidential election year—and Hicks made a second demand of Hatfield prior to publication. The author had to come clean about his past in order to make the rerelease of the book about Bush and not about the book's author. Hatfield agreed, going so far as to write a foreword that explained his version of what had happened back in 1987 that had landed him in the federal penitentiary. As the publication date approached, Hatfield and Hicks braced themselves, since *Fortunate Son*'s rerelease was deemed so newsworthy that it merited a feature segment on *60 Minutes* reported by Lesley Stahl.

Hatfield may have detailed his criminal past in his new foreword, but Stahl gave the nation the television version. "You paid someone to murder someone," Stahl said to Hatfield on camera. "Well, it's a very complicated story," Hatfield replied. To which Stahl said, in a voiceover, "Complicated all right. It involved the attempted car bombing of a female co-worker in 1987. The bomb went off, but the intended victim walked away unharmed." Then, on camera, Stahl fixed her sights on Hatfield: "You hired a man [and] paid him $5,000 to have her killed." "Yes," Hatfield said." "Wow," Stahl answered.[20]

The problem with the version of events in the foreword, at least according to Lawrence R. Burk (Hatfield's boss at the time) and Delores Kay Burrow (the woman Hatfield said Burk wanted him to have killed because she was blackmailing him about a past extramarital affair), was that it was libelous. Burrow contended in her lawsuit that Hatfield wanted her dead because she had discovered he was embezzling money. Burrow and Burk's resulting lawsuit against Hatfield, Soft Skull Press, Barnes and Noble, Borders, and Amazon effectively led to the second recall of *Fortunate Son*. The book was out of print for months, long enough that when Sander Hicks had sorted out the legal problems—he had to withdraw the foreword—the election was over.

Months later, when Hicks released yet another edition of the book, he revealed Hatfield's unnamed sources to try to give the book some credibility. To prove Rove was a source, Hicks produced telephone records showing that Hatfield had Rove's unlisted home telephone number in Ingram, Texas, his fax machine number, as well as other unlisted numbers belonging to him. That proof did little to impress journalists—or the public—who remained skeptical. Sales of the book did not take off, Curtis was unable to line up new contracts for Hatfield, and Hatfield's financial circumstances turned dire. Eventually, unable to make a living and battling chronic emotional distress, Hatfield committed suicide in a motel room in Springfield, not far from his home in Bentonville.

Karl Rove would never comment publicly about the death of James Hatfield.

4.

"Very early in the race," Craig Crawford says, "back in 1999 when Bush started running, I was editing the Hotline, the Washington subscriber-only Web site, and I thought Bush was called Bush Junior. So, at Hotline, because we needed a device in our headlines to delineate him from Bush Senior we were just calling him Bush Junior. Well, one day I picked up the phone and there was this person screaming at me on the other end. It was just nonstop yelling. It was Karl Rove and I mean he tore my head off over our calling Bush Bush Junior. I don't remember his exact words; I just remember a lot of yelling. It was very clear they were trying to put the kibosh on him being compared to the father. I guess Junior is a kind of belittling term. 'It's better than Shrub,' I think I said to Rove at some point. But I got his message. I didn't want any more phone calls like that one. I also determined Rove was someone not worth dealing with, so I made [it] a point never to talk to him again. I never tried to and I never wanted to. In addition, I figured out the Bush campaign was stealing their Hotline subscription through a law firm, so I made them subscribe for the campaign itself. But we did stop calling Bush Bush Junior."[21]

This haughtiness may have resulted from a feeling within the campaign that was becoming apparent to the press. With its money and endorsements, the campaign—and in particular Bush—had begun to display an arrogance that bordered on cockiness. On the Fourth of July, in 1999, the *Washington Post* observed that the Bush campaign lacked "the real substance of a presidential platform."[22] Maybe, but that didn't seem to matter, at least not to Bush. The newspaper noted: "Candidate Bush is supremely confident, even cocky. Last Wednesday afternoon he was calling signals at a football camp in Sacramento, California. 'Sixty-two,' he barked. 'Seventy-seven. Thirty-six-point-two-five.' The crowd broke up in laughter. The last number was a reference to the amount of money ($36.25 million) his campaign had just announced it had raised. At another stop last week, Bush referred to himself as 'the president of the United States' before correcting himself. 'Soon-to-be president,' he said."

This attitude was beginning to translate into bigger problems. During the fall, one campaign official after another in New Hampshire told Rove that, because of the way Bush was campaigning in the state, he was going to have trouble winning there. New Hampshire voters like to have access to presidential candidates. They insist on a candidate being humble enough to come to the state and engage in old-fashioned retail politics, going door to door to meet voters, shaking hands along the way. But Rove had decided that Bush was not going to make himself available in the way candidates traditionally do in the state. Because he thought the nomination was inevitable, mostly due to the staggering amounts of money flooding in, Rove concluded that Bush did not have to participate in any debates until January, only weeks before the primary.

"For the second time in six days," the *Washington Post* reported on October 29, "Bush skipped a candidate forum here, staying in Texas to attend a ceremony honoring his wife, Laura. In his absence, Bush's rivals mostly sought to take the opportunity to boost their standing by concentrating on their own campaign themes, rather than criticizing one another. . . . It took the final questioner to change the tone. Noting that she preferred to put her query directly to Bush, who has [now] raised about $60 million, the questioner wondered how anyone could stop the money spiral in politics. . . . Noting that Bush had skipped some campaign events in favor of fund-raisers, [candidate Steve] Forbes quipped, 'Perhaps in the future at a forum like this, if we called it a fund-raiser he might show up.'"[23]

Rove was beginning to realize he had a problem. Prior to the forum in which a questioner had finally asked where Bush was, Rove had requested that the station broadcasting the forum interview Bush two hours before the event began. In that interview Bush did little to dispel criticism of his arrogance. Pointing out that his campaign was spending huge sums of money to advertise on the station that was carrying the interview, he said, "I hope your station appreciates it." Then, later, when asked about his campaign in New Hampshire, Bush boasted, "It seems the people of New Hampshire accept my vision and they want me to be the nominee." In fact, opinion polls were showing that Bush was beginning to falter.

Under increasing pressure from advisers in New Hampshire, Rove broke down and allowed Bush to participate in three debates toward the end of 1999, but that only created the feeling that Bush was gracing the debates with his presence—an air of entitlement that infuriated New Hampshire voters. What's more, because Bush's main rival, Senator John McCain of Arizona, was skipping the Iowa caucus due to his steadfast opposition to the federal funding of ethanol—a make-or-break issue in Iowa since corn, the state's main crop, is used to produce it—New Hampshire was shaping up to be the first state in which the two top-tier Republican candidates were going to meet. Unlike Bush, McCain had held some 100 town hall meetings. He could not have made himself more available to the voters of New Hampshire.

Thanks to what the media called a "sound-bite style" of campaigning, a strategy largely urged on Bush by Rove in part to disguise how uninformed Bush was, Bush had tremendously damaged his chances of winning New Hampshire. In November, the press began to ask openly if Bush's overconfidence had allowed McCain to make a race of it in New Hampshire. By midmonth, the Bush campaign was answering McCain's growing popularity by spending money. They said they would run more television and radio ads, send out more direct mail, make more phone calls—all as a way to distract from the fact that Bush still was not accessible to the voters of New Hampshire at the level they expected. Bush's chances had been so damaged that by December, former governor Stephen E. Merrill told the *New York Times*, "The Bush campaign believed it was the front-runner in New Hampshire. There's no such thing as the front-runner in New Hampshire. . . . I love this guy. He'd make a great president. That's what's so frustrating. There is no inevitability in any presidential primary. The great irony is that the candidate understands that. I'm not sure everybody else does."[24] In this case "everybody else" certainly included Karl Rove. If Rove continued to handle the New Hampshire primary the way he had from the start, Bush was going to lose. By December, Bush had to acknowledge reality. McCain "may very well be the front-runner now in New Hampshire," he said in the wake of a series of opinion polls that showed McCain on the rise.[25]

During the primary season, Rove made other missteps, and not just in New Hampshire. For example, he wasted money opening regional headquarters to prove the Bush campaign was going to be national in scope, even going so far as to open a campaign office in Guam, a first in presidential politics. Instead of worrying about New Hampshire, Rove appeared to be worrying about territories literally outside of the country.

Nor was Bush helped overall, but particularly in New Hampshire, by his marginal win in the Iowa caucus on January 24. Taking just 41 percent of the vote, Bush watched Forbes come in a strong second, with

30 percent. However, Bush appeared undeterred by his less-than-stellar performance in Iowa, when he stood before supporters beaming about his "record-shattering victory" that spelled "the beginning of the end of the Clinton era."[26] Then, as if to seal Bush's fate in New Hampshire, during the final days before the primary, Rove brought in Bush's parents for the weekend and, in front of a crowd of supporters and with the national press corps recording it all, Bush Senior referred to Bush as his "boy"—hardly the term a campaign would have chosen to describe their presidential candidate.

Finally, on election night, February 1, 2000, disaster struck. In a stunning upset, McCain defeated Bush by a staggering 19 points, with McCain receiving 49 percent of the vote and Bush, only 30 percent. It was, according to the *Washington Post*, "the worst defeat suffered by a front-runner of either party in the modern history of the New Hampshire primary."[27] What was supposed to have been a victory celebration for Bush on the campus of a college in Manchester instead had the feeling of a wake. Hot dogs and sodas may have been served to the gathered crowd to set the theme of a Texas-style picnic, but there was no celebrating going on. The Bush camp was crushed; many were disheartened by the size of the loss. "I think that almost any other campaign would not have survived that defeat," Mark McKinnon, a media consultant for the campaign, would say. "We lost by 19 points. Guys that worked with me in that campaign who have worked on other presidential campaigns were literally packing their bags."[28]

The local Bush advisers had been right: If you go to New Hampshire flaunting an air of inevitability, the voters will destroy you. That's what they did to Bush, and for that defeat the blame can only be placed on Rove. He may have been the architect of two victories in Texas, but in New Hampshire, his arrogance and his justifiable fear that Bush was not ready to enter the presidential race without being protected as much as possible caused him to meet with failure. In their first head-on contest,

McCain had defeated Bush in a crushing landslide. If he won in the South Carolina primary less than three weeks after New Hampshire, McCain could become the new front-runner. No doubt that was why, on the flight out of New Hampshire following his drubbing, Bush found Rove on the plane and gave him one order—and one order only. "Do whatever you have to do to win in South Carolina." That's what Bush told Rove.

⇌

First, Rove had to appeal to the conservative base in South Carolina, so he scheduled Bush to make a speech about values at Bob Jones University in Greenville, an institution that was openly anti-Semitic and banned interracial dating on campus. Among the colleges and universities in the United States, Bob Jones University might not be "compassionate," but there was no doubt it was conservative.

Bush also weighed in on another touchstone issue in the state. He came out in favor of the state government being able to continue flying the Confederate flag over the capitol. But solidifying Bush's conservative credentials in a state where conservatism is supreme was not enough. He had to take out McCain. He did this by unleashing one of the most aggressive, pervasive, and ultimately effective smear campaigns ever inflicted upon a political candidate. In the days between the New Hampshire and South Carolina primaries, McCain, his wife, and his family were subjected to one of the most brutal character assassinations ever carried out in American politics.

In South Carolina, McCain became the object of an unrelenting attack. A Bush surrogate, J. Thomas Burch Jr., chairman of the National Vietnam and Gulf War Committee, claimed that McCain was weak on issues important to veterans, saying at one public appearance he made with Bush, "McCain had the power to help . . . veterans. He came home, forgot us."[29] There was also a whisper campaign, the subject of which made its way into push calls, that said McCain had fathered an illegitimate black child. (Cindy and John McCain *had* adopted a child from Mother Teresa's orphanage in Bangladesh, so McCain was indeed the father of a black child. They had rescued her from sure death since, when Cindy found her, the baby girl had suffered from a cleft palate so severe it would have proved fatal.) There was also gossip about Cindy McCain's drug abuse, which did have a grain of truth to it, since she had admitted to having been addicted to painkillers after a misdiagnosed, untreated medical condition caused chronic pain in her lower back. The pain was eventually cured when, under her gynecologist's orders, she underwent a hysterectomy. There were even stories about John McCain being the "fag" candidate.[30]

The spectacle of the smear was daunting. In the final 48 hours before the South Carolina primary, Georgette Mosbacher, one of the national cochairs of McCain for President, drove around the state in a rental car and listened to the radio. Never had she heard such an unrelenting barrage of negativity directed toward one candidate. No matter what radio station she turned to, no matter what hour of the day or night it was, there was a constant assault perpetrated on McCain either by callers or hosts commenting on radio programs or campaign commercials running on those same stations. In all the years she had been in politics—she was both the former wife of Robert Mosbacher, who was George H. W. Bush's secretary of commerce, and the former chairperson of the Republican Governors Association, for which she had been one of its most successful fund-raisers—she had never witnessed such a thorough annihilation of a candidate. The assault was just as bad on television. In all, the Bush campaign spent $3 million on an advertising onslaught guaranteed to overcome Bush's New Hampshire defeat.

Rove's attack on McCain was no doubt made even more satisfying for Rove because the McCain campaign was being run by his old rival, John Weaver. Only now, the roles were reversed. Rove was the most important consultant in the presidential race, with Weaver falling to second place. All Bush had to do was win the South Carolina primary, and he would become the front-runner again. On February 19, the smear campaign paid off when Bush defeated McCain by a comfortable margin. The victory all but reversed the disaster of New Hampshire and put Bush back on top. "South Carolina has spoken," Bush said in his victory speech in Columbia, "and tonight there are only 263 days more to the end of Clinton–Gore." After a close call, Rove had redeemed himself. Years before, Lee Atwater had made South Carolina the "fire wall" for the front-runner of the Republican Party, and in 2000 the man who claimed to be Atwater's protégé had used his invention as if it were his own—and saved his candidate in the process.

McCain did continue to pick up victories here and there, such as one in the Michigan primary three days after the South Carolina defeat, but for all intents and purposes his chances of winning the nomination ended in South Carolina. The final blow for McCain came when Bush was the big winner on Super Tuesday, all but eliminating him. A *New York Times* reporter followed Rove around the victory celebration being held in Austin at the Four Seasons Hotel. "And when I brought up the talk about his experience being too provincial," the reporter wrote on May 14, "his response again was pretty macho: 'No, I haven't run a national campaign, but who has? Jim Baker?' This he said as if being James Baker, who reluctantly ran President Bush's 1992 campaign, is maybe not such a good thing." Earlier that evening, the reporter had overheard Rove on the telephone, telling Bush about the McCain "meltdown": "'It's not pretty, they say. . . . It's not pretty how the numbers are being received. He's going to Arizona, and the scuttlebutt is he's going to his cabin and nobody thinks he can continue. Yeah, recriminations, finger-pointing. No, over there. Oh, big time. It's unbelievable.'" About Rick Davis, McCain's campaign manger, Rove had had especially harsh words: "'Yeah, he is a bad guy. This guy was a lobbyist for Imelda Marcos and General Abacha of Nigeria! Just the consummate inside-D.C. thug. He needs adult supervision.' (Davis's firm, though not Davis himself, did some work for Marcos and for Nigeria when Abacha was in power.)"[31]

While the Bush campaign wanted to create the appearance of harmony between the candidate and his adviser, the *Times* article—a kind of profile of Rove—hinted at the possibility that Bush could be jealous of Rove. This was how the *New York Times* ended its article about Super Tuesday and Rove: "Finally, the candidate did leave this phone message for me," the reporter wrote. "'This is Governor George Bush. I understand you're writing an article on Karl. I've known Karl a long time, since about 1972. I know him as a friend, and I've been in combat with him, political combat, on more than one occasion. I think—I know—he's brilliant. He is very witty and fun to be around. He's well read and an all-around good man. Thank you for your interest'—long pause—'in Karl.'"

Ultimately, McCain did suspend his campaign, meaning that Bush had wrapped up the nomination. Since Rove had orchestrated the nomination of a first-time presidential candidate, he was now worthy of more media coverage. Other articles followed. One contained language that would prove to be prophetic. In the summer of 2000, David M. Shribman traveled to Austin to interview Rove for a profile for the *Boston Globe*. The interview took place in Rove's office, located, to quote Shribman, "just a few blocks down Congress Street from the Capitol, on the second floor of the sort of steel-and-glass palace that has sprouted around this booming city."[32] The writer and Rove discussed a variety of topics, but when he published his article on July 23 it was the questions not asked that proved to be forebodings. "Here," Shribman wrote, "are the questions, mostly unfair but all with a kernel of truth in them, that Rove desperately hopes do not come up in our conversation: Is there a place where George W. Bush ends and Karl Rove begins? Are you the wizard behind the curtain of George W.? Are you worldly and experienced enough to keep pace with the battle-tested Gore team? Is W. too dependent upon you? And, worst of all: Are you George W. Bush's brain?"

In the future the credit for the ugliness of the campaign—in particular the smear on McCain and his family—would fall to Rove, elevating him into the same league as his guru Lee Atwater, but some observers believe Bush should be given at least as much credit, if not more. "All candidates control their campaigns," John Dean would say, "and if they don't want such activity, it doesn't occur. [Bush] is a highly sophisticated political operator. . . . Rove gets the credit for being Bush's political brain. It's an arrangement both men like, because it raises Rove's importance as a political operator, and lowers Bush's exposure. In truth, Bush is probably more politically savvy than Rove. Both men learned their politics from Lee Atwater, who ran Bush senior's 1988 campaign. Atwater made dirty politics into an art form, by which I mean he provided those for whom dirty deeds were done deniability while Atwater's people tore up an opponent's pea-patch and everything else."[33]

So that was the debate. Who was more important, Bush or Rove? Was Bush as uninformed as he sometimes appeared to be? Given some of the blunders he had already made, was Rove as brilliant as he wanted the press to believe? In the end it might be that Bush really was as savvy as some suspected, because he was smart enough to let Rove be out front, absorbing criticism that could sometimes have been directed at the candidate. Bush would also allow Rove to remain out front until he had to put him in his place—or until he didn't need him anymore.

5.

With the presidential nomination wrapped up, Bush turned his sights on the Democratic nominee, Al Gore. The first decision Bush had to make was who would be his vice presidential running mate. In March, not long after Super Tuesday, Bush had approached Richard Cheney, an old friend of the family who was the CEO of the Dallas-based oil service company Halliburton, but at the time Cheney had said no. On April 25, Bush asked Cheney to head up his vice presidential screening committee, which Cheney agreed to do. As Bush went about interviewing the candidates Cheney had vetted—Senator Chuck Hagel of Nebraska, Senator John Danforth of Missouri, Governor George Pataki of New York—he knew he still wanted Cheney. Finally, over the Fourth of July weekend, as they discussed the potential running mates, Bush asked Cheney one more time— and much to his surprise, this time Cheney agreed. Within Bush's small circle of advisers, however—Karen Hughes, Joe Allbaugh, and Karl Rove— it was Rove who was opposed to the selection of Cheney. At the time Rove refused to comment on the choice, but years later he was to the point. "Selecting Daddy's top foreign policy guru ran counter to message," Rove would say. "It was worse than a safe pick—it was needy."[34] As it happened, Rove was right about Cheney, though not for the reason he stated. It would be decisions Cheney made about foreign policy—those that Bush agreed with and refused to admit were misguided—that would harm Bush in ways only history will be able to determine.

He had made mistakes in the primary season, and Rove continued to miscalculate during the fall campaign. In true Rove fashion, there would be the dirty trick leading up to the all-vital presidential debates. In an echo of the discovery of the bug in his office during the 1986 Clements campaign, a woman who worked for the media company producing ads for the Bush campaign—named Maverick Media, the outfit was set up to make commercials for no other candidate but Bush—was indicted for allegedly sending a Gore campaign adviser a copy of a videotape of Bush rehearsing for his debate performances. Not only that, the woman, or whoever sent the package, included a 120-page briefing book documenting what Bush had to do in the debates to defeat Gore. In retrospect, it was a sideshow created to take attention away from the debate between the candidates. It was vintage Rove, a classic sidestep away from the actual drama taking place on the political stage, and, as always, no one could prove he was behind the ploy.

But Rove made more costly mistakes. As of August, Rove had scheduled Bush on seven campaign swings through California, where he'd been consistently behind in the polls, and the trips continued through the fall. Later, Rove justified his actions by claiming he wanted to increase Bush's chances of winning the popular vote. Getting as many votes in California as possible could only help. But in order to win the presidency, as Bush would soon discover, you didn't need to win the popular vote, only the Electoral College.

Bush did not help Rove either, regularly committing verbal and social gaffes. When he called a reporter an asshole on stage during a campaign appearance, it was picked up by a camera crew. "His personal qualities had so much to do with his ascent on the national stage," one Republican strategist said at the time, "and he needs to take great care in preserving those."[35] But there were bigger problems with Bush: his apparent inability to pronounce some words properly, his limited knowledge of world politics and leaders as evidenced during a television interview when he did not know the names of the leaders of important countries like Pakistan, and his innate ability to mutilate the English language. "Is our children learning?" Bush asked at one campaign stop.

Rove could not control Bush's ineptitude, but he could control the campaign's schedule, tone, and demeanor, and rarely did someone make as many mistakes as he did in the campaign's final days. That appeared to be true in part, again, because of Rove's arrogance. In mid-October, at a time when most pundits were predicting the race would be one of the closest in history, Rove boasted that he felt no pressure at all. "We have the resources and the volunteer enthusiasm to conduct an aggressive air and ground game in all the battleground states and then some," he said. "The people who are left out there, available to both sides, are going to move begrudgingly.[36] He believed, not surprisingly, that they were going to move to Bush.

In the final days of the campaign Rove had Bush making moves that were illogical by almost any standard. The Sunday before the final weekend of the campaign, while Gore was campaigning around the clock, Rove scheduled a day off for Bush. There was a mere week and a day left before the election and Bush spent the day resting—a move that, in and of itself, could have cost Bush a margin of victory. Then, even though he had little or no chance of winning California, Rove sent Bush to the state one more time in the final days; he also scheduled him to appear in New Jersey, a state Gore ended up winning with 56 percent of the vote. Apparently, Rove felt he had the battleground states so wrapped up that he could waste his candidate's time campaigning in states where Gore was all but sure to win—not just New Jersey and California, but Oregon and Washington as well.

One development that should have concerned Rove was the revelation during the final weekend of the race that, years before in Maine, Bush had been arrested for driving while intoxicated. It was the kind of October surprise that could sink a campaign, and it's up to the campaign to anticipate such surprises and to manage expectations with careful predictions. Instead of voicing apprehension, Rove stuck with a tone of confidence bordering on cockiness. For example, one state Rove had no doubt Bush would win was Florida. Two days before the election, Rove told a reporter for the *New York Times*, "We're here in Miami, man. It's going pretty wild!" Could Bush win the election without Florida? "It's a hypothetical not worth writing about because we're going to carry Florida," Rove said. Not only was he supremely confident that

Bush was going to take Florida, Rove believed Bush would win the general election by a six- or seven-point margin, he told the reporter, and pick up as many as 320 votes in the Electoral College. It was an ill-advised prediction to make, even if he believed it, and the political community received it that way when it appeared in the paper.[37] A campaign wants to lower expectations just before an election, not *raise* them, if for no other reason than to motivate core voters.

As it turned out, Rove could not have been more off the mark. On the night of the election, Florida was too close to call. Rove was so out of touch with reality that he had calculated one scenario in which Bush could have been put over the top to victory by the electoral vote in Maine. As election night unfolded and it became clear that a winner was not going to be declared—first the networks called Florida for Gore, then they withdrew it, then they called the state for Bush, then they just gave up—Rove sat at his computer at Bush election central and had a meltdown. He had been wrong about the six- or seven-point victory. He had been wrong about the Electoral College. It was now clear that Bush was even going to lose the popular vote—and by as much as a half-million votes. Even so, Rove would not admit he had miscalculated. Like Bush, he would never be quick to concede he was wrong about anything. He accused the networks of bias in their reporting of the election instead of admitting he was off in his calculations.

"Karl Rove is not a man to whose lips the words 'I made a mistake' spring easily," the *New Yorker* would report, "and, as regards the 2000 election, he has often pointed out . . . that his candidate far outper-formed all those predictive models that posited Al Gore, as the nominee of the party in power during peaceful and prosperous times, as unbeat-able. Still, Rove was heard during the last month of the campaign saying that Bush was going to win by six points. That the election was, instead, a tie seems to have come as a surprise to him. 'I don't know what we were going to win by,' he said. . . . 'I mean, toward the end it was bravado. But particularly after that last, after the D.U.I.'—the revelation during the campaign's last week that Bush had been arrested in Maine for drunk driving years earlier—'it was closing, as these things tend to anyway, and then that just accelerated it.' He added that the Republicans had been 'grossly outspent' by groups affiliated with the Democratic Party."[38] As for the drunk-driving story, Rove would later claim he believed the revelation cost Bush as many as 4 million votes, a number that may seem high but that's hard to dismiss since so much of Bush's political base was made up of Christians who would have been turned off by such revelations.

In the end it was not Rove who was put in charge of the Florida recount, but James Baker. When the Bush family needed a confidant working on their behalf to make sure they won an election that was literally up for grabs, they turned to a protégé of Bush Senior's who had proved his ability to maneuver through complicated political situations many times in the past. "Rove was not sent down to Florida because he had his head in the toilet," says Roger Stone, who joined the effort to win the Florida recount for Bush at Baker's behest. "Karl had predicted that the election would be a cakewalk for Bush. He was quite confident. He was so sure Bush was going to win that when the election ended up the way it did, he had a physical attack. He couldn't stop throwing up from nerves. It was so bad that Little Bush had to call Baker, who went to Florida and overwhelmed Bill Daley [Gore's campaign manager, who helped to represent Gore in the recount]. Warren Christopher [the US secretary of state under Bill Clinton and another Gore representative in Florida] looked old and dried up. Daley looked like a buffoon. Baker simply took over. He ended up being the dominant figure in the Florida recount. He, more than anyone else, was the reason why the recount proceeded as it did."[39] In no time, Baker was overseeing a staff of 100, with representatives in all 67 Florida counties. Rove was not among the staff. He had virtually nothing to do with the recount.

In the end, of course, after 36 days the US Supreme Court decided the contested election in a five-to-four decision that awarded the presidency to Bush. In a real way, Rove had little if anything to do with the fact that the recount was decided in Bush's favor. Regardless, as soon as the Supreme Court had settled the election and Bush began to assemble his White House staff, one of the first people he appointed to a position in his administration was Rove. Rove's title would be senior adviser and assistant to the president. Rove was "one of the reasons why I was elected governor, and one of the reasons why I was elected president," Bush said in naming him to his job. "People have been saying, 'Hey, great job,'" Rove would tell a reporter in early January 2001. "And I say, If it was such a great job, why did it take 36 days?"[40]

That might have been true, but the Bush administration—and in particular Rove—headed to Washington seeming to feel not as if they had won the one of the closest presidential races in American history, but as if they were finally being given the chance to do what they had been planning to do for years. Or at least *Rove* had been making plans for years. Ever since he had gotten into politics as a career, perhaps ever since he had been a teenage nerd back in Utah, he had had a dream of making a difference on the national political scene. Now that his opportunity had become a reality, Rove knew what he wanted to try to achieve: a legacy that would be historic, lasting, permanent.

6.

"Karl is not interested in permanent *issues*," Tom Pauken says. "He's interested in power. The lobbyists and big boys take on big roles because there's a lot of money and power there. Ideas get in the way because sometimes you've got to roll people and if you have too many policy guys they may not want to go along all the time. You want people to salute. It's very Nixon-esque."[41] Loyalty was vital, but that loyalty was important only for what it could achieve for Rove and the Bush administration. Right from the start, within the Bush inner circle, it became apparent that Rove wanted to create a situation whereby the Republicans could control the power in Washington for the foreseeable future. Rove enjoyed likening his goal to the kind of majority the Democrats sustained under Franklin Roosevelt.

"The real prize [for Rove]," the New Yorker would report, "is creating a Republican majority that would be as solid as, say, the Democratic coalition that Franklin Roosevelt created—a majority that would last for a generation and that, as it played itself out over time, would wind up profoundly changing the relationship between citizen and state in this country. 'I think we're at a point where the two major parties have sort of exhausted their governing agendas,' Rove [said]. 'We had agendas that were originally formed, for the Democrats, in the New Deal, and, for the Republicans, in opposition to the New Deal—modified by the Cold War and further modified by the changes in the 1960s, the Great Society and societal and cultural changes. It's sort of like the exhaustion of two boxers fighting it out in the middle of the ring. This periodically happens. This happened in 1896, where the Civil War party system was in decline and the parties were in rough parity and somebody came along and figured it out and helped create a governing coalition that really lasted for the next some-odd years. Similarly, somebody will come along and figure out a new governing scheme through which people could view things and could, conceivably, enjoy a similar period of dominance.' Karl Rove clearly wants to be that somebody, and his relentless pressing for every possible specific advantage is in service of the larger goal."[42]

This would be historic. "When Karl got to the White House, he immediately started putting together a plan for what was essentially the Third Reich of Republican majority in this country," says Mark Sanders, a longtime Republican strategist in Texas. "That was absolutely his plan, a Republican majority domination not just of the US House, the US Senate, and the presidency, but also state legislatures across the country. This was not just a pie-in-the-sky dream that Karl had. He wanted to see the Republican Party rule for the next 30 to 40 years."[43]

It's hard to believe that a consultant whose candidate had just eked out one of the closest races in history could have such lofty plans, but he did, and he began to implement the plans as soon as he got to Washington. "The ugly little thing nobody cares about is, it's all about redistricting," Sanders says. "If you get control of state legislatures around the country and you get to redraw congressional districts it is almost impossible not to elect a Republican from that district, and if you have Republican control of Congress then Republicans are controlling the White House. Redistricting was the whole game. It was the key. If you are Karl, you are the power broker who did it. You are the go-to guy. You orchestrated it all. He likes that credit. If you are the guy who made America Republican for 30 to 40 years, you'd be in the history books."

Indeed, as the *Atlantic Monthly* later reported, "Rove's idea was to use the levers of government to create an effect that ordinarily occurs only in the most tumultuous periods in American history. He believed he could force a realignment himself through a series of far-reaching policies. Rove's plan had five major components: establish education standards, pass a 'faith-based initiative' directing government funds to religious organizations, partially privatize Social Security, offer private health-savings accounts as an alternative to Medicare, and reform immigration laws to appeal to the growing Hispanic population. Each of these, if enacted, would weaken the Democratic Party by drawing some of its core supporters into the Republican column. His plan would lead, he believed, to a period of Republican dominance like the one that followed McKinley's election."[44]

Finally, years later, Rove himself would go on the record: "I believe," he said, "we are entering a new political system—a new structure in which one party tends to dominate politics, as Democrats did in the New Deal system. We're entering this new political structure in a much different way than the sharp shifts we've seen before. You can see it not only in the presidential and Congressional elections, where reapportionment will strengthen the GOP in the coming years but also in the change in state legislatures. For the last several elections Republicans have been at or near the highest number of state legislative seats that we've had since the 1920s. And remember, in the '20s there were no Republicans in the South—literally a handful of Republican elected officials in Winston County, Alabama, eastern Tennessee, western North Carolina, the German hill country of Texas, and scattered remnants in West Virginia."[45]

Some observers saw a permanent majority in darker tones. "Karl's plan was to transform American politics into a fascist regime," says George Shipley, a longtime player in Texas politics and Ann Richards's gubernatorial campaign adviser. "As soon as they got into the White House, Bush allowed him to wander into the policy areas. It got worse as time went on because the Bush administration didn't realize the vastness of what they could do. They didn't know enough. They wanted to put into place the American equivalent of the 1,000 Year Reich and they got caught. What ultimately caught them was their own error in the misdirected war against Iraq."[46]

The problem that would arise for the Bush administration and Rove was the balance between politics and policy. Simply put, there would *be* no difference—a flaw that would ultimately prove to be fatal. "We've never had a White House as political as the Bush White House," Matt Towery says about the administration that was about to descend upon Washington. "With very few policy goals, their main intent was merely to win the next election and the election after that. The person in charge of that agenda, such as it was, was Karl Rove."[47]

CHAPTER FIVE

MR. ROVE GOES TO WASHINGTON

1.

"I noticed what they were doing from day one," says Gordon Hamel, a career bureaucrat who worked in various areas of the federal government, including the White House. "The telltale sign of what the crowd was going to be like was the way Bush was appointing politicals early on. He was putting tons of unqualified politicals into positions. One of the things I noticed the most was the inspectors general. He was filling all of the IG positions with former Secret Service agents. It had nothing to do with their skills. A Secret Service agent does two things: Protect the president and chase counterfeiters. Unless you were a manager, you were one of the geeks standing at the door talking into your sleeve. So how are you qualified to go from that into an executive position that requires manager and policy-making skills? But these Secret Service agents were the ones who had guarded Daddy Bush and Bush and Rove knew it. The agents were loyal Bushies."[1]

The appointment of former Secret Service agents to IG positions was important for a second reason. There are 86 inspectors general in the federal government; each department or program has an inspector general appointed to be in charge of detecting waste, fraud, and abuse. By appointing unqualified personnel to positions of oversight—personnel who were loyal to Bush but not necessarily to the government—the Bush administration could guarantee it could manage the reporting of waste, fraud, and abuse within the government. Should unethical activity occur, it would be up to the IGs to report it first to members of the administration and, with their approval, to the press and the public. However, if the administration did not want the waste, fraud, or abuse to be reported, the IGs could be kept silent.

Moreover, the Bush administration was not selective in choosing what areas of the government would be overseen by these unqualified former Secret Service agents. For example, the agents were appointed even to the Transportation Safety Administration, the agency in charge of security at airports nationwide. It would be hard to determine the chilling effect created by placing an IG unfamiliar with the inner workings of the TSA in a position of authority at that agency. It would also be hard to imagine that the integrity of the organization was not compromised during this vital period of time—after the 1993 attack on the World Trade Center, after the 2000 bombing of the USS *Cole*, after a foiled attack on the Los Angeles International Airport by a terrorist who planned to detonate a bomb in the facility—when terrorism, and, consequently, safety at airports, was becoming a more urgent topic.

"Another thing that really troubled me was the way they closed down all the avenues of communication between the White House and all the agencies," Hamel says. "Each department had a political appointment from the White House and immediately these agencies, which control billions and billions of dollars, started to cease giving contracts to Democrats. Alfonso Jackson, the deputy secretary of the Department of Housing and Urban Development, even said he purposefully did not give contracts to Democrats. At the same time, there were very few [initiatives] coming out from the White House except from a handful of people. Things that were being done by dozens and dozens of people in the past were now being done by a few—Karen Hughes, [White House chief of staff] Andy Card, and, of course, Karl Rove. They had an incredible grasp on everything that went on in government, and they were thumbing their noses at the Democrats. They essentially hijacked the Congress by having a couple of key players like Tom DeLay"—the congressman from Sugar Land, Texas, and the Republican whip—"rolling people over. While they were pissing on the legislature, Bush was starting to load down the courts with very conservative judges, so if they were to lose an argument in the legislature and it went to the courts, they would have their people in place."

This handful of people, Rove central among them, assumed virtually total control of the government within the first months of Bush taking office in January 2001. "I had never seen this level of control over the government or disregard for the other branches of government," Hamel says. "They were forming a government within the government. The level of organization of this was clearly unique to George W. Bush. They were extremely efficient at appointing people who were unqualified. It's an oxymoron, but they did it. And Karl Rove was the ringmaster."

For individuals within the government who were looking on, especially career workers, it became clear how Rove and the rest of the inner circle maintained control over their government within a government. From the beginning, Rove held weekly meetings with the chiefs of staff from all of the government agencies to keep the administration on message. On a regular basis, he held PowerPoint slide meetings with representatives from various departments to coordinate how the resources of the federal government could be used to help Republicans get elected in 2002 and 2004. The plan was to increase the appeal of Republicans among minorities and unions, as well as with technology voters such as those in Silicon Valley. This involved coordinating administration officials to make public appearances or announce funding with Republicans who were running in various districts, particularly those where a Democrat might pose a serious challenge to a Republican.

The meetings, organized by the White House, featured Rove. One of the first occurred on March 12, 2001, only weeks after the president had been sworn in. An invitation to the meeting contained the declaration "How we can work together." The purpose was to overlap visits by cabinet members to make high-profile public appearances or announcements of funding with races in states or districts that were important to Republicans in upcoming elections. Rove was so aware of the potentially unethical nature of the meetings that he carefully consulted White House lawyers on an ongoing basis about how to comply with the Hatch Act, the law that forbids the use of federal resources for political purposes. Rove supposedly remained in compliance with the Hatch Act, over the coming years, as he held 100 or more of these how-we-can-work-together meetings, although some critics of the Bush administration would later question the legality of Rove's tactics.

On the issue of communication, the Bush administration did something no other administration had done, something that was questionable if not outright illegal. At the start of Bush's presidency, an e-mail system was installed at the White House that was separate from the official White House system, which, because it was owned by the federal government, was required to make its content a part of the public record. The Republican National Committee installed the separate system, so e-mail sent through it was considered private and not subject to the laws governing information produced by the federal government. In essence, members of the Bush administration could e-mail one another through the private RNC system knowing that anything they said would remain private, even if it pertained to government business. Eighty-eight White House officials had RNC accounts, including Rove. While these accounts were private, the RNC did in fact save the e-mails generated in the system. Over the several years that Rove used his RNC account, the committee saved at least 140,000 e-mails that had been sent to or by Rove. Those e-mails would constitute an electronic paper trail of much of his activity while he was at the White House, but because they were sent through a private system, their ownership would be open to debate.

This was just a single example of why the Bush administration would be seen as one of the most secretive in history. Many types of documents that had regularly been made public by previous administrations would be opened by the Bush administration only after legal pressure or the Freedom of Information Act had been applied. The ownership of and need to release to the public even documentation as innocuous as pictures taken by staff photographers at White House events would be questioned. "I have never seen a White House as secretive and difficult to deal with as the Bush White House," says a source close to a White House official who has served in a number of administrations. "Oddly enough, the Bush people seemed to know how secretive they were, and they didn't care."[2]

As for Rove, from the start he was a central figure in the administration. Rove took as his office in the West Wing the one occupied by Hillary Rodham Clinton during her years as First Lady; she was the first First Lady to situate her office in the West Wing instead of the East Wing. Stories would be leaked to the press about Rove bringing in spiritual consultants to cleanse the office of evil spirits—stories leaked, one can assume, so Rove could deny them. As in the past, a story would be leaked to the press and though Rove would be conveniently positioned at its center, he would deny any involvement.

As he continued to create a myth about himself, Rove included in his office certain artifacts that ended up being mentioned in articles about him. The office would be described by one publication as a "meticulously neat room with a view of the Washington Monument." Although his role model for Bush had been William McKinley, who placed Roosevelt on the ticket as vice president in 1900 against the wishes of Mark Hanna, Rove's office was said to have on its walls pictures of Abraham Lincoln and Theodore Roosevelt, whom one can assume to be Rove's Republican heroes. In addition, one wall featured a James Madison autograph, framed and displayed in a place of prominence. Finally—and here was a real nod to mythmaking—Rove had on display pages from *Great Moments in History*, the first book he contended that he remembered reading. Such a touch could be seen as having a kind of flair to it—or a fake sentimentality that bordered on the cynical. In the world of authentic political thinkers, who would reduce himself on an intellectual level to displaying on the walls of his White House office pages from the first book he said he read, which was conveniently a children's book about history? It smacked of opportunism and carefully manipulated public relations: Put it on the wall of your office in the White House and reporters will write about it—and they did.

Besides his title of senior adviser and assistant to the president, Rove was in charge of the Office of Strategic Initiatives, a research operation in the White House. In a sense, then, Rove was in a league of his own. "Rove's unique role [was] that he [was] a political guy making policy decisions for political reasons," John Dean later said. "Decisions made in the Bush White House [were] made not based on what [was] best for the public interest, rather what [would] get the president the most mileage with his base, and the best political advantage. Not since Nixon's so-called responsiveness program—which was uncovered during the Watergate investigation—have we had such overt political decision-making."[3] In an obvious attempt to reward an important segment of Bush's base, one of the first moves Rove made was to establish within the White House an entity entitled the Office of Faith-Based and Community Initiatives. This was a blatant effort to appease the Christian community, which had been central to Bush's election in 2000.

From the start, critics were suspicious about Rove's ability to make policy. "Being opposed to Karl in the legislative area was easier than in a political area," says Bill Miller, who had worked both for and against Rove on issues in the Texas legislature. "His gift for winning elections is strong. His expertise in legislative matters is weak; his strategic skills are weaker. On elections, he's a genius; on the other, he's back to earth."[4] Or as Roger Stone puts it, "Karl was supposed to provide the political component to policy decisions. He was supposed to say that this is a good idea or that this is a bad idea for our coalition. As it turned out, Karl was heavy on the political, weak on policy. Or even worse. Policy was left lacking in lieu of politics."[5]

Some decisions the Bush administration made early on to please interest groups Bush was beholden to dented Bush's popularity. To further placate the Christian community, especially the right-wing fundamentalists who had turned out in massive numbers to vote for Bush, Bush took a firm stance against federal funding of stem cell research. The religious right did not have as visceral a reaction to stem cell research as it did to abortion, but it was close, and Bush would not risk alienating the religious right by not strongly stating his belief in limiting the federal funding of that research. Rove convinced Bush to take the position he did because he was also worried about losing the Catholic vote, and the Catholic community was a voting bloc that Rove wanted to cultivate. Not only was Rove repaying the base for its support, he was looking toward the future. "I think Karl was bound and determined he was not going to repeat the mistakes of the father," Ed Rollins says, "which is sort of the formula they were using: to reinforce the conservative base, which the father never had any claim to."[6]

Besides the religious right, Bush was indebted to the energy business. So, right away, Bush had Cheney hold secret meetings with a task force that would develop the administration's energy policy, one the energy community in the United States could embrace. Rarely if ever has an administration brought in leaders from an industry to develop a White House policy that would be in the best interests not of the public, but of that industry. In the case of the Bush administration, with Rove's approval, that was exactly what happened. Then, for good measure, Bush withdrew the United States from the Kyoto Treaty, an accord signed by almost every nation in the civilized world that would limit the emission of greenhouse gases in order to reduce global warming. Bush withdrew the United States from the treaty because the science, he argued, was not conclusive. Bush was uncertain, he said, whether global warming was occurring and, if it was, whether man-made greenhouse gas emissions were helping to cause it. But the main reason Bush withdrew from the Kyoto Treaty was this: The energy industry wanted him to, and that was more than acceptable to Rove.

⩦

The Bush loyalists were systematic about how they went about their business, too. If government employees threatened to break ranks, especially if they had witnessed misconduct and tried to do something about it, they were pressured either to be silent or to resign. Sometimes the episodes took on an air of intimidation that was alien to the way business had historically been conducted in the federal government.

Here is how one government employee—known to be a Democrat and therefore considered not to be loyal to the Bush administration—says he was treated by administration officials when he tried to bring to light gross waste and corruption at the Department of Housing and Urban Development during the first year of the Bush administration. "When I arrived for my appointment," the worker would reveal about a meeting that had been set up so he could give one of the inspectors general documented evidence of waste and corruption, "I told the receptionist I was there for a 10:00 a.m. appointment with the IG. She immediately got up and went into the office behind her, closing the door. I began to get the feeling something wasn't right. Within about one minute the receptionist came out of the office and directed me to follow her to a conference room, saying, 'He'll be with you in a moment.' I sat down at the conference table and took the folder of documents out of my briefcase"—the proof of the waste and mismanagement—"that I intended to give the IG.

Moments after I sat down, [two] deputy IGs came out of the office that the receptionist had gone into and closed the door. The one deputy IG came into the conference room and introduced himself. He sat down, looked at me, and said that the IG would not be attending the meeting but that he would handle it. I told him there must be a mistake because my meeting was at the IG's direction. [The inspector general had personally set up the meeting with the worker only days before.] With that I stood up and began to put my papers back into my briefcase.

"At that point, the deputy IG pointed to me and ordered me to 'sit down' in a very stern and agitated tone. I ignored his command and made a profane comment to him as I finished putting my files into my briefcase. Again, in a stern and very agitated voice, the deputy stated, 'Look, you don't dictate. . . .' He was unable to finish his statement because I interrupted, saying, 'You're right. I don't dictate. I'm leaving.' At that point the deputy IG stood up, put his hand on my shoulder, and pushed me toward a door that was not the one I came in. My initial thought was that he was pushing me into a room full of hostile agents and I resisted. I told him I was going out the door I came in. He quickly moved back to the door I was trying to exit by, blocking my way. He put his hands on both of my shoulders and again ordered me to leave by the other door. At that point, I felt I had put up with enough of his abuse and attempt to intimidate me, and I told him to remove his hands from my shoulders or I would have him arrested.

"Suddenly, he got such a cold look in his eye that for a split second I thought he was going to hit me. He became extremely agitated (his hand was shaking violently) and again pointed his finger directly into my face, stating, 'I know all about your reputation in the IG community and you're a joke.' I was embarrassed and humiliated, but I kept my composure [and] stepped around him, exiting the room."[7]

Later, in reflecting on the incident, the worker remembered that the deputy IG clearly knew who he was—that is to say, he knew that he was a Democrat, not a loyal Bushie. In his years of working for the federal government, the worker had never been threatened physically by someone in a position of authority. It was behavior that did not seem to him appropriate to the American system of government.

⬌

In this culture of secrecy, intimidation, suppression, and payback-for-supporters-at-any-cost, the first accomplishment of the Bush administration was pushing through Congress a new education bill entitled No Child Left Behind, a back-to-basics program that mandated better funding of public schools and based the advancement of students not on social promotion but on passing heavily monitored, mandatory standardized tests. The bill was passed by the House of Representatives on May 23, 2001, and signed into law by the president several months later. Although some critics maintained that the program emphasized testing over learning, it was nonetheless a major achievement for the Bush administration and fulfilled one of Bush's campaign promises. However, after the bill was passed, Bush administration officials offended a Republican senator who had devoted much of his career to advancing educational issues. Senator James Jeffords of Vermont was a little-known figure outside his home state of Vermont, but when the Bush administration angered him by not funding special education in the new education bill and, some observed at the time, by not inviting him to a Teacher of the Year ceremony at the White House—staffers reportedly felt that because the Rockefeller Republican's liberal leanings were out of step with Bush's bedrock right-wing values, he needed to be punished by isolating him—he did the unexpected just to get even with the administration. A progressive Republican, Jeffords had been disappointed with Bush's right-leaning politics, but the pettiness of the administration pushed him to the breaking point, so he decided to leave the party.[8]

After the 2000 election, the Republicans controlled the House of

Representatives comfortably, but it held the Senate by the slimmest of margins—50 Republicans to 50 Democrats, with Cheney breaking any tie votes to give the Republicans control. (The vice president, as stated in the Constitution, is president of the Senate, and when a vote is tied, his vote is required to break it.) When Jeffords changed his party affiliation from Republican to Independent, he shifted the balance of power in the Senate from the Republicans to the Democrats, who then had 51 members to the Republicans' 49. The desertion took Bush officials off guard, and members of Bush's inner circle were livid, particularly Rove.

In the end, Jeffords's defection opened Rove to intense criticism from fellow Republicans who believed he should have been more aware of the senator's unhappiness and taken actions to prevent him from leaving the party. "One of the things the Bush administration didn't do effectively," Ed Rollins says, "is they never built a congressional liaison operation. They were heavy-handed with the Republicans in the House and the Senate and expected them to do whatever they wanted them to do. Karl didn't have direct control over congressional relations, but, certainly, in his position as the political guy, he had control over whatever he wanted to have control over."[9]

"Many prominent Republicans," the *New York Times* reported on July 2, 2001, "who once marveled at the Bush administration's agility say the president's lieutenants are increasingly stumbling in ways that are not merely embarrassing but also perilous to Mr. Bush's political standing. . . . They point to the arguably clumsy way the administration handled the global warming issue and the initial rollout of its energy plan, the defection of Senator James M. Jeffords of Vermont from the Republican Party and the meeting of a senior administration official with executives from a company in which he owned more than $100,000 worth of stock. And they note that these and other episodes have at times made the administration seem alternatively arrogant, sloppy, unethical, and out of touch."[10] The unnamed Bush official who had met with representatives of a company in which he owned stock was Rove.[11] Generally speaking, some Republicans were coming to believe that, within the administration, Rove had too much power and, moreover, he was heavy-handed in the way he wielded that power. Equally troubling, it was thought that by allowing him to wander unchecked through the realms of both politics and policy, Bush had given Rove too much leeway over policy decisions and the political motivations that seemed increasingly to be behind them.

But these concerns seemed to be lost on Rove and others in the Bush administration. Instead, their focus had turned, for instance, to the various ways Jeffords could be punished, now that he had committed the sin of being disloyal to the president. It never occurred to the Bush loyalists that they might have been responsible for forcing from their ranks a man who had been a Republican Party member throughout his career. At the same time, Rove began to zero in on what he had to do to win back the Senate in the 2002 midterm election. Here was his plan of attack: Ignore what could have been achieved by gracefully acknowledging errors in judgment that had offended a party regular like Jeffords and fixate on using force to retake the Senate and on punishing the Bush administration's political enemies along the way.

But, then again, Rove had started thinking about the midterm election as soon as he got into the White House. Once it was apparent that Bush had won the 2000 election, Rove had hired the campaign's field director, Ken Mehlman, to begin planning how they were going to increase the number of Republican seats in the House and the Senate. Throughout the spring of 2001, as Bush was making one decision after another that hurt him with the general electorate but helped him with his base, Rove and others met regularly in a dining room at La Brasserie to plot out their plans for the midterm. These meetings took on an air of giddiness. "Sometimes we're in a meeting talking to each other and

BlackBerrying each other at the same time," one participant later said.[12] The meetings continued during the year, until late summer of 2001, when most of the major players in the administration went on vacation. Then, just after the vacations ended, the unthinkable happened.

2.

On the night before September 11, George W. Bush had dinner with his brother Jeb, the governor of Florida, at a resort on the Florida coast. The next morning, a Tuesday, Bush woke up around six o'clock at the Colony, a hotel located in Longboat Key. Bush's first public event of the day was an appearance in a second-grade classroom at an elementary school in Sarasota to promote his education agenda. He arrived at the school just before nine o'clock. At the school, Rove, who was traveling with Bush as he frequently did, whispered some disturbing news into Bush's ear. An airplane had crashed into the upper floors of the North Tower of the World Trade Center. Details of the crash were sketchy, so it was not clear what had happened, but it appeared to be a tragic accident, or so it was implied to Bush. For good measure, Bush was briefed by telephone from the White House by Condoleezza Rice, the national security adviser. Previously, Rice and Bush had both been given a national security memo generated by the FBI dated August 6, 2001, that was entitled "Bin Laden Determined to Strike in U.S." The memo even spelled out that Osama bin Laden and his al Qaeda followers planned to "bring the fight to America" in retaliation for the United States having bombed their bases in Afghanistan during the Clinton administration. The last time bin Laden's group had attacked the United States had been in 1993, and his target had been the World Trade Center—the very building that had just been hit by an airplane not five weeks after the FBI had issued its memo. But Bush and his advisers did not seem to make the connection between the memo and that morning's airplane crash. Regardless of what had happened in New York, Bush decided—and Rove concurred—he should continue with his plans for the morning. So he entered the classroom, where he proceeded to meet with the children.

"President Bush was sitting in a second-grade classroom in Sarasota, Florida, on Tuesday morning, his eyes and his smile fixed on 7-year-olds showing off their reading skills," one report would state. "But his mind was clearly fixed on the news he had heard just moments before: a passenger jet had crashed into one of the World Trade Center towers. At 9:05 a.m., the White House chief of staff, Andrew H. Card Jr., stepped into the classroom and whispered into the president's right ear, 'A second plane hit the other tower, and America's under attack.' "[13]

It was now, as countless critics of Bush would observe in the future, that the president seemed to be at a loss for what to do. Having just heard a piece of news more disturbing than any president had received since Franklin Roosevelt was told about the bombing of Pearl Harbor or John Kennedy was informed about the Bay of Pigs and a looming nuclear holocaust, Bush did nothing. "Really good readers, whew," Bush said to the children. "This must be sixth grade." Then, inexplicably, he sat with the children for another six minutes still doing nothing, another fact his critics would underscore. In one of the most bizarre interludes in presidential history, while the Twin Towers of the World Trade Center burned in lower Manhattan, while the United States homeland was under attack, Bush sat in a second-grade classroom in Florida and didn't move—for six full minutes. But, then again, neither did anyone on his staff, including Andrew Card and Karl Rove, both of whom were standing nearby watching the president. If at any point in his career Rove should have been able to advise Bush, it was now, and he did nothing. The apparatus of the presidency stopped—for six full minutes. No one entered the classroom to escort the president out. No one made any signal that he should leave. Finally, at 9:12, in a move as strange as his sitting still for six minutes, Bush stood up, turned on his heel, and walked out. At least the president would not be sitting in a grammar school classroom before television cameras when the third airplane hit the Pentagon and the fourth crashed in a field in Pennsylvania.

By 9:55, Bush, still accompanied by Rove, was aboard Air Force One, where he got on the telephone with Dick Cheney. It was not apparent, however, exactly where the president was going. Cheney was at the White House, where he and others—Laura Bush and Condoleezza Rice among them—had been taken to a secure location, a private, fortified bunker beneath the White House. So, not knowing where the president should go, Bush officials decided that Air Force One would fly to Barksdale Air Force Base in Shreveport, Louisiana. There, Bush held an impromptu press conference at which he made a statement, but took no questions. Rove had staged countless press appearances for Bush in the past, but he could not have failed more thoroughly with his staging of this one. "Bush appeared before the reporters for just two minutes," the *New York Times* reported, "declaring, 'Freedom itself was attacked this morning by a faceless coward.' But he looked nervous, and the tape of the appearance was jumpy and grainy."[14] By no means was it Bush's finest hour. Indeed, Bush's appearance did more to unsettle the public than calm it. He seemed scared, uncertain, unqualified to lead at this moment in history.

From Louisiana, Air Force One took Bush, seemingly at random, to Offutt Air Force Base near Omaha, Nebraska, where he held a national security meeting that ended at four o'clock in the afternoon. It was later said that Bush then made it clear that he wanted to go back to the White House, although there would be no evidence that this was the case. Supposedly, the Secret Service responded—for the second time that day—that Bush could not return to Washington. Yet it was unclear when Bush had demanded to return to the White House earlier in the day. Finally, after looking as if he had been on the run from enemies for hours, Bush did fly back to Washington around 7:00 that evening so he could properly address the nation from the Oval Office at 8:30. Rove was with Bush as he made his speech. So far, Bush had given the worst performance he could have as a president under pressure, and the man who had been the architect of his ascent to the highest position of power in the country had been with him throughout the debacle. Finally, with the speech from the Oval Office, which at least made Bush look as if he were in charge, Rove had begun to correct the damage he had allowed Bush to sustain during the day.

On September 12, Bush was criticized because he had not returned to Washington right away after the attacks. Fearing that Bush might sustain severe political damage because of questions being raised about his behavior, the administration issued a cover story, no doubt approved by Rove, that said that Bush had not gone back to the White House because there was credible evidence that Air Force One was a target of the terrorists. According to this story, the White House received a call saying, "Air Force One is next," after which the caller used code words that indicated he or she was familiar with White House procedures. "We are talking about specific and credible intelligence, not vague suspicions," Rove said, although he never gave any indication of what that "specific and credible intelligence" was. Rove added that Bush had wanted to return to Washington twice—once in the morning, immediately after the second plane hit, and once in the afternoon—but the Secret Service would not let him. Rove never explained why it was the Secret Service and not the president who had decided when he should return to Washington.[15]

Soon, Bush's behavior was being openly questioned by the press. "But Karl Rove, Mr. Bush's political strategist, is in the middle of our national security crisis," columnist Maureen Dowd wrote on September 23. "First, he called around town, trying to sell reporters the story—now widely discredited—that Mr. Bush didn't immediately return to Washington on September 11 because the plane that was headed for the Pentagon may have really been targeting the White House, and that Air Force One was in jeopardy, too. Then Mr. Rove apparently grew livid when Dick Cheney's dramatic retelling of the scene in the White House"—which Cheney offered to Tim Russert on *Meet the Press* on the Sunday after the attacks—"relegated the president to a footnote."[16] Rove had never liked Cheney and had argued against his being put on the ticket as vice president, and now this: Cheney was making himself out to be the major player in this pivotal moment in history when it should have been the president.

In the meantime, on September 17, in a move calculated to restore the country to some kind of normalcy, Bush dispatched Rove to representatives of Major League Baseball and the National Football League to convince them to have their teams resume their regular schedules. Looking back, this would seem a bit odd, since, for example, in Britain, officials postponed for an entire year the Ryder Cup golf tournament; played every other year and slated to commence on September 28 at a golf course in Belfry, it was, according to tournament officials, inappropriate to stage the event in the wake of such a horrific tragedy.

Bush tried to regain some credibility by giving a speech to a joint session of Congress on the evening of September 20. In that speech, he announced the creation of a new federal agency, the Office of Homeland Security. To be headed by Pennsylvania governor Tom Ridge, a decorated Vietnam War veteran, the agency would provide a way for the divergent law enforcement agencies within the government to establish a united front against threats to the homeland.

⇌

On October 7, the United States and its allies, mainly the United Kingdom, began an all-out ground and air attack on Afghanistan. Their purpose was to destroy the Taliban government that had been harboring Osama bin Laden, the mastermind behind the hijacking of the planes on September 11. Using cruise missiles and long-range bombers against a country that had no national military, but rather a network of warlords controlling different regions, the allied forces toppled the existing government with little or no resistance. The military might of the allied forces made the victory quick and unequivocal, and, because it was generally agreed that Afghanistan had been protecting bin Laden—providing him with a home base from which to enlist and train terrorists—the community of nations was supportive of the military action.

By the following month, the issue of September 11 and the war in Afghanistan seemed at times to have become detached from Rove's thinking. On October 18, ambassadors were invited to Washington for a luncheon briefing with Rove at Blair House. Naturally, the political community thought the topic of the briefing would be politics in a post-September 11 world. The day of the luncheon arrived, and the ambassadors showed up in large numbers. They had all come to hear what Rove, speaking on behalf of the administration, had to say about what might happen next on the political front as a result of the attacks of September 11 and the military action taking place in Afghanistan. Instead, Rove stood before the luncheon audience and made a speech about, to quote the *Washington Post*, "the nature of party politics, how to win, the history of the Republican Party's opposition to slavery, the importance of the black vote, and so on."[17] The paper quoted one ambassador as saying, "It was so surreal, it was difficult to keep a straight face. I was expecting something on military targets achieved, plans for ground troops in Afghanistan, anthrax, anything but what we heard."[18]

Then, in early November, Bush ordered Rove to fly to Los Angeles to meet with television and motion picture executives to explore how Hollywood could help create films and television shows that would support the war effort. Jack Valenti, the head of the Motion Picture Association of America who had once worked in the Johnson administration, set up the meeting between Rove and the executives; Valenti said that he wouldn't mind if Hollywood made movies like they did after the start of World War II. It was never made public what, specifically, was discussed. Whatever it was did not come to fruition, because few if any films or television shows were produced that promoted the United States' efforts against terrorism or in the war in Afghanistan.

Immediately after September 11, the Bush administration was able to push through Congress the USA PATRIOT Act, which passed so quickly that many members of the House and Senate, especially the Democrats, did not fully understand some of the flaws in the bill, such as a provision that allowed for the temporary appointment of some government officials—US attorneys, to name one group—on an interim basis. Critics of the bill would argue that aspects of it infringed on the civil rights of American citizens under the guise of protecting the country from terrorism. Then, by the beginning of 2002, which was, after all, a midterm election year, Rove found a way to use the attacks of September 11 as a political wedge issue. In a speech before the Republican National Committee in January 2002, Rove argued for the first time in public that Republicans could use what the Bush administration had come to call the "war on terrorism" to their advantage in the midterm election. Republican candidates could "go to the country on this issue," Rove told the assembled politicos, because American citizens "trust the Republican Party to do a better job of protecting and strengthening America's military might and thereby protecting America."

What was never made clear in the speech, or during political debates afterward, was why the Republicans should be considered the party to protect America when it had been a Republican president and a Republican administration—warned by its own intelligence agencies—that had allowed the terrorist attacks to occur in the first place. If Bush could not prevent the attacks from happening, especially when he had been warned that an attack was being planned and the World Trade Center had already been the target of such an attack in 1993, it should have been apparent that his ability to wage a war on terrorism was suspect. But the Bush administration's ability to sell this piece of nonlogic to the public was excellent, and, in many ways, Rove's strategy would end up working.

There was no doubt about it. In the aftermath of September 11, once the stories had been released to cover Bush's bumbling on the day of the tragedy, and then as a result of the quick and successful invasion of Afghanistan, the country rallied around the president, whose approval ratings, which had been slumping in the months leading up to September 11, began to soar. At one point following the attacks, Bush enjoyed ratings in the low 90s, among the highest ever achieved by a president and matched only by those of his father following the successful war in the Gulf in 1991. The Bush staff acted to use this popularity in various ways, at times intimidating and punishing their enemies. They were apparently more than willing to attack Republicans, not just Democrats, as evidenced in the way Rove dealt with Congressman Tom Tancredo of Colorado, who did not always vote in lockstep with Bush, which in Rove parlance meant he was disloyal.

≡

One morning in April 2002, Congressman Tom Tancredo, who represented a district in the southern Denver metropolitan region—one of the state's most Republican areas—got into his car outside his home in Alexandria, Virginia, and headed for his office on Capitol Hill. No sooner had he pulled out of his driveway than his cell phone began to ring. When he looked to see who the caller was, the phone's small screen flashed "The White House." This was the first time the White House had called him on his cell phone since he became a congressman in 1998, so, rather startled, Tancredo answered the call at once. A woman on the other end of the line said, "Hold for Mr. Rove."

Upon hearing Rove's name, Tancredo knew exactly what the call was about. The day before, he had held a long luncheon interview with the editorial board of the *Washington Times*, the right-leaning alternative to the *Washington Post*, and much of the discussion had addressed a topic that was of deep concern to Tancredo—immigration. A Goldwater–Reagan conservative who was opposed to what he considered to be the federal government's liberal—that is to say, in his view, dangerously lax—treatment of the issue of illegal immigration, Tancredo had been purposefully provocative in the interview. If in the future the country suffered another event similar to the attacks of September 11, if the event were perpetrated by someone who "waltzed across our borders" without any law enforcement agency knowing about it, and if the government had done no more to secure the borders than it had as of April 2002, then "the blood of every American killed," to quote what he had told the editorial board, "will be on the hands of the Congress and the president of the United States."[19]

The newspaper had been anxious to run Tancredo's interview about the government's "open-door" policy on immigration and the prospects of terrorists in pursuit of American "blood," and it had that morning. So, even though he had not yet read the newspaper, Tancredo knew why Rove was calling. It was not long before Rove got on the phone.

"Karl," Tancredo said, "how are you doing?"

"I was doing a lot better until I read this morning's paper," Rove shot back.

"Well, I haven't read the papers yet but I'm sure I know what you're referring to."

This exchange began a conversation that became more and more animated and lasted throughout Tancredo's 30-minute drive from his home in Alexandria to Capitol Hill. During the call, Rove became increasingly incensed.

"I don't know how you could have said a thing like that," Rove said. "You're a traitor to the president."

It occurred to Tancredo that his oath of office required him to support and defend not the president or even his party, but the Constitution. Even so, he did not mention that fact to Rove. "Let's walk through it," Tancredo said instead. "If it goes the way I outlined it—if we have another attack like September 11, if it is carried out by someone who has crossed our borders, and if we have not done anything to strengthen our border security, who do you think the American public *should* blame? The Elks Club? Who is in charge of our security?"

"We've put smart borders in place," Rove replied.

"When was the last time you were actually on the border?" Tancredo asked.

"I've been in Texas for . . . "

"I'm not talking about Crawford," Tancredo interrupted. "I'm talking about being on the border."

"You are wrong about the border," Rove said. "We've done something about the border. And *you* had better muzzle it."

Tancredo could hardly believe what he had just heard. The president's chief political adviser was threatening a member of Congress over the phone about an interview he had given to a newspaper—*and* warning him not to speak out again.

"Well, I'm not going to muzzle it until you secure the borders," Tancredo said.

"Then you better never darken the doorsteps of this White House," Rove said, livid.

"I don't ever remember the welcome mat being out for me, to tell you the truth," Tancredo said. "And besides, *it is not your house!*"

Though the president won in a squeaker election, the Bush administration frequently governed as if it had won in a landslide. Many individuals within the administration, including department heads, conducted themselves as if they were somehow above recrimination and not subject to the laws that govern ordinary citizens. So after they had packed the government with unqualified personnel who could easily be controlled, some of the figures of authority in the Bush administration went about abusing their power with impunity, in part because they knew their subordinates would not dare challenge them. Consider Mel Martinez, the secretary of the Department of Housing and Urban Development. He routinely used his government SUV, driven by members of his security detail, to run a carpool for his son—a practice that violated government codes. Martinez was so flagrant about this misuse that he even documented it. On September 11, 2002, Jessica E. Clark, the secretary's director of scheduling, sent an e-mail to Robert E. Langston, his head of security, with copies routed to six members of the secretary's security staff.

On the one-year anniversary of the worst terrorist attacks on our country, when concern about security for officials in government was at its highest, Martinez's staff was concerned not so much about protecting the secretary from terrorists as about getting the secretary's son Andrew to school on time. In an e-mail bearing the subject line "Morning Pickups," Clark wrote: "FYI . . . when I list 'please use the suburban' in the notes section on the Secretary's schedule that means (typically) that the Secretary will need to take Andrew and the other carpool kids to school that day. You've probably already figured that out, but just in case. . . ."[20]

3.

By now, Rove was well into his effort to win both the House and the Senate for the Republicans in the midterm election. It would be a rare accomplishment for a sitting president, but Rove believed he could pull it off since Bush, thanks to the rallying around the flag that had continued since September 11, had maintained his historically high approval ratings. Back in June, there had been the now-expected moment of strategic confusion when a copy of a PowerPoint presentation detailing Republican plans for the midterm election was found on a bench in Lafayette Park, supposedly left there by an intern. It was yet another classic misdirection that was becoming routinely associated with Rove-run political operations. Then, in July, there was a shake-up at the White House when Karen Hughes, the counselor to the president, a member of Bush's Iron Triangle along with Rove and Joe Allbaugh and the person who had been Bush's public voice for almost a decade, decided to leave her post in the administration. Officially, she was resigning because her family wanted to go home to Texas, but rumors persisted in Washington gossip channels that Hughes and Rove, no longer getting along, were locked in a power struggle over the control of Bush's public image. Hughes wanted Bush to try to maintain a more moderate image, as he had attempted to do during the presidential campaign; Rove hoped to move Bush farther to the right in an effort to motivate the Republican base. Apparently, Rove won, or so it would be said after Dan Bartlett, a protégé of Rove's since the age of 22, was named as Hughes's replacement. Now Rove had more control than ever. The tone of the administration became harsher and Bush's appeal to the party's conservative base became more blatant—the latter a move Hughes had long resisted.

In conjunction with Ken Mehlman, Rove had also developed a strategy he called the 72-Hour Task Force, which in theory was a grassroots get-out-the-vote effort that could win a campaign for the Republicans in the race's last three days. The plan was simple and old-fashioned: Have workers make personal phone calls instead of automated ones at the same time that they hit neighborhoods on foot, knocking on doors to ask for votes. But the big debate going into the 2002 midterm elections was how to use Bush in the congressional races. Traditionally, the president did not actively campaign in midterm races, choosing to stay above the fray in the White House. But Bush was different. From the beginning, Rove had played such a pivotal role in the daily decision making at the White House that the Bush administration had never even attempted to separate politics from policy. "There are few decisions, from tax cuts to judicial nominations to human cloning, in which Rove is not directly involved," *Time* noted about the administration. "'It's not a real meeting if Karl isn't there,' says a senior member of the domestic-policy staff."[21] So when the final decision had to be made about the president's participation in the midterm races, it was easy: Yes, Bush would be used in whatever way possible to help the Republicans shore up their dominance in the House and regain control of the Senate.

Indeed, with the House securely under Republican rule, Rove was focusing on the Senate, particularly the races in South Dakota, Minnesota, Iowa, Missouri, Colorado, and Georgia. Of those contests, the one that seemed almost to obsess Rove was the race in Georgia, where incumbent Max Cleland, the Vietnam veteran who had lost three limbs in an accident during the war, was being challenged by Saxby Chambliss, a congressman from the state. Chambliss had agreed to give up his House seat and run for the Senate only if Rove could guarantee him extensive support from the president, in terms of both fund-raising and stumping for him in his state. As it turned out, the Georgia race would be one of the dirtiest of the midterm election cycle, with all of the classic earmarks of a Rove-run campaign.

≡

"Karl Rove came down to Georgia and personally recruited my opponent, Saxby Chambliss," Max Cleland says. "Rove made the proposition.

That's how badly the White House wanted to take me out. Bush had everything except the Senate. Senator Jeffords had changed parties and decided to caucus with the Democrats, which changed the balance of power in the Senate. Tom Daschle became the majority leader. The goal of the White House was to unify their control in Washington. I was one of the people standing in their way."[22]

Rove targeted Cleland because Rove felt he could be defeated. "I had gotten something like 49 percent of the vote in 1996 in a very tight race, so Rove looked at me as vulnerable," Cleland says. "Because of that, they came after me. Rove was the ultimate political assassin, hired by Bush to do his dirty work. Ralph Reed was chairman of the Republican Party here; he worked closely with Rove. They were all out of the Lee Atwater cloth where the goal of a campaign is to drive your opponent's negatives up."

To do that, Rove decided to launch an all-out assault on Cleland, and using the Rove tried-and-true tactic of attacking opponents not on their weaknesses but on their strengths, he decided to focus on Cleland's patriotism and support of protecting America's homeland as a means of defeating him. In Vietnam, during a combat mission, Cleland had lost both legs and an arm in an explosion. In the years since then, he had often quipped, "I have only one more limb to give to this country." Rove saw Cleland's personal history—and all that it represented about his service to the country—as an asset that had to be destroyed. Cleland says, "The White House had begun using September 11 as a wedge issue to show what they always try to show: Democrats are weak and Republicans are strong. Republicans tried to use this in the 1950s, when Eisenhower was president. Now they were trying to say Democratic candidates were soft on terrorism."

At one point in the campaign, Chambliss actually accused Cleland of treason because he broke "his oath to protect and defend the Constitution." Cleland's crime? He had refused to vote for the bill establishing the Department of Homeland Security. But the reason Cleland had voted against the bill—actually, he had voted against amendments to the bill—and the way Rove used his votes against him is illustrative of Rove's tactics.

"I was on the General Services Committee in the Senate," Cleland says, "and Joe Lieberman and I began to push in the early spring of 2002 for a Department of Homeland Security." The Office of Homeland Security, established by Bush just after the attacks of September 11, was not a cabinet-level agency; Cleland and Lieberman began the effort to elevate the agency to the cabinet level, making it a department, not a mere office. "Early on, Rove and the White House said, 'No, we don't need a Department of Homeland Security. The office with Tom Ridge is sufficient.' The office had 12 to 15 people working in it. When our bill got some steam behind it and it looked like it was going to pass, Rove and the White House had a change of mind. They supported our idea and in committee tried to scuttle our bill so it would be theirs that passed. The Republican amendments to try to scuttle the bill Lieberman and I coauthored were the amendments I voted against. I had been in favor of the Department of Homeland Security for months and had helped write the original legislation, so in the fall if you are Karl Rove and you want to use this against me, what do you do? You lie."

Specifically, the Chambliss campaign ran a television ad in which Cleland's face appeared alongside those of Osama bin Laden and Saddam Hussein. "I had actually fought the Communists in Vietnam," Cleland says, "while Saxby Chambliss, who had never served in the American military, got out of going to Vietnam with a trick knee. But here they were using September 11 as a wedge issue and putting my picture up in an ad next to pictures of Osama bin Laden and Saddam Hussein, with the ad saying I had voted against Bush's Homeland Security bill 12 times. Bush didn't even *have* a Homeland Security bill until Lieberman and I wrote ours! And I never voted against the bill, I voted against the Republican amendments to the bill I had coauthored. In order to distort my record, they had to lie about it, and they lied visually. Somehow, Osama bin Laden and Saddam Hussein and Max Cleland had something in common. I had voted to weaken the country."

The Rove-orchestrated smear against Cleland very much resembled the one he had effected in South Carolina against John McCain, another war hero. That both Rove and Bush had done all they could to avoid active military service—through draft-dodging deferments (Rove) or pulling family strings to get admitted to the Texas Air National Guard at a time when the Guard did not go overseas to fight (Bush)—was lost on Georgia's voting public in a race that would become notorious for its ugliness.

Rove did not keep Bush away from the mudslinging. Anything but. Ten days before the election Chambliss needed help, so he asked Bush to come to Georgia twice, once for a stop in Marietta, once in Savannah. Bush agreed to make both appearances, on November 2. Three days later, Chambliss won the election, and political observers agreed that, in the final analysis, Bush's last-minute stumping for Chambliss was what put him over the top after the ad campaign had smeared and discredited Cleland so badly that he could be defeated.

Georgia was not the only state in which Bush campaigned. At Rove's urging, Bush traveled 10,000 miles to 15 states, touching down in 17 cities in the final five days before the election. Rove even scheduled Bush to stump for Norman Coleman in Minnesota only days after incumbent Democratic senator Paul Wellstone had died in a plane crash. With this last 10-day campaign push, Bush became the most ambitious sitting president ever to work for his party in the midterm elections.

⬢

Bush started out election day by voting at a volunteer fire station near his ranch in Crawford, but that night, after having dinner with Laura and friends, Bush watched the returns with Republican leaders and their wives in the living quarters of the White House. Rove kept Bush posted with updates from an election war room. Once all the results were in, Bush and Rove had much to celebrate. In the House of Representatives, the Republicans ended up with 229 seats to 205 for the Democrats (with one Independent). The Republicans took back the Senate, too, securing 51 seats to the Democrats' 48 and 1 Independent. In addition to Georgia, they won in states like Minnesota and South Dakota, where Rove also had handpicked the candidates. An old Rove client, John Cornyn, won a Senate seat in Texas.

Not surprisingly, the accolades poured in for Rove. "His name was not on any ballot," the *New York Times* observed on November 7, "but Karl Rove, the West Wing mastermind who has plotted for years to bring George W. Bush and the Republican Party to dominance, emerged as one of the biggest winners in the midterm elections of 2002."[23] This, from *Time*: "He woke up Wednesday morning in a new political world, one step closer to the grand, gauzy vision Rove has been touting for the past three years: that together he and Bush are forging a new Republican majority that will rule the land for a generation." Rove himself told *Time*, "'It's not going to be a dramatic realignment of American politics in which one day it's deadlocked and the next day it's a blowout. The changes are gradual, but they're persistent.'"[24]

Others tried to put the election—and what it meant not just to Rove but also to Bush—into historic perspective. "For the first time since 1934 (in FDR's first term), a president led his party to gains in both chambers of Congress two years into his first term," *Newsweek* reported. "His Democratic opposition was left divided and confused, groping for ways to oppose a leader they had dismissed as a dimwitted usurper after the disputed election of 2000. And his domestic victory was only half of the story. Three days after the election, following two months of prodding, the U.N. Security Council unanimously supported a sternly worded resolution that gave Bush wide latitude to attack Saddam Hussein if the Iraqi dictator doesn't disarm by next February. Even Syria voted yes. 'He had the equivalent of two presidencies in one week,' crowed chief of staff Andy Card. 'On Tuesday, he showed he is leading the country,' said another top administration aide. The United Nations vote 'showed he is leading the world.'"[25]

A week later, Rove himself weighed in on the historic significance of the midterm election. He was speaking at the University of Utah, one of the institutions of higher learning he had attended but had not graduated from, and his topic was the American presidency. "'Things are moving in a new direction,'" Rove said. "'It's not just that Republicans picked up three seats in the Senate or six or seven or eight seats in the House. It's something else more fundamental, but we'll only know what it is in another two years or four years.'"[26]

In the meantime, Rove had the next two years to think about. Rove's agenda, which would be detailed in Bush's State of the Union address in early 2003, would focus intently on tax reform, perhaps the most important overall issue to his base. The Bush administration had already passed tax cuts in 2001 and 2002. "Rove had pushed through the tax cuts," Matt Towery says. "In reality it was—and would be—the only thing the administration passed of real substance. Whether you liked the tax cuts or not, the economy did improve. Now, arguably the economy might have improved whether you had a tax cut or not, but we'll never know. And Rove was responsible for the tax cuts. To that extent, he served the president well."[27] Rove continued to push for more tax cuts, which were enacted in 2003. The effect of the cuts was drastic, in both the short- and the long-term. The country had rarely—if ever—seen such a great accumulation of wealth among such a small group of people as it did under the Bush administration. While the rest of the population struggled, the top one-half of the top 1 percent of Americans would see their worth soar, and the

Bush tax cuts were responsible for a vital part of that wealth realignment.

But other special interest groups aligned with Bush needed accommodating as well. Bush was so determined to pass the Medicare bill to appease his corporate supporters in both the insurance and the health care industries that, when it was being voted on in the House, he personally made phone calls from Air Force One while flying back from London, where he had been a house guest of Queen Elizabeth II. He had also made calls from Buckingham Palace itself. Then, as soon as he got off the plane in Washington, he gave a speech supporting his Medicare bill on the tarmac before returning to the White House. He continued to make calls into the wee hours of the morning. Bush was pushing for passage of the Medicare bill, despite the fact that rank-and-file conservatives in the party were opposed to it.

"They called my wife to try to find out where I was because I wasn't answering my phone anymore," Tom Tancredo says. "I had gone to sleep and turned everything off. They called her at, like, one in the morning. But they were relentless all because of Medicare. We held that vote open until they got the last vote and they slammed it down and we went home. It was Chinese water torture on your principles. You can come into the Congress like the Rock of Gibraltar and you go out like a pebble. We passed that Medicare [bill] twice. It was the first time that was awful. But Bush needed it. He had to pay back the people who had supported him."[28]

It would not be the only pay-for-play legislation Bush would get passed during the second half of his first term, as he headed into the reelection campaign. From the moment when Bush was finally declared the winner in 2000, Rove had been scheming about how he was going to get Bush reelected. Now, with the Republicans in control of both chambers of Congress, Rove would set his sights on the victory that would further advance his pursuit of a permanent Republican majority, the achievement that, once and for all, would get him into the history books.

CHAPTER SIX

THE ARCHITECT

1.

In the wake of the Gulf War in 1991, the United Nations passed Security Council Resolution 687, which forbade Iraq from using or even developing chemical, biological, or nuclear weapons—weapons of mass destruction. For years, the UN Special Commission on Iraq's weapons inspectors had monitored the situation until inspectors had finally left the country in 1998 in response to Saddam Hussein's failure to cooperate. After September 11, 2001, Bush and his administration decided that, besides defeating the Taliban in Afghanistan and destroying al Qaeda's bases of operation there, they were going to target Iraq. The Bush administration argued that Saddam was developing weapons of mass destruction that could be used to hit the eastern seaboard of the United States. Just as egregious, these Bush officials said, Saddam had been working with al Qaeda and may have played a part in the planning and execution of September 11. The Bush officials made this assertion even though George Tenet, director of the Central Intelligence Agency, had made it clear in his daily security briefings with the president that there was no connection between Saddam and Osama bin Laden. In fact, the two men didn't even agree with each other on basic political and religious issues. Bin Laden viewed Saddam as an infidel; Saddam saw bin Laden as an extremist who was a threat to his government.

Nonetheless, the Bush administration concocted what amounted to a public relations scheme to sell an invasion of Iraq to the American public. That scheme included an appearance before the United Nations by Secretary of State Colin Powell that Powell and senior members of his staff would later admit contained false information. Vice President Cheney, the administration official most in favor of an attack, engaged in behavior that eventually would call into question the motives of some journalists. Routinely, a Cheney staffer would leak information to a journalist, often Judith Miller of the *New York Times*, whose resulting article would then become front-page news that Cheney would in turn cite as a reason for going to war. As it turned out, much of the Cheney-generated information leaked to reporters was suspect, having been gathered from dubious informants or simply fabricated, as was a good portion of a presentation the Bush administration made in late 2002 to members of the United States Senate, which then authorized the president to use force against Saddam.

In early 2003, Bush declared Iraq to be in noncompliance with the United Nations resolutions and demanded that Saddam leave his country. When he refused, the United States, along with some 40 allies known as the Coalition of the Willing—mainly Great Britain, Spain, and Australia—invaded Iraq on March 20, 2003. Under the command of General Tommy Franks, the initial wave of the attack, with its overwhelming airpower and dramatic display of unrelenting bombing, became known as "shock and awe"—and it *was* an awesome sight to watch on television, for the invasion had been carefully scripted for broadcast around the world. Encountering little organized armed resistance by the Iraqis, the allied forces advanced quickly. On April 9, Baghdad fell to the allies, symbolized by a group of Iraqi citizens, with help from US troops, tearing down an iron statue of Saddam in a prominent public square. In the following days, one development caused alarm if not at the White House then among critics of the invasion: No weapons of mass destruction were found, contrary to the rationale the Bush administration had used to justify its invasion of Iraq in the first place.

This detail did not stop Bush from declaring victory. On May 1, he climbed into the cockpit of a fighter jet in San Diego, even though he reportedly was no longer qualified to fly an airplane (and no doubt the reason he was accompanied by a military pilot who *did* know how to fly), flew a short distance out into the Pacific Ocean to the USS *Abraham Lincoln*, landed on the aircraft carrier's flight deck, emerged for the cameras wearing his flight suit, greeted servicemen, and—once he had changed into appropriate attire—delivered a speech to the assembled audience of active military personnel. In his remarks Bush announced the defeat of the Iraqi forces and a victory for the allies. Behind him hung a huge banner declaring "Mission Accomplished." Unfortunately, while the conventional Iraqi army might have been defeated, the insurgent forces had not, and over the coming months and years the United States—eventually virtually only the United States, as one ally after another dropped out of the "Coalition of the Willing"—became bogged down in a military morass that would be described at various times as a ongoing insurgency or a civil war, but never as a victory for the United States.

Throughout this debacle, while the driving force behind the invasion was Cheney, Rove was lurking in the background trying to find ways to use the war to benefit Bush and his effort to get reelected. "I do not know what role Rove played getting us into the mess in Iraq," Tom Tancredo says, "but I'll bet it wasn't insignificant."[1] That might be because, according to *The Prince*, the book by 16th-century politician Niccolò Machiavelli that Rove claimed was his bible in his early years in politics, one of the best ways for a leader to hold on to power is to take his nation into a war. One fact seems certain. According to sources, while he would not be instrumental in planning the military action itself, Rove was involved in staging the landing of the fighter jet on the USS *Abraham Lincoln*, when

Bush announced as a victory what turned out to be merely the first wave of military action. There was no doubt it was pure Rove, but one potential political problem should have been obvious: What would the administration's fallback position be if the invasion of Iraq did not end with an all-but-immediate military victory? That is to say, what would happen if the conflict dragged on and turned into a prolonged military and political morass not unlike the one the United States had found itself in in Vietnam in the 1960s and 1970s? That does not appear to have been a scenario the Bush administration anticipated.

2.

On the morning of February 24, 2004, in the Roosevelt Room at the White House, Bush stepped up to a podium to read a prepared comment. "Eight years ago, Congress passed, and President Clinton signed, the Defense of Marriage Act," Bush said, his voice controlled and even, almost emotionless, as if he were reading a statement he had no choice but to read and about which he felt no passion, "which defined marriage for purposes of federal law as the legal union between one man and one woman as husband and wife. . . . In recent months, however, some activist judges and local officials have made an aggressive attempt to redefine marriage." Bush went on to cite cases in Massachusetts, San Francisco, and New Mexico, where marriage licenses were being issued to same-sex couples. "On a matter of such importance, the voice of the people must be heard. Activist courts have left the people with one recourse. If we are to prevent the meaning of marriage from being changed forever, our nation must enact a constitutional amendment to protect marriage in America. Decisive and democratic action is needed, because attempts to redefine marriage in a single state or city could have serious consequences throughout the country."

Finally, Bush challenged the Congress. He wanted the House of Representatives and the Senate "to promptly pass, and to send to the states for ratification, an amendment to our Constitution defining and protecting marriage as a union of man and woman as husband and wife." As soon as Bush finished his remarks, he hurriedly departed. He did not take questions from the pool of reporters who had gathered to listen to his announcement, an event that had been scripted by Rove and the operatives working for Rove.

As a matter of fact, Bush had no choice but to do what he did. The war in Iraq was now a year old—it had been almost 10 months since his boastful declaration of "Mission Accomplished" on the *Abraham Lincoln*—and the allied forces were no closer to securing the country and setting up an independent Iraqi government than they had been at the time of the shock-and-awe invasion. In short, the war in Iraq was not going the way members of the Bush administration, such as the vice president, Secretary of Defense Donald Rumsfeld, and Defense Department Deputy Secretary Paul Wolfowitz, had predicted it would. The United States and its allies had not been greeted by grateful Iraqi citizens throwing flowers at the allied servicemen who had come to liberate the country from the dictator Saddam. Instead, the United States was being viewed as an aggressor nation that had invaded Iraq without proper cause and was now an occupying force that should leave. This sentiment was also beginning to be reflected in the domestic polls in the United States; the president's overall approval rating had slipped from a historic high in the low 90s following September 11 to somewhere in the mid-40s. In fact, the situation in Iraq appeared to be deteriorating, and the Bush administration did not anticipate that the situation would improve in the near future.

As a result, it was going to be hard to get Bush reelected to a second term, Rove realized, if all he had to run on was the war. The subject was quickly becoming a losing proposition for Bush, and that was also why there was a growing sense of tension between Rove and Cheney. Cheney was the war's strongest proponent, so Rove blamed Cheney, at least in part, for Bush's falling poll numbers. However, Bush had a base group he could count on in the religious right. Though presently somewhat disenchanted with Bush because they felt he had not done enough on issues important to them, they would help Rove reelect Bush if the administration made a few concessions.

For some time, Donald Wildmon, the Mississippi-based founder of the American Family Association, had been vocal about his wish that Bush advance the idea of a constitutional amendment proclaiming marriage to be between a man and a woman. Around the time of the State of the Union address in 2004, several high-profile ministers approached Rove about their desire for such a constitutional amendment. In the State of the Union speech Bush made a passing reference to the constitutional "process," but this did not placate Christian leaders. In fact, it prompted James D. Dobson, of Focus on the Family, to send his 2½ million followers a stinging e-mail pointedly addressing the issue of an amendment. "The homosexual activist movement . . . ," Dobson's e-mail read, "is poised to administer a devastating and potentially fatal blow to the traditional family. And sadly, very few Christians in positions of responsibility are willing to use their influence to save it."[2]

If Dobson considered Rove to be among those unwilling Christians in positions of responsibility, he would have been wrong, for Rove, even though he often placated the religious right in order to get their votes for his candidates, and in particular for Bush, was not a Christian. "I know something, which is known to few but is not a secret," journalist Christopher Hitchens later said. "Karl Rove is not a believer, and he doesn't shout it from the rooftops, but when asked, he answers quite honestly. I think the way he puts it is, 'I'm not fortunate enough to be a person of faith.'"[3]

Rove himself was not threatened by the gay community. In fact, over the years, he had remained close to his stepfather even after he had begun to live an openly gay lifestyle. "I knew Louis Rove both in Los Angeles and when we retired to Palm Springs," Joe Koons says. "I lived on Camino Real and Louis lived nearby. We were very close friends. He was my strongest friend at the time. We were like brothers. He was a remarkable gentleman in every sense of the word. We both loved classical music, although Louis didn't love it as much as I did. We both enjoyed our cocktails. I know there were a few occasions when we over-indulged, but it was not something that was very common. As for his son Karl, Louis and Karl had a pleasant father–son relationship—very close. I would see Karl coming and going at Louis's house when he visited him, particularly in Palm Springs. We would chat, Karl and I, often about politics. Karl knew his father was gay, of course. There was a group of us. For the most part, the men were very intelligent, well-to-do people, Louis among them. In fact, Louis was very socially prominent, mostly because of his job. Louis did have relationships through the years. He had one or two people on a strong basis. I would meet his friends, since Louis and I were who we were, best friends."[4]

While it was not Rove Dobson had referred to in his e-mail blast, Rove was the person Dobson's colleagues often turned to when they wanted to put the Bush administration on the spot, which they did with a conference call to the White House in late January 2004. It was Rove with whom they conferred. During the call, Richard Land, of the Southern Baptist Convention, demanded to know when Bush was going to fight for a constitutional amendment banning gay marriage with the same fervor he had shown when he pushed through Medicare reform. If he could fight for his supporters in the corporate health industry, why could he not do the same for the Christians? Rove assured the Christian leaders that Bush would make a public statement on the subject at an appropriate time in the near future.

Then Rove, the nonreligious stepson of a gay man, saw one of his wedge issues for the upcoming presidential race materialize before his eyes—an issue that could help divert attention away from the fact that conditions in Iraq were shaping up to be a political and military nightmare. Rove had used homosexuality as a wedge issue before, and now he needed it more than ever. In short, Rove's pragmatism took over. Bush would make a public appeal to Congress to commence the process for a constitutional amendment protecting traditional marriage, and because statewide votes must be held on such matters, his move would prompt state groups to put initiatives banning gay marriage on their ballots during the presidential election. An anti-gay-marriage initiative would motivate Christians to vote for it, and while they were in the booth they would pull the lever for Bush, the man who had proposed the constitutional amendment. Hence Bush's appearance in the Roosevelt Room on February 24, a month after the conference call between Rove and the Christian leaders.

⇌

For much of the early stages of the 2004 presidential election cycle, Bush was not the subject of heavy media coverage since he was running unopposed for the Republican nomination. In the spring, his opponent was determined to be Senator John Kerry of Massachusetts. During the primary season for the Democrats, the contest had been hotly contested, with the front-runners being Kerry, Governor Howard Dean of Vermont, Senator John Edwards of North Carolina, and Congressman Richard Gephardt of Missouri. Because he had assembled an impressive Internet fund-raising operation and, more to the point, because he had become the media darling—so much so that magazine after magazine had put him on its cover—Dean, who had based much of his reason for running for president on his opposition to the war in Iraq, was expected to win the nomination. There was one drawback. While he had brought new voters into the process, in particular younger people who responded to a message that said it was time for the everyday Americans to take back the Democratic Party from the corporations and special interests, Dean did not appeal to the traditional rank-and-file Democrats. So, on the night of the caucus in Iowa, not only did Dean not win, he finished in third place behind Edwards, who had performed better than expected, and Kerry, who had won the caucus by a comfortable margin. When he won the New Hampshire primary days later, Kerry solidified his role as front-runner and proceeded to pursue the nomination with little or no competition. He had the nomination locked up by Super Tuesday.

Rove could not have been more pleased that Kerry would be Bush's opponent. Here was a Massachusetts liberal who had a 20-year voting history in the United States Senate—a record Rove could easily find ways to use against him. In addition, Kerry was hated by many members of the press in Massachusetts. When one reporter was assigned to write a presidential profile about Kerry for a national magazine, a staff member from the *Boston Globe* called and offered to supply him with all the negative material possible, because the staff at the newspaper disliked Kerry so much they would help in any way to discredit him.[5] What's more, Kerry could be downright strange. As soon as he had secured the nomination, he became fixated on the idea that to win the election he needed to take a bold step that no candidate had ever attempted, at least not in modern American politics. For his vice presidential running mate, Kerry wanted to select a Republican, and not just any Republican, but John McCain, the man whom Rove had slandered in the 2000 primary season in order to win the nomination for Bush.

To get McCain to join the ticket, Kerry began an all-out behind-the-scenes campaign to convince him it was in the best interests of the country for him to run as his vice president. Kerry approached McCain on more than one occasion and asked him, without making the offer directly, what McCain would do if Kerry were to ask him officially to consider being his running mate. McCain's answer was always the same. He was not interested in going on the ticket with Kerry. At one point Kerry even offered to create a hybrid position of vice president and secretary of state as a way to make the position more powerful, and potentially more appealing. But the answer was still no. According to a source, Kerry went so far as to telephone Cindy McCain to see if she would lobby her husband.[6] A Kerry staffer called a journalist who had written extensively about McCain in the past to see if he could help determine McCain's thinking. The journalist was told by a close friend of McCain's what McCain had been insisting to Kerry himself: McCain was a Republican and, as such, he was not willing to run on a ticket with Kerry, even if there would be an attempt to present their pairing as a bipartisan team destined to change the direction of American politics.

Part of McCain's appeal was his background as a military hero. It would be unique, and Kerry believed uniquely appealing, to have two Vietnam veterans running on the same ticket. When McCain made it clear that his answer would remain no, Kerry caved in to party pressure and chose not Richard Gephardt, who would have brought him at least the state of Missouri, if not others, in the Electoral College plus the support of the country's union voters, but instead John Edwards, a politician who was not going to run for reelection to the Senate because he knew he would lose. Kerry picked Edwards because the party was worried that he would not be able to raise campaign contributions, and Edwards, a proponent for trial lawyers since he was one himself, would at least be able to bring financial support to the Kerry campaign. In the end, Edwards was not needed to bring in cash. Kerry raised more money than any Democratic presidential candidate in history to date.

But Kerry had made a calculated decision. Even without McCain as his running mate, he was going to mount a campaign that highlighted his service in Vietnam, hoping, presumably, to bring attention to the fact that Bush, when given the chance to serve during the Vietnam War, had chosen instead to seek asylum in the National Guard. So, at the Democratic National Convention that summer, Kerry built his whole presentation of himself around his service in Vietnam. He did not mention that, after he had returned home, he had been a member of and spokesman for Vietnam Veterans Against the War and had appeared as a witness at a Senate hearing in which he asked two rhetorical questions that would come to symbolize the antiwar movement in the country: "How do you ask a man to be the last man to die in Vietnam? How do you ask a man to be the last man to die for a mistake?" Nor could he reveal his darkest secret. He may have been proud of his military service, but after Vietnam he suffered from a case of post-traumatic stress disorder so severe that he would wake up at night, jolted from sleep by hellish nightmares of what had happened to him in Vietnam. If the charge were ever leveled against him that he suffered from this potentially debilitating emotional disorder, he would be hard-pressed to argue that he didn't. The existence of the post-traumatic stress disorder was documented in his military medical files, according to a confidential source familiar with the file.[7] He had never allowed the complete file to be made available to the public.

Either from firsthand knowledge or by instinct, Rove knew the psychological disorder was Kerry's weakness. He also knew Kerry planned to make his military service a cornerstone of his campaign. Therefore, Rove understood that he had to do what he had done to McCain in 2000 and Cleland in 2002. He had to attack Kerry's perceived strength, that is, his military service. Kerry would be no problem, since, unlike McCain and Cleland, he had come back and spoken out against the war, turning many veterans against him.

If Kerry had wanted to goad his opponents—and telegraph what he thought would be an asset of his campaign—he did it right off, in April. He said Cheney and Rove were people "who went out of their way to avoid their chance to serve when they had a chance." "These people in the White House today," he continued, "[have] twisted ethics and morality," referring to the attacks on heroic veterans like McCain and Cleland. Kerry added, "I went. I'm not going to listen to them talk to me about patriotism and how asking questions about the direction of our country somehow challenges patriotism"—he was now referring to the administration's response to Kerry's opposition to the course of the war in Iraq—"because asking questions about the direction of our country *is* patriotism."[8]

＝

The Bush campaign—that is to say, Rove—made it clear that unlike past Augusts in presidential election years, the month would not be a slow one this time. They were going to use the month to go on the offensive against Kerry. The campaign put together a week-by-week attack plan, downplaying his service in Vietnam and highlighting what was going to be described as his liberal voting record and his tendency to "flip-flop" on issues. All of this was a preamble to the Republican National Convention, being held in New York City late in the campaign season, on August 30 through September 2. "This gives us a chance to lay out an agenda, to tell people what [Kerry] wants to do over the next four years," Rove told the *New York Times*. "We need, as we go into the convention, to put more of an emphasis on our agenda. But we still need to explain the war on terror and we need to offer a contrast with Senator Kerry."[9]

For the Bush campaign, the laying out of that contrast, at least on the subject of Vietnam, would be helped considerably by a political action committee named the Swift Boat Veterans for Truth. During his service in Vietnam, for which he was awarded the Bronze Star, the Silver Star, and three Purple Hearts, Kerry was a commanding officer of a swift boat, the small, motorboat-size craft the United States Navy used to patrol the Mekong Delta, among other waterways in Vietnam. To be on a swift boat at the peak of the war was, to put it mildly, a harrowing assignment, for sailors riding the boats never knew when or from where the next attack would come. Kerry had performed with honor during his time on the delta. It was one of the proudest accomplishments of his life. Because the public might view Kerry's military service as admirable, in a campaign in which Rove represented the opponent, there could be only one tactic: That service had to be attacked. That's where the Swift Boat Veterans for Truth came in.

The plan began around the time Kerry was wrapping up the nomination. Roy F. Hoffmann, a retired rear admiral, put in a call to Adrian L. Lonsdale, another Vietnam veteran, to ask if he had seen *Tour of Duty*, a book about Kerry's military service written by Douglas Brinkley, the respected journalist and presidential biographer. Both men had read the book and felt they had been portrayed inaccurately; one report would note that in the book some "veterans compared Mr. Hoffmann to the bloodthirsty colonel in the film *Apocalypse Now*—the one who loves the smell of Napalm in the morning."[10] The two men were determined to fight back, and they decided to make Kerry the target of their campaign. Soon Hoffmann called John E. O'Neill, a prominent Houston attorney who had been a swift boat commander and who, after he and Kerry had returned stateside, had famously debated the merits of the war with Kerry on the *Dick Cavett Show*. O'Neill had ended up supporting the Vietnam War as strongly as Kerry opposed it.

O'Neill was sympathetic to Hoffmann and Lonsdale. The three brought in other Vietnam veterans supportive of their position, and as a group they decided to put together a multimedia assault on Kerry that would feature television commercials, appearances on radio and television talk and news programs, and a book entitled *Unfit for Command: Swift Boat Veterans Speak Out Against Kerry.* According to published reports, it was O'Neill who knew two people the group brought in to be key financial supporters, Harlan Crow and Bob J. Perry. Later, it would be argued it was mere coincidence that Perry, who gave the group $200,000, had donated $46,000 to Bush's two campaigns for governor and had been close friends with Rove for years, dating all the way back to 1986 when they both worked on the Clements campaign. Crow, a member of the family that owns one of the country's largest real estate firms, Trammell Crow, had supported the Bush family so strongly over the years that he had been named a trustee of the George H. W. Bush Presidential Library Foundation. With these men and others putting up seed money for the organization, the Swift Boat Veterans for Truth hired a political advertising company to produce the commercials they would air; that company happened to be Stevens Reed Curcio and Potholm, of Alexandria, Virginia, which had created the notorious "tank" commercial in 1988. Who could forget the shots of Michael Dukakis driving around in a tank, wearing an ill-fitting helmet that made him look silly and unpresidential? That commercial was generally considered to be one of the reasons Dukakis lost the election to George H. W. Bush.

The book as well as the series of commercials, which featured a dozen or more Vietnam veterans, were based on one concept: Here were men who had served in Vietnam at the time Kerry was there and they were calling Kerry's credibility into question. Their claims were varied and damaging. Kerry had received one Purple Heart because he had wounded himself trying to fire a grenade, they said. Kerry had won one of his stars, they said, by turning his boat to attack an enemy soldier on the riverbank who turned out to be a teenager in "a loin cloth." In Kerry's most praiseworthy mission, when under enemy fire he had guided his swift boat to rescue an American serviceman who had fallen in the delta, the intense firefight—remembered by Kerry crewmates in grim detail even decades later—never even occurred, or so said the Swift Boat Veterans for Truth.

This was the problem with the book and commercials: According to all four crewmen who had served with Kerry on the swift boat he commanded, the version of events as described by the members of the Swift Boat Veterans for Truth simply was not accurate. So what was their motivation? Were the Swift Boat Veterans for Truth so angry over *Tour of Duty* that they would fabricate events to contradict what the book was saying? Were these men still furious with Kerry because he had come back from Vietnam and spoken out against the war? Or was there some other, perhaps political, motivation at play? Once the attack on Kerry began, the Bush campaign argued that it had nothing to do with either the book or the commercials, even though one of the initial financial supporters of the group's efforts was a close friend of Rove's. But finally, in August, during the month the Bush campaign had said it would attack Kerry on his military service, it was revealed that the attorney for the veterans' group, Benjamin Ginsberg, also worked for the Bush campaign as its chief outside counsel. Ginsberg had even been involved in the 2000 Florida recount.

Many believed that Ginsberg, one of the most savvy lawyers working in politics, was the conduit between the Bush campaign and the political action committee that had been set up to attack Kerry's military record in August, as promised by Rove. "The truth is," Ginsberg said at the time the connection was discovered, "there are very few lawyers who work in this area. It's sort of natural that people do come to the few of us for the work."[11] Apparently, it never occurred to Ginsberg—or so he would argue—that his representing both the Bush campaign and the Swift Boat Veterans for Truth might pose a conflict of interest. As soon as Ginsberg's connection was made public, he resigned from the Bush campaign. But he wasn't the only person connected to both the campaign and the political action committee. Kenneth Cordier, who had served on a veterans' advisory committee for the Bush campaign, had appeared in one of the television commercials for the Swift Boat Veterans for Truth. Cordier also distanced himself from the campaign. But the links had been established, and they might have been used to show the Swift Boat Veterans for Truth for what it was: a front for the Bush campaign, the type of third-party smear operation Rove had come to specialize in using.

The damage inflicted on Kerry was severe. He had structured much of his campaign around his military service, and now a group of Vietnam veterans—few, if any, of whom had served directly with Kerry in Vietnam—were calling into question that service. The damage was not helped by Kerry's response. He took the advice of his chief political consultant, Robert Shrum, who had never run a successful presidential campaign and had quit Jimmy Carter for President after 10 days, later telling Carter, "I don't believe you stand for anything other than yourself."[12] Shrum advised Kerry not to respond to the allegations made by the Swift Boat Veterans for Truth. Shrum's line of thinking went like this: The public will not buy the charges, and if the group is ignored the allegations will go away. Shrum had even devised some strange notion that the controversy was only being covered by the cable television shows, as opposed to the networks, and as long as it remained on the cable shows Kerry would not be hurt.[13]

When a reporter appeared on the *Early Show* on CBS to debate John O'Neill over the merits (or lack thereof) of the group's allegations against Kerry, David Wade, the press secretary for John Kerry for President, admonished him during a telephone call for appearing on the show. "We're trying to keep the story on the cables," Wade said. "You just put it on a network morning show." It did not seem to occur to the

Kerry brain trust that the combined audience of the television ads and appearances by swift boat veterans was already massive, not to mention that the book, an immediate bestseller, was reaching its own wide audience. It had stopped being a "cable" story as soon as the first ad aired and the first book landed in a store. So by the time Kerry finally responded to the attack, after more than three weeks, it was too late. The perception had been created in the public consciousness that Kerry had lied about his military record, thus discrediting his service—which was what Rove had said he wanted to achieve when he had announced that August would be the month the Bush campaign would attack Kerry. He could never have anticipated that he would be assisted in the destruction of the Kerry candidacy by Kerry's own chief political consultant.

Political observers would later agree that the most damaging single development in the 2004 campaign was the attack on Kerry by the Swift Boat Veterans for Truth and Kerry's failure to answer the charges. "The swift boat attack was very important," Roger Stone says. "The lesson of the 1988 election was to take the other guy apart. The swift boat attack deconstructed John Kerry and destroyed him. It was the Atwater playbook, which was the Nixon playbook. You have to go on the attack to win the election."[14]

The incident would even become part of the political lexicon. Candidates would be said to be "swiftboating" other candidates when they launched all-out assaults on them that called into question their character or their beliefs. But the swiftboating of Kerry would not have worked had Kerry not remained silent. So why did he do it? There was the bad advice from Shrum, but there was also this: In order to answer some of the charges, Kerry would have had to release his military medical record, which he could not do since the record contains documentation of his post-traumatic stress disorder. Kerry remained silent in part because he had no choice.

No sooner had the intense coverage of the Swift Boat Veterans for Truth's accusations died down than another service-related controversy erupted. Since he had first entered the national political arena in 1999, questions had repeatedly been asked about George W. Bush's military experience. He had graduated from Yale University in 1968, at the height of the Vietnam War, and instead of volunteering for active military service like so many young men his age had—for a role model he had to look no further than his own father, who had served honorably as a Navy pilot during World War II—Bush decided to join the National Guard. "It was seen as an escape route from Vietnam by many men his age," the *Washington Post* reported.[15] To reduce his chances further, when asked on his application if he wanted to serve overseas, he checked "do not volunteer."[16] At the time, as might be expected, the waiting lists for the various state Guards could be long, especially in large states like Texas. So Bush's father, a congressman from Houston, pulled strings, which allowed him to leapfrog over the other names on the list. To accomplish this, Bush had a member of his staff telephone Ben Barnes, the lieutenant governor of Texas, who instructed a member of his staff to contact the leadership of the Guard, and the arrangements were made.

Bush's service in the National Guard had first been raised when he ran for governor against Ann Richards in 1994, but at the time he had been able to sidestep the issue. At that time and later, too, Bush contended that no one from his family had used their influence to get him admitted to the Guard. By the time Bush was running for president in 1999, Barnes had for years been approached by reporters who wanted him to tell the real story of how Bush had enlisted. The issue had relevance, too. If Bush had not wanted to serve in the active military, he should have just said so; Bill Clinton had pulled no punches when he revealed that he used influence to avoid the draft because he was opposed to the Vietnam War. But Bush would not admit to what had really happened. His contention was that he had joined the National Guard because he had wanted to learn how to fly airplanes "like my father," that he would have been willing to serve in Vietnam had his unit been deployed there (which would have been improbable since the million-plus American servicemen who had been sent there included only about 15,000 guardsmen), and the reason he hadn't served in Vietnam was simply that his unit was never called up. He did not mention the detail that on his National Guard application form, in answer to the question of whether he wanted to serve overseas, he had checked "do not volunteer."

Barnes could have answered questions about Bush's enlistment in the Guard, as well as an array of additional questions, but, out of fear or some other motivating factor, he steadfastly refused to speak to reporters. In the summer of 1999, when a journalist for a national publication offered to submit to him a paragraph detailing how he had pulled strings to get Bush into the Guard, a paragraph in which he would not be quoted but asked only to confirm the details of the events as a background source, Barnes did not respond. Then, finally, during the 2004 presidential cycle, Barnes decided that, at last, he would break his silence. After being approached repeatedly by CBS News, Barnes agreed to sit down for an interview with Dan Rather to reveal publicly for the first time his involvement in a story that had been circulating in political circles for a decade and a half. "Those of us who had known the true facts of the story were elated," says a source close to Barnes. "We thought that after all of these years Bush would finally have to answer the question about how he had gotten into the Texas Air National Guard— and tell the truth. He had certainly not told the truth up until then."[17]

The interview between Rather and Barnes, the interview journalists following Bush had been eagerly awaiting for years, occurred in early

September for a show scheduled to be broadcast on CBS's *60 Minutes II* on September 8. The segment, entitled "For the Record," aired as announced and Barnes confirmed what had been rumored for years: He had indeed facilitated George W. Bush's entrance into the Texas Air National Guard at the request of Bush's father. To many, that revelation would have been enough. At a time when the average American college graduate had had to worry about being drafted into the service, Bush had used his family's pull to make sure he was not. It was more than relevant that the man who wanted to be known as a "war president" had had his father make sure he didn't have to serve in the active military. That was the kind of story that could have had an effect on the upcoming election.

But Dan Rather and his producer Mary Mapes did not present the Barnes interview as they could have, in a manner that could have been debated but not refuted: an important political figure finally comes forward to give relevant information about the president for the record. They did not simply broadcast their "get" interview. With it, they included, much to the concern of sources following the story at the time, memos supposedly written by Bush's squadron commander, the late Lieutenant Colonel Jerry Killian, detailing Bush's behavior in the National Guard during the years 1972 and 1973. The memos documented Killian's observation that Bush had not met the standards expected of members of the Texas Air National Guard, as well as his dissatisfaction that Bush had failed to undergo required medical examinations.

No one could authenticate beyond any doubt that the memos had been written by Killian, now deceased, because they were typed documents. His widow, his son, and one colleague were questioned, but they could not verify the authenticity of the documents. Still, Rather and Mapes decided to run with them. Rather reported in the piece that the documents "were taken from Colonel Killian's personal files," which was not accurate. As would be determined later, CBS had obtained them from a former guardsman named Lieutenant Colonel Bill Burkett, supposedly an enemy of Bush's. Within hours of the show's airing, right-wing bloggers began to question the veracity of four of the six memos included in the piece, noting that certain font styles used in typing the memos were not available in the early 1970s, when Killian was said to have written them.

For the next two weeks, CBS, and in particular Dan Rather, defended the documents. On September 10, Rather went so far as to say, "I know that this story is true. I believe that the witnesses and the documents are authentic. We wouldn't have gone to air if they would not have been." The criticism of the report, spearheaded by a conservative Atlanta-based lawyer named Harry W. MacDougald, was relentless—and effective. To complicate matters, Killian's secretary, Marian Carr Knox, 86 years old in 2004, came forward to say that the content of the memos was true— "We did discuss Bush's conduct and it was a problem Killian was concerned about," Knox was quoted as saying—but that she did not think she had typed the memos, which contained phrasing neither she nor Killian would have used.[18] Finally, Burkett himself revealed that the documents had not come from Killian's personal files, but instead had been given to him by, as the *New York Times* would describe the person, "some hard-to-find mystery woman."[19] If what Burkett was saying was true, it would not be at all difficult to imagine that he had been set up and had then, unwittingly or not, perpetrated the fraud onto CBS.

Finally, on September 20, CBS admitted that the documents could not be authenticated by either handwriting experts (to prove Killian had at least signed the memos) or by technicians familiar with typewriters from the early 1970s. At that point, Rather was forced to admit, "If I knew then what I know now I would not have gone ahead with the story as it was aired, and I certainly would not have used the documents in question."[20] The issue was that he *had* gone ahead with the story and he *had* used the documents, in spite of the fact that the only part of the story that was true beyond doubt was Barnes's revelations. Rather's blunder was, according to the *New York Times*, a "shattering error at the twilight of his career."[21]

"I knew that what Barnes told Rather in the interview was true," says the source close to Barnes. "But as soon as I heard there were documents involved, I got worried. I mean, this is Texas and in 2004 we were living in a post-Rove world down here and you can never be sure where pieces of paper come from unless you can authenticate them beyond any shadow of a doubt. The Rovian way is to destroy the primary story by creating a second story that makes your guy look good. That is exactly what happened with the CBS piece. The relevant facts provided by Barnes about Bush getting himself into the National Guard was damaging, but they were obscured by the bigger story of the fake memos. Pure Rove, I'm telling you. Pure Rove."[22]

Terry McAuliffe, the chairman of the Democratic Party, made the allegations in public. "It has become crystal clear that the president has lied to the American public about his military service," McAuliffe said. "I can tell you that nobody at the Democratic National Committee or groups associated with us were involved in any way with these documents. I'm just saying that I would ask Karl Rove the same question."[23] To this charge, Scott McClellan, the White House spokesperson, replied, "The documents do not change the facts. The president met his obligations and was honorably discharged. And the one thing that is clear is the timing and the coordination going on here. There is an orchestrated effort by Democrats and the Kerry campaign to tear down the president because of the direction the polls are moving."

Actually, the coverage of the flawed CBS News piece did achieve something for Bush. In all that was written about the Rather piece, the fact that finally, after almost 15 years, Ben Barnes had told the truth about how Bush was admitted into the National Guard was totally overshadowed by the haze of controversy surrounding the potentially fraudulent documents. The media did not press the Bush campaign to respond to Barnes's revelations and, for all intents and purposes, the issue, so hotly debated for so long, disappeared once the truth of the situation was known. The debate shifted from how Bush got in the Guard and what he did once he got there to whether or not CBS had aired fraudulent documents and whether or not Dan Rather was biased in his reporting, as his critics had alleged for years.

＊

Another weird episode would occur in the campaign, this one during the debates. *Salon* first reported the story. Here is a press account, published on October 9, of the *Salon* item: "What was that bulge in the back of President Bush's suit jacket at the presidential debate in Miami last week? According to rumors racing across the Internet this week, the rectangular bulge visible between Mr. Bush's shoulder blades was a radio receiver, getting answers from an offstage counselor into a hidden presidential earpiece. The prime suspect was Karl Rove. . . . When the online magazine *Salon* published an article about the rumors on Friday, the speculation reached such a pitch that the White House and campaign officials were inundated with calls."[24] The mystery of the bulge on the president's back would never be solved. Of everyone involved in the 2004 race, however, it would be Rove, more than anyone, who would attempt to keep alive the rumor that he was feeding Bush answers through a radio transmitter. At a stop near the end of the campaign, he stood apart from the assembled crowd during the president's stump speech, cupped his hand to his mouth, and recited words and phrases from the speech just before Bush uttered them. If the box so clearly strapped to Bush's back had not been a radio transmitter Rove was using to relay answers to him, Rove certainly wanted the national press corps to *believe* it had been.

3.

On Thursday, October 28, with five days left before an election that looked to be extremely close, a Web site named CommonDreams.org reprinted an article by Russ Baker from another site, GNN.tv, entitled "Two Years Before 9/11, Candidate Bush was Already Talking Privately About Attacking Iraq, According to His Former Ghost Writer." The ghostwriter referred to was Mickey Herskowitz, and the article was based on conversations between Herskowitz and Baker, conversations Herskowitz did not believe were going to be made public. Herskowitz had considered the conversations to be part of Baker's preliminary research, and he had intended to review his memories of his Bush interviews before allowing his comments about those interviews to go on the record.

But that's not what happened. The article appeared. The headline— and the article's lead—was an interpretation of a comment Bush made to Herskowitz during their interviews for *A Charge to Keep* on how he would have handled the first Gulf War differently than his father had. Bush had answered a hypothetical question about whether he would have taken out Saddam in 1991—yes, he would have—but, after reading Baker's article, one would have concluded that Bush had been plotting his own eventual invasion of Iraq all the way back in 1999, or even in 1991, neither of which was true.

"My comments appeared on the Internet," Herskowitz says, "and the White House got calls from the *New York Times,* the *Washington Post*, and the wire services. When they all contacted me, I told them the remark was taken out of context. It really wasn't what they were looking for in terms of a headline: that Bush was planning to invade Iraq as far back as 1999. So the legitimate publications backed off. But the White House was in a dither over it because I got a call from someone on the president's staff asking me if I would take a call from Karl Rove. It was a delicious moment of irony, I thought. I said I would be happy to talk to Karl."[25]

But after Herskowitz assured the White House staffer he would not be a source for any future articles on the subject, meaning that the story would likely not make its way from the Internet into the mainstream media, Rove never called.

⇔

At a rally in Albuquerque, New Mexico, on the Monday night before election day, Rove was asked what he would do if Bush lost Ohio. His response was strange, but typical of Rove. He offered to the assembled group of reporters an answer that was telling and, ultimately, prophetic. "We're winning Ohio," he said, and then he launched into a sort of Rovian chant. "And we will win Ohio. We will win Ohio. We will win Ohio. We will win Ohio. We will win Ohio. We will win Ohio." That seemed to be the overriding question: Could Bush win the battleground states, Ohio principal among them? Recalling the blunder he had made in 2000, when he had offered his boastful predictions in the hours before the election and all of them had turned out to be wrong, Rove refused to speculate heading into the final hours of the race, with the exception that Bush would win Ohio. He would not guess at the number of Electoral College votes Bush would win. He would not speculate about the margin by which Bush might defeat Kerry. He didn't even hint that he believed that this time, should Bush win, he would carry the popular vote. No, for once, Rove was relatively quiet. "It was Mr. Rove who said four years ago that Mr. Bush would easily beat Al Gore in the Electoral College," the *New York Times* reported, "a prediction that reporters like to bring up to torture him. . . . Mr. Rove said he was making no such predictions this time around."[26]

On election day, as the Bush campaign's inner circle traveled on Air Force One, Rove began to get the early exit poll numbers by telephone, and they were not good. According to what Rove was seeing, Kerry was going to win in a landslide. When one journalist received an e-mail that day from David Wade, Kerry's press secretary, he was startled by the confidence Kerry's campaign displayed. "Winning comfortably," the e-mail stated. While Rove was initially upset by the early numbers, according to published reports, he felt reassured once he realized that the Republicans' 72-Hour Plan was in place. Sanctioned by the Republican National Committee, the plan featured as its core element a highly organized army of "activist" volunteers whose goal was to get voters to the polls on election day through individualized phone calls and personal contact.[27] Those volunteers were at work nationwide even as the exit-poll numbers were being released. The polls may have been predicting a Kerry win, but the race was not over, not by any means. Rove took to e-mailing key Republicans, telling them not to believe the exit polls and reminding them that those same polls had been wrong in 2000. He also suggested, in no uncertain terms, that now was the time to redouble their efforts in getting out the vote.

At the White House that evening, Rove continued to crunch numbers. In the living quarters, Bush had 30 friends and family members over for a buffet dinner, after which they all settled in front of a television to watch the election returns, with Rove giving them updates from downstairs in what he called his "bat cave," an old dining room that had been turned into a war room for the evening. Bush remained optimistic. Around 10:30, Rove determined that Bush would win both Florida and Ohio, meaning that he would win reelection. When he gave Bush the news, he warned him not to give an acceptance speech until Kerry had conceded. Even so, Rove announced to his staff that they had won. At 12:45, the Fox News Network and NBC announced that Bush had won Ohio—the one state, it became apparent as the evening had gone along, that he had to win to win the election. This development triggered Bush's speechwriters to start finishing the victory speech they had been working on. A motorcade was prepared to take Bush from the White House to the Ronald Reagan Building and International Trade Center on Pennsylvania Avenue, where he would deliver his acceptance speech. But the upbeat feeling in the family quarters turned to anger when Kerry refused to concede. Because of reports of massive voter irregularities in Ohio, Kerry was not convinced that Bush had won the state. Because of this, in the early morning hours of Wednesday he sent John Edwards out into the drizzle falling on Boston to make a brief speech to the dwindling crowd in a commons park across the street from Kerry's hotel. Edwards told the supporters that the Kerry campaign would not give up until "every vote is counted." The campaign would fight on.

The Democratic Party had been so sure that there would be voter irregularities, especially in Ohio, that the day before election day word had gone out to trusted major Democratic contributors that a fleet of private jets would be needed at Logan Airport in Boston to fly lawyers to wherever they needed to go at a moment's notice. By the end of the day on Monday, the day before the election, the fleet of private jets was at Logan. The prospect of voter fraud was also the reason that, in the final stretch of the campaign, Kerry had held back $14 million of the campaign's money. It would be used to finance recounts, if necessary.

A month before the election, when a reporter had asked David Wade about suggestions that there would be polling problems in Ohio not unlike those that had plagued the 2000 race in Florida, Wade's answer could not have been clearer: "We have that covered."[28] Indeed, the campaign did: It had the money to finance recounts and the jets to fly lawyers around the country as needed. At some point after Edwards had made his statement in the early morning, Kerry had decided what he would do. According to sources familiar with the Kerry campaign, two key members of his inner circle—John Edwards and Teresa Heinz Kerry, his wife—had lobbied strongly that Kerry himself should fly to Ohio to demand a recount. But others, political staffers such as Bob Shrum, had argued that the vote tallies were not close enough and that to preserve his ability to run for president in the future—as Nixon did in 1968 after losing a close election to Kennedy in 1960—he should concede. Kerry had consistently listened to Shrum's bad advice, and he didn't stop now. Early on Wednesday morning, Kerry concluded that he would not travel to Ohio and challenge the election, but instead would concede the race to Bush.

Meanwhile, at the White House, Bush had gone to bed around five o'clock in the morning, only to wake up two hours later. By 8:00, he was in the Oval Office, where he had a conversation with his father. Then, at 11:02, once Bush had been joined by a group of aides, his personal secretary, Ashley Estes, entered the office to announce that he had a call from John Kerry. Bush took the call while standing behind his desk. In the short conversation, Kerry conceded the election. "I think you were an admirable, worthy opponent," Bush would later be reported as having told Kerry. "You waged one tough campaign. I hope you are proud of the effort you put in. You should be."[29] After the telephone call, Bush went around the room hugging his aides, among them Dan Bartlett and, of course, Rove. Then Bush proceeded down to Cheney's office where, bumping into one another in the hallway, the two men congratulated each other.

Finally, in the afternoon, Bush was able to proceed the three blocks from the White House to the Ronald Reagan Building to make the speech he had wanted to give the night before. With his family, staff, the vice president, and the Cheney family by his side, Bush offered his remarks. "America has spoken, and I'm humbled by the trust and the confidence of my fellow citizens. With that trust comes a duty to serve all Americans, and I will do my best to fulfill that duty every day as your president."[30] In his speech Bush thanked the people he considered essential to his victory. Of those he mentioned, he singled out one, Karl Rove, "the architect." It was a moment Rove had been waiting for for years. In his field, on this day, at this moment in history, Rove had reached the pinnacle.

It was an impressive achievement. "In 2004, given the fact that the Iraq situation had begun to deteriorate," says conservative commentator Monica Crowley, an assistant to Richard Nixon just before his death, "it was a rather perfect storm for Democrats to win. And yet, Rove managed to pull the rabbit out of the hat for a second time, despite the fact that all the trends were going in the other direction. That was a huge accomplishment."[31] Even the *New York Times* gushed: "Victory may have a thousand fathers, but if President Bush's triumph . . . had a Big Daddy it was indisputably Karl Rove—the seer, strategist and serious student of politics and the presidency that a grateful Mr. Bush himself referred to as the architect of his winning campaign. And with Mr. Bush's re-election, Mr. Rove has not only cemented his reputation as one of the canniest campaign gurus in a generation but has also put himself in position to shape second-term policies that could help realize his longtime goal of consolidating a broad Republican electoral majority for a generation to come."[32]

Was there one determining factor? In Rove's view, it may have been the anti-gay-marriage constitutional amendments on ballots in 11 states across the country. "This is an issue on which there is a broad consensus," Rove said following the election. "In all 11 states, it won by considerable margins. People do not like the idea or the concept of marriage as being a union between a man and a woman being uprooted and overturned by a few activist judges or a couple of activist local officials."[33] Of the 11 states in which proposed amendments appeared, many were in battleground states, Ohio included. As it turned out, it now seemed that when he had caved in to the demands of the Christian leaders on the conference call following Bush's State of the Union address, Rove had known exactly what he was doing.

$$\rightleftharpoons$$

On the Thursday after the election, Todd Purdum got a phone call from Rove. Purdum had coauthored the article in that day's *New York Times* praising Rove and attempting to place him in a historical context. In the *Times* article, Purdum compared Rove, as journalists had been doing for years, to Mark Hanna, the McKinley protégé.[34] In the past, Rove had embraced the comparison. Now, though, Rove had changed his mind. "Rove said he had not idolized Hanna," Purdum would write, "whom he described as merely 'the Don Evans of the McKinley campaign,' referring to George W. Bush's old oil-patch friend, leading fund-raiser, and first secretary of commerce. Instead, Rove cited a more intriguing idol, one hinting at grander ambition, erudition, and complexity. His real hero, he said, was another McKinley campaign strategist, Charles G. Dawes, who went on to become Calvin Coolidge's vice president and Herbert Hoover's ambassador to Britain. Dawes was a banker and utility executive who shared a Nobel Peace Prize for his efforts to rebuild Europe after World War I."[35] Rove did attempt to hedge his new grandiosity, however. In talking to Purdum on that Thursday morning after Bush's victory, now only a day old, Rove had said of Dawes, "But I'll never live up to his reputation!"

CHAPTER SEVEN

ERRORS OF JUDGMENT

Even though the Electoral College count was razor close, Bush won the popular vote in 2004 by 3.5 million votes, a noteworthy accomplishment since he had lost the popular vote to Al Gore by a half-million votes four years earlier. "President Bush ran forthrightly on a clear agenda for this nation's future, and the nation responded by giving him a mandate," Cheney had said in his acceptance speech at the Ronald Reagan Building, using a word Bush himself had been reluctant to utter that day— "mandate." Others in the administration were even more forthcoming in their pronouncement of a mandate for Bush. As Rove put it a month later while addressing a conservative group, "Next time one of your smarty-pants liberal friends says to you, 'Well, he didn't have a mandate,' you tell him this delicious fact: This president got a higher percentage of the vote than any Democrat candidate for president since 1964."[1]

In an election as close as the one in 2004 was—had Kerry carried Ohio, he would have been president, which was the reason that the leaders of the Democratic Party had wanted him to challenge the vote there—it is hard to believe anyone could have seriously viewed the results as offering a mandate, but Cheney and Rove did. Within 24 hours of giving his acceptance speech, Bush still held off on using the word "mandate." (As he did with so many other aspects of his administration, he let others say publicly what he himself believed.) However, in

a press conference at the White House the newly elected president convened with no prompting from his staff—a rarity for a president
who hated press conferences—he said his election, with its impressive
popular-vote victory, meant he had "political capital"—that was the
phrase he wanted to use—and in the coming years he intended to spend
it. In retrospect, this may have been a example of Bush's hubris, which
ultimately helped turn his second term into a political disaster. "I think,"
Ed Rollins says, "at the end of the day, after the 2004 election, where the
Bush administration made the mistake is, they declared a much bigger
victory than they had. Karl got a little beyond himself, when he started
talking about a legacy: 'We're going to be a permanent majority.' "[2]

With the second term came a new role for Rove in the administration.
No sooner was Bush sworn in than he made the bold move of promoting
Rove into a more powerful position. In early February, Rove was named
deputy chief of staff for policy. He also maintained his title of senior
adviser to the president, which included responsibility for intergovern-
mental and political affairs and strategy. In his new capacity, Rove would
work with the National Economic Council, the Domestic Policy Council,
the National Security Council, and the Homeland Security Council—a
much larger domestic and international portfolio than he had managed
during the first term. "[Rove] is one of the president's most trusted advisers," Scott McClellan said of the appointment, "who has played an inte-
gral role in the strategy and policy development for a long time. So now
he has a more expanded role."[3] That role saw Rove move into a new office
in the White House, just feet from the Oval Office. Rove was now at the
very heart of the Bush administration, a unique position for a political
consultant to be in, especially considering that, after his second presidential victory, Bush would not be running for public office again.

Perhaps it was now, with his expanded title and new office, that Rove
felt emboldened. "The president made a powerful case in the inaugural

speech and before," Rove said in mid-February during his appearance at the 2005 annual meeting of the Conservative Political Action Conference, "for spreading human liberty and preserving human dignity. . . . We are seizing the mantle of idealism."[4] Certainly, this renewed confidence may have been partially responsible for helping to produce the string of politically fatal errors of judgment that would be the hallmark of the second four years of the Bush administration.

⪧

The Social Security program is known as "the third rail" of American politics because touching it means sure death, at least as far as a politician's future is concerned. As a result, although politicians had talked about trying to reform Social Security for years, arguing that the trust fund was going bankrupt and the federal government would soon be unable to meet its obligation to American citizens, no one had been successful in making any kind of fundamental changes in the way the Social Security system was run. Most Americans, as it turns out, have been happy with Social Security and do not want the program to be altered in any drastic way.

On a basic level, at the start of Bush's second term, Rove did not realize that Social Security was a program most Americans felt was untouchable. He had gotten Bush to where he was—a reelected Republican president, which neither Bush's father nor Gerald Ford had been able to do—by paying back his supporters. One of the promises Bush had made to the financial services industry, which had consistently funded him, was to try to privatize all, or at least part, of the Social Security program. Bush would never have a better time to make his move than now, in his second term. He had political capital, he said; he was going to spend it.

In addition, Rove argued to Bush that he believed, after looking at previous second-term presidencies, that Bush needed to make a bold move at the very beginning of his second term. There could be no bolder move on the domestic front than reforming Social Security. Bush went along. In February, the Bush administration rolled out a new initiative it entitled "Strengthening Social Security," a plan that called for younger workers to be able to voluntarily invest part of their Social Security taxes in private accounts in lieu of receiving guaranteed benefits.

The effort to sell the initiative to the public had the feeling of a political campaign to it, complete with town hall appearances by the president, advertising buys in the national and local media paid for by major sponsors, phone banks getting out the message, and a mention in the State of the Union address. Rove brought in outside organizations to help—the Republican National Committee, corporations, conservative think tanks, Republican lobbyists, various public relations firms, and grassroots outfits—all with the goal of wresting from the federal government the Social Security trust fund, worth countless billions of dollars, and turning it over to Wall Street and the financial services industry. As he had in earlier political campaigns, Rove took his place as the point person in the operation, marshalling a budget of $200 million to advance his cause, while Bush went out front to sell it.

"The Bushies hate that this element of the New Deal is a great example of public solidarity, of Americans helping Americans," says Glenn Smith, a political consultant in Austin who first met Bush and Rove in the 1980s. "We contribute our money so the rest of Americans don't end up sleeping under the bridge. Social Security is the most successful and popular public care initiative ever, and because it's so successful and popular, they hate it. In their worldview, if you get old and you don't have any money, too damn bad. What they miscalculated was just how popular Social Security was."[5]

Rove and Bush may have miscalculated, but members of Congress did not. Even Republicans, who had all but given Bush a blank check to set policy as he pleased in his first term, balked at getting involved in changing Social Security. Bush might be willing to touch the third rail, but they were not; they had to run again in two years, unlike him. As soon as Bush had announced his initiative, congressmen returned to Washington from visits to their home states complaining that as many as 80 percent of their constituents were opposed to Bush's plan. That number was especially daunting since the public rarely agrees on any issue with such plurality. The position of both Republicans and Democrats in Congress was simple: "Strengthening Social Security" was a nonstarter. They didn't want to have anything to do with it, mandate or no mandate.

"You've got to basically sit down," Ed Rollins says, "with your team—the Republicans in the House and the Senate—and say, 'All right—what is it that you want? Here's what I want. What are your priorities? How do we get this through?' As opposed to saying, 'You know, this is what I want. You've got to do it.' Had Bush or Rove sat down with members of Congress, those members would have told them what the public felt, but the Bush administration consistently felt they did not have to consult Congress. They simply declared what they wanted—now they wanted Social Security reform—and Congress had to go along. Forget that the public didn't want it."[6]

The plan may have been dead, but week after week Bush and the apparatus that Rove had put together ground out their message. Rove even hit back at opponents of the Bush plan, including AARP, one of the most powerful organizations in the country not only because of its massive membership (nearly 38 million in early 2007), but also because of its ability to lobby successfully for its members. With its massive influence, it would be foolish to attack AARP, but that's what Rove did, with both television ads and mailings. Those attacks, implying that AARP was somehow biased against the president, did little to help Rove advance his cause.

Rove also staged a huge public relations campaign designed to sell

Bush's program. For example, John Snow, secretary of the treasury, held an event to sell Social Security privatization, even though he had had little involvement in developing the new plan. Snow invited 25 talk radio hosts to come to Washington at their own expense and broadcast their shows from the Treasury Department. Two who took him up on it were G. Gordon Liddy and Hoppy Kercheval (from West Virginia). Snow gave five morning-drive-time interviews and four afternoon-drive-time interviews. In addition, the Treasury Department had lined up hundreds of similar interviews with surrogates, including Rove, commerce secretary Carlos Gutierrez, and Office of Management and Budget director Joshua Bolten, plus four other Treasury officials. The message was summed up by Snow, who told one reporter, "Social Security has served us well. Unfortunately, the safety net is now frayed."[7] Rove put it this way to a Seattle station: "We should be concerned about the guy at the bottom of the scale. Why should we say that he shouldn't have access to the wealth-making capacity of the American market? Why should we say, 'You're stuck with Social Security and you're getting 2 percent on your money'?"[8] By relaxing regulations on Social Security, the argument went, an individual could invest all or part of his Social Security account in markets that could yield higher returns. Of course, those investments would then be at risk in a way a traditional Social Security account is not.

Meanwhile, Bush too was doing his part to sell the proposal. By early March, he had traveled to nine states, with more scheduled for later that month. On Friday, April 15, Bush went to Ohio, where he praised the substitute system for Social Security that the state used for many of its public employees and suggested that the Ohio system could be turned into a national model. In Ohio, the public employees could opt out of Social Security, he noted, and put their money into portfolios of stocks and bonds. In Ohio with Bush, Rove was vocal, too. "It did so well that it quickly expanded beyond the professors," he said of the Ohio plan, which had started with professors at the state university. "It's a model worth studying."[9]

Bush seemed blissfully unaware that his ideas about privatizing Social Security were not resonating with the American public at all. As of late May, when he appeared at a highly produced town hall meeting in Greece, New York, before an audience that was preselected and assembled on stage as if they were at a presidential campaign event, he sold his Social Security plan with the same zeal he'd used when making a stump speech during an election campaign. The audiences the White House assembled for events such as this one—attendees were usually handpicked by local Republicans and given tickets to keep any protesters out—may have cheered on cue, as had the audiences who had been selected to attend so many Bush appearances in the past, but they were little more than stage dressing for a photo op. They did not represent the majority of the American public. "Every time the president went out to make a speech on Social Security, he lost ground," Rollins says. "He went backwards in the polls."[10] In the weeks Bush pushed Social Security reform, his numbers on that subject slipped from the mid-40s into the mid-30s.

As he continued to make appearances that featured adoring fans and campaignlike paraphernalia, Bush did not seem to understand that he was preaching a message the country did not want to hear. For a candidate who had based his political life on an ability to practice retail politics, which is based on keeping in touch with ordinary voters to see what is really on their minds, Bush was out of touch. Ironically, even if Bush didn't yet know what the initiative's fate was, Rove and other staffers *had* come to the realization that it was doomed, though they had not clued in the president. They felt if they pushed the initiative long enough they could turn around public opinion, or at least convince members of Congress that the public had come to view the president's plan differently. "They kept Bush out there long after they knew it was a failure," Smith says. "It was a mistake. Early on, they knew they had to bluff, and

ERRORS OF JUDGMENT

179

the bluff failed."[11] Indeed, the attempt to privatize Social Security constituted what the *Washington Post* would call "the biggest domestic policy failure of Bush's presidency."[12]

Since 2003, Bush had been able to sell an increasingly unpopular war in Iraq in part because, with the combat taking place a world away, it had little impact on the everyday lives of ordinary Americans. Now, however, in trying to seize control of Social Security, a popular program that touches almost every family in the country, he was losing credibility. "When Karl became the deputy chief of staff, in charge of policy and everything else, and he laid out Social Security as the major second-term agenda, it was a disaster," Rollins says. "There's not a Republican anywhere who wouldn't tell you that selling Social Security is always difficult. It always works against Republicans. The Democrats have very effectively used it against us in the past. It was almost like Karl had no history and certainly didn't have any real history relative to Washington, or what had gone on before."[13]

If pushing Social Security privatization ended up being a major error in judgment for Rove, it would not be the only error in judgment he would make in the first six months of Bush's second term.

≋

On the evening of June 22, 2005, Rove gave a speech in Manhattan at a fund-raiser for the Conservative Party of New York State. As he stood at the podium reading his prepared text, he made statements he believed would resonate in the midterm elections of 2006. In the last presidential election, Bush had been able to win, despite the fact that the war in Iraq was becoming a severe political liability, because he—and Rove—had been able to convince the American public that Bush would be better able to protect the country against terrorism than Kerry. That theme had apparently worked, and now Rove hoped to build on it as Republicans started looking ahead to the midterm elections. So, on this evening, he said something designed to be provocative.

"Conservatives," Rove declared to his highly receptive audience, "saw the savagery of 9/11 in the attacks and prepared for war; liberals saw the savagery of the 9/11 attacks and wanted to prepare indictments and offer therapy and understanding for our attackers. In the wake of the terrorist attacks, conservatives believed it was time to unleash the might and power of the United States military against the Taliban; in the wake of 9/11, liberals believed it was time to submit a petition."[14] Rove didn't care that this was untrue. Polling data gathered in the wake of September 11 indicated, according to *Salon*, that 84 percent of liberals were in favor of taking military action against Afghanistan and 80 percent of Democrats nationwide supported such action.[15] Indeed, the vast majority of Democrats in the Congress had authorized the president to use military force. But the truth had never gotten in the way of a good speech for Rove. "I don't know about you," Rove told the crowd, "but moderation and restraint is not what I felt when I watched the twin towers crumble to the ground, a side of the Pentagon destroyed, and almost 3,000 of our fellow citizens perish in flames and rubble." Not surprisingly, the conservatives in the room burst into applause, happy with Rove's red-meat rhetoric and unconcerned that his facts were wrong.

This time, the mainstream press, which during Bush's first term had often given his administration the benefit of the doubt, responded strongly. Writing for *Salon* on June 24, Joe Conason answered Rove's remarks. "The other night," Conason declared, "Rove lied about the liberal reaction to the September 11 attacks and again exploited patriotism for narrow partisan advantage in a time of war. He seeks to divert public opinion from the failures of the Bush administration by suppressing dissent, stigmatizing 'liberals' and returning to the same old tactics that the Republican far right has used ever since the McCarthy era. His unhinged rhetoric is a sign of deep worry within the White House, of course, as polls continue to show deepening public alienation from the president. . . . Moreover, Rove must cope with Republicans as well as Democrats who are openly dissenting from the administration line, not only regarding Iraq but on the Bolton nomination and Social Security privatization."[16]

The nomination reference was to John Bolton, whom Bush had nominated for ambassador to the United Nations—a nomination that had no chance of passing the Senate because of Bolton's right-wing isolationist politics—just what was *not* needed at the United Nations—and his insulting and abrasive handling of staff. But Bolton was not the only nominee Bush had named to an important position who had run into trouble. Not long after he had been inaugurated for his second term, Bush had tapped Bernard Kerik to be his new secretary of Homeland Security, replacing Tom Ridge. Kerik, a former New York City police commissioner, had been L. Paul Bremer's senior policy adviser and interim minister of the interior in Iraq in 2003. In the ensuing controversy surrounding ethical concerns about both his public and his private life, Kerik was forced to withdraw his nomination, which was a major embarrassment for Bush. Eventually, Bush nominated US Circuit Court judge Michael Chertoff, who was confirmed by the Senate. In his role as deputy chief of staff for policy, Rove would have had input into the selection of both nominees.

If Rove was aware that he had created problems with the speech he had given to the Conservative Party of New York State or with the cabinet-level nominations he had championed with dubious results, he would have even bigger problems to contend with in the near future. In only a matter of weeks, a storm would hit the Gulf Coast of the United States that would change the fortunes of the Bush administration forever.

CHAPTER EIGHT

KATRINA

On Monday, August 29, 2005, at about 6:00 a.m., Hurricane Katrina slammed into the coasts of Louisiana, Mississippi, and Alabama. A category 5 hurricane until just before landfall, it was one of the worst storms ever to hit the Gulf Coast. Kathleen Blanco, the governor of Louisiana, had been briefed extensively about what to expect when the storm hit, which was why, on the Friday night before the storm reached the coast, she signed papers declaring Louisiana to be in a state of emergency. Based on what she had been told by her advisers and what she knew from being a native Louisianan, she understood that Katrina, creeping gradually toward land with sustained winds of a strength rarely seen in a hurricane, could prove to be catastrophic for Louisiana, and particularly for New Orleans.

Over the weekend, Blanco and her staff monitored the storm from an emergency headquarters in Baton Rouge. As the storm was hitting on Monday morning, Michael Brown, the head of the Federal Emergency Management Agency, met with the governor and her staff. Brown had arrived in Louisiana the night before, supposedly ready to deal with the disaster. When he got to the headquarters that morning, Brown told Blanco he was prepared to help. "He showed up Monday morning," says Bob Mann, a senior aide to Blanco, "and gave us the feeling we would have everything we wanted and needed. He was nothing if not an effective bullshitter."[1]

Specifically, there was talk of FEMA buses. "Michael Brown told me he had 500 buses," Blanco says. "They were staged and ready to roll in."[2]

Meanwhile, as a deadly storm of historic proportions ripped into three Gulf Coast states that Monday, Bush, on a working vacation at his ranch in Crawford, stuck to his schedule for the day. He traveled to Arizona, where he gave a stay-the-course speech about the war in Iraq. He even made himself available for a photo op after the speech, posing with a guitar next to someone wearing a sombrero, seemingly unaware that the Gulf Coast of the United States was in the throes of a horrific natural disaster perhaps unparalleled in the nation's history. For a president who often seemed to care more about developments in Iraq than those at home, here was a singular moment. Never had Bush appeared to be so out of sync, at least when it came to events unfolding in the homeland. To make matters worse, in this case the disaster was not happening on the other side of the world or even the other side of the country, but in a state next door to Texas.

"From what I can tell," US senator Mary Landrieu of Louisiana says, "from being right there in the center of almost everything, the Bush administration was caught completely off guard. The staff could not get the president's attention on this. He was in Crawford. Condoleezza Rice was traveling. Michael Chertoff [secretary of the Department of Homeland Security] was giving a speech somewhere. I do know [Maine senator] Susan Collins was in a cabin in Maine because I called her myself. I said, 'Do you have a television?' She said, 'No.' I said, 'You need to get to one and turn it on.' I'm not blaming Susan Collins, but she was the Republican leader of the Homeland Security committee in the Senate. It was August, so everyone was gone. I was home in the city where I should be—my home that literally got blown away. The edge of the storm went right over my house. I had been evacuated with my children."[3]

With parts of Alabama and particularly Mississippi devastated but Louisiana seemingly spared the utter destruction the storm could have delivered, the unthinkable then happened in New Orleans. Levees broke in two places and within hours 80 percent of the city was flooded with water from Lake Pontchartrain. Some neighborhoods were under 20 feet of water. Landrieu was in the executive room with Blanco and members of the US Army Corps of Engineers when the levees broke. The group of officials was listening to reports coming in over the squawk box.

"The 17th Street Canal just broke," Landrieu heard the voice say.

"On what side?" she asked.

"The New Orleans side," the voice said.

"Then the whole city is going under right now."

Members of the Corps of Engineers told Landrieu there was no confirmation of that.

"You don't *need* any confirmation of that, for God Almighty's sake," Landrieu said. "All you need to know is the city."

In fact, members of the Corps of Engineers *didn't* know the city. The deputy administrator of the corps didn't even know where the 17th Street Canal was located. This was not the only government agency that seemed unprepared. FEMA was not ready to kick into action either, contrary to Michael Brown's promise. Brown and FEMA officials were at a loss for what to do, and one of the first mysteries to emerge was the whereabouts of those 500 FEMA buses. When it was time for the buses to roll into action, none materialized.

On Tuesday, Bush was still out of touch with what was happening and seemingly unaware of the seriousness of the events unfolding on the Gulf Coast, especially in New Orleans. A major American city had filled up with water, but Bush had not departed from his planned schedule. In Coronado, California, at a naval base near the USS *Ronald Reagan*, Bush delivered a speech to commemorate the 60th anniversary of the defeat of the Japanese in World War II. But Bush used the occasion, as he had repeatedly of late, to give yet another stay-the-course speech about Iraq.

On this day, he compared the ongoing military action in Iraq to the allied struggle against German fascism and Japanese imperialism in terms of its moral significance. "The terrorists of our century are making the same mistake that the followers of other totalitarian ideologies made in the last century," Bush said. "They believe that democracies are inherently weak and corrupt and can be brought to their knees." It was not terrorists who had brought three states in the American South to their knees, but an act of nature that, judging from his actions on Monday and Tuesday, had not fully engaged the attention of the president.

As it turned out, the federal government's attempts to respond to the storm and flooding appeared frozen by inadequacy and ineptitude. Thousands of people were stranded in their homes, unable to make a better escape than to their rooftops to wave for help and hope emergency personnel in helicopters might rescue them. Tens of thousands of refugees were holed up downtown in the Convention Center and the Superdome, yet FEMA was unable to bring in even food, water, or ice, not to mention buses to evacuate them. Touring the Superdome on Tuesday night, Blanco was disturbed by what she witnessed: in short, no federal assistance whatsoever. All she saw was the Louisiana National Guard and the Louisiana State Police—certainly not enough of a law enforcement presence to be able to maintain order without additional guardsmen and troops.

If Bush had not seen what was taking place by Tuesday, Karl Rove had. The first evidence of Rove's involvement in the Katrina disaster occurred on Tuesday afternoon. "Rove understood what a nightmare this was for the president," Landrieu says, "so he went into high gear on the spin thing they're so good at in the White House. Rove had David Vitter, the Republican senator from Louisiana. I was at a press conference and David Vitter walked up to the mike and said, 'I just got off the phone with Karl Rove.' I looked at the governor and she looked at me, like, 'Why is David Vitter on the phone with Karl Rove?' I mean, he could have been talking to generals, the president himself, but Rove is just a political hatchet man."[4] Instead of dealing with Bush, his chief of staff, or the secretary of Homeland Security, all officials in the expected chain of command for a natural disaster, Vitter was communicating with the administration's political mastermind—and by announcing it at a press conference he wanted to make sure the media *knew* that was who he was talking to. So whether he wanted to or not, he had brought politics into the situation.

As it turned out, despite his expertise being politics, the administration had made Rove a central player in the handling of the disaster. "A light switch in the White House didn't get turned on without going through Rove," says Adam Sharp, a Landrieu aide. "It was clear that Rove was the point person for the White House on this disaster."[5] That fact was proven precisely by what Vitter had done and said at the press conference. "As soon as Vitter said he had just gotten off the phone with Rove and other Republican officials," Landrieu says, "he started in on the first talking point to come out of the ordeal. I said to myself, 'Oh my God, I can't believe the White House has already given David Vitter talking points to talk about this.' We weren't going to blame anyone. We weren't going to blame the president. I mean, is there a Republican talking point for how to get people water? But that was Karl Rove."[6] Privately, Vitter delivered a message from Rove to Blanco. Rove suggested the governor consider federalizing Louisiana or imposing martial law.[7] Blanco was opposed to either idea.

On Wednesday morning, Blanco put in a call to Bush, who had now cut short his vacation to return to the White House, but he did not take her call. Undeterred, Blanco called Andy Card, the White House chief of staff; he too refused to talk to her. "About Wednesday," Mann says, "things started to turn and it had a lot to do with the fact that something was going on in the White House. They were realizing the political jeopardy the administration, and especially the president, was in because of the way they were bungling the response to the hurricane."[8] So they began hatching a plan. Instead of supplying relief to the city, Rove had devised a scheme whereby he could blame the failure of government to take action on someone besides Bush. "They looked around," Landrieu says, "and they found a Democratic governor and an African American Democratic mayor who had never held office before in his life before he was mayor of New Orleans—someone they knew they could manipulate. Ray Nagin had never held public office and here he was the mayor of New Orleans and it was going underwater."[9]

In short, Rove was going to blame Blanco for the failure of the response in Louisiana, and to do that he was going to use Nagin. He had already set the plan in motion on Tuesday with Nagin, who, even though he was a Democrat, was so close to the Republican Party that some members of the African American community in New Orleans called him "Ray Reagan." In 2000, Nagin had actually contributed $2,000 to Bush's campaign when he ran for president. Rove knew of Nagin's ties to the Republican Party, so more than likely Nagin could be convinced to level his criticism at Blanco and to support Bush when he could. Here was Rove's strategy: Praise Haley Barbour, the Republican governor of Mississippi; praise Michael Brown and FEMA; blame Blanco, the Democrat. It was not a stretch for Nagin. He and Blanco so disliked each other that in Blanco's last race Nagin had endorsed her opponent.

Rove and Nagin were communicating through e-mail. "I heard Nagin was bragging about being in touch with The Man," Blanco says. "Nagin took the position that they were the people who could help the most to do what he wanted. People get highly complimented when they have contact with the White House."[10] In this case the trade-off for Nagin was his willingness to cooperate with Rove. "I knew Ray Nagin could be easily manipulated," Landrieu says. "I could feel it. We were all working together in a relatively small building. We were in close proximity. But I could see where Rove was going. Blame Blanco. Blame the levee board. Blame the corruption in New Orleans. 'The reason the city is going underwater is because the city is corrupt,' Rove was saying. 'But don't blame the Republicans or George W. Bush or David Vitter. We are the white guys in shining armor, and we are going to come in and save the city from years of corruption.' That was their story and they sold it very well."[11]

Rove sold the story, as he had in the past, through the media. On Wednesday, while Blanco was trying to get help from the White House, her staff began receiving calls from reporters questioning her handling of the disaster, almost all of them citing as their sources unnamed senior White House officials. "One story," Mann recalls, "would say the governor was so incompetent she had not even gotten around to declaring a state of emergency when she had actually done so three days before the storm. It was obvious to us who was behind this attack based on inaccurate information [that was] being shoveled to Washington reporters who were identifying their sources as senior Bush administration officials."[12] Blanco adds, "People at *Newsweek* told me the White House called them to say I had delayed signing the disaster declaration. The assumption was that their source was the political director—Karl Rove." Not only was the attack on Blanco in print, it was also on television. "All of a sudden," Blanco says, "a whole lot of talking heads showed up on television repeating the misinformation over and over, making it the truth."[13]

On Wednesday afternoon, Blanco again called Bush, who now took her call. She told him she needed "everything you've got." Since Bush promised to help, Blanco believed that assistance was arriving in the person of Army lieutenant general Russel Honore, who met with the governor. After a long and cordial discussion, Blanco asked Honore how many troops he had brought with him to Louisiana at the order of the president. "Just a handful of staffers," Blanco heard him say, much to her amazement. "I am here in an advisory capacity."

On Thursday, as New Orleans remained underwater, with countless thousands of people stranded in their homes, on their rooftops, or at the Convention Center or Superdome, there was still no federal help. What continued unabated, though, was the assault on Blanco, questioning her handling of the disaster. "We were in life-and-death mode and every minute counted," Blanco says. "I found my staff having to do public relations in the middle of the most disastrous days Louisiana has ever experienced. The talking heads had been turned on. My staff was saying, 'My God, governor, they are crucifying you politically.' I finally pulled all of my staff together and said, 'We are wasting our energy. We do not have a stable of talking heads. We cannot control the national media. We have lifesaving missions to accomplish, so let's do it.' My staff was upset with me."[14]

Blanco sought out Michael Chertoff. She found him in one of the emergency headquarters trailers. "Turn off the talking heads," she told him point-blank. "People are dying while you people are playing politics. Turn them off." It was Thursday, and so far the FEMA buses had still not arrived to help evacuate people from the Convention Center and Superdome, nor had Bush sent any federal troops, who were desperately needed in the search-and-rescue efforts. Instead of sending help, the administration had come up with a ploy. "I was on the conference call with the White House," Adam Sharp says, "where they were saying: If you want any help, you have to turn over all control of your state to the president. We won't help until you give us control of your National Guard and your law enforcement agencies, until Louisiana becomes a federal territory. They were using this as the excuse for their delaying on the issues. They kept trying to put it on Blanco. But no governor would ever give control of her state to the president."[15]

On Friday, Bush finally traveled south. His first stop was Mobile, Alabama, where he met with Bob Riley, the Republican governor whose associates were engaged in a collaboration with Karl Rove to destroy politically Don Siegelman, the Democratic former governor. During the stop in Mobile, Bush went out of his way to congratulate Michael Brown, saying, "Brownie, you're doing a heck of a job." Bush was willing to make such a public statement in support of Brown, carefully staged in a holding area for a national press corps that included a wall of television cameras. It was especially perplexing that he would make this statement now because the day before Bush had read a news report, handed to him by an aide, that contained information about events on the ground in New Orleans that Michael Chertoff had not shared with him that very morning in his briefing. Chertoff himself had been briefed by Brown. Worse still, Brown had at first been unaware that 25,000 people had gathered at the Convention Center—a fact so disturbing that some Republicans had begun to call for his firing, a move Bush seemed unable to make. "Mr. Brown," the *New York Times* later reported, "had become a symbol of President Bush's own hesitant response."[16]

From Alabama, it was on to Mississippi for Bush. There, he met with an old friend, Haley Barbour, the Republican governor. Significantly, Bush had nothing but praise for Riley and Barbour, neither of whom he asked to consider federalizing their National Guard troops. Finally, Bush traveled to Louisiana, still in the throes of disaster five days into the crisis—and still receiving no help from the federal government. In New Orleans, Bush met with Nagin and Blanco, along with other officials, aboard Air Force One at the Louis Armstrong international airport. The events aboard Air Force One began with a meeting of several officials, including Landrieu, Vitter, Nagin, and Blanco, as well as selected congressmen and staff members. Rove was onboard, too, "lurking," as Blanco would put it, "around the halls." In the meeting Nagin, extremely agitated, kept insisting, "Do something! Do something!" It was not clear exactly what he wanted done or who he wanted to do it, nor was it evident whether Nagin had any idea that his clandestine e-mail communications with Rove during the week may have contributed to the Bush administration's lack of response. They certainly had not helped. Finally, Bush asked to meet with Blanco alone in his office on Air Force One.

"Kathleen," Bush said in their meeting, which was attended by Joe Hagen from Bush's staff but no one from Blanco's staff—a fact that troubled Blanco—"I'm going to need you to sign a waiver that the Louisiana National Guard needs to be turned over to the federal government. I can't take them from you but I'm going to need you to federalize them."[17]

Blanco had no intention of signing a waiver. She was concerned about a variety of legal ramifications that could result from her signing over her National Guard, but her main fear was that, without the leverage Blanco had as a free agent in what had now turned into a protracted negotiation with the administration, she would have no means to force Bush to provide any assistance at all. Blanco told Bush she would not sign a waiver. "You need to give General Honore some soldiers," Blanco told Bush. "Where has the federal government been for five days? If I sign this, it's going to look like I've been wrong."

Bush appeared to be confused by what Blanco was saying.

"Well, I have no intention of turning over my National Guard to you," Blanco said. "Anyway, the evacuation of the Superdome is now well underway and after that we will begin finishing the evacuation of the Convention Center." This was true. While the administration had bickered over politics, Blanco had expanded the size of her National Guard by accepting deployments of guardsmen from all of the other 49 states. As she was meeting with Bush, she was the commander in chief of the largest deployment of National Guard troops in history. Since the federal government was not going to do the job, her expanded National Guard would carry out the evacuation of the Convention Center and the Superdome, the two missions of the most pressing urgency at the moment.

Bush again acted confused. He asked Blanco how it would work if he deployed troops to Louisiana if he was not in charge of her National Guard.

"It'll work perfectly," she said. "I need 40,000 soldiers in any combination of Guard and regular service. Your soldiers will stay under Honore's command. Mine will stay under my command."

Bush still seemed puzzled, as if he didn't know what Blanco was talking about. But Blanco would not back down; she refused to sign the waiver. It was a pivotal moment in the week's drama, for, if she had agreed, Rove would have been able to proceed with his strategy of smearing Blanco to defend Bush. By federalizing her guardsmen, Blanco would have been admitting that it was the state that was unable to handle the disaster, not the federal government. The Bush administration could have argued that they had had to save the day for Blanco because she was not up to the task. However, if Blanco did *not* take the bait, the scheme was dead. Blanco wondered about Bush's confusion. Was he really confused or just trying to get her to sign the waiver?

It didn't matter. Not only did Blanco refuse to sign, she gave Bush a two-page letter detailing everything the state needed to cope with the disaster—troops, buses, supplies, money, and more. It would not be until several days later, when Blanco's aides released the letter to the press and got frantic phone calls from Rove's aide Maggie Grant, that it became clear that Bush had taken the letter Blanco had personally handed to him—and lost it.

Finally, that day on Air Force One, when it became apparent that Bush would not be able to manipulate Blanco, he ended the meeting. Then, he took a private meeting with Nagin, who had taken his first shower since the storm hit on Air Force One. Afterward, Bush was taken on a tour of the city by helicopter, which included a visit to the 17th Street Canal.

Blanco accompanied Bush in his helicopter, along with Nagin. Landrieu, Vitter, and Rove had followed in a second helicopter. Behind them in a third was a pool of reporters from the national press corps.

"We landed at the 17th Street Canal," Landrieu says. "The story that day Karl Rove was feeding was: 'The president is on the job, the president has taken control, the president is going to rebuild, and despite the fact that the government and all these babbling fools down here can't do anything, the Corps of Engineers is on the job.' So we landed at the canal, five minutes from my house. I was so excited because they were finally doing something. The Corps of Engineers was there, and they had dump trucks and sandbags. All the cameras were there for the president, who was doing one of his famous press conferences about how he was going to do everything. So I thought, 'At least the guy is doing something, so show your manners and be good and smile.'"[18]

⇌

Once Bush and Rove flew back to Washington, though, their efforts to wrestle control from Blanco continued. On Friday night, after Bush had retuned to the White House, Blanco was approached by Lieutenant General H. Steven Blum of the National Guard on the subject of federalizing her guardsmen. When the topic had been brought up two nights before, Blum had told Blanco in person that he thought it was a bad idea. By Friday, he was back in Washington. "General Blum called from the White House," Blanco says, "asked if I had a fax machine, I said yes, and he said, 'I'm sending you some papers to sign and I need them back in five minutes.' I said I would not sign them without my lawyer and executive council looking them over carefully. I said I would not sign them in five minutes."[19] Obviously, Blum had had a change of heart from his earlier advice to Blanco. "They had dragged Blum into the White House and put a gun to his head," Bob Mann says, "and he was on the phone trying to persuade the governor to do what he had discouraged her to do two nights earlier. Later, Blum admitted he had gotten what he called a 'goat screwing,' which was his way of saying he was coerced."[20] Reportedly, while Blum was on the phone with Blanco, Rove was going in and out of the conference room from which Blum was making the call.

Blanco still would not give in. Done with Blum, she got Andy Card on the phone. Blum had been told he was not going to be able to leave the White House until he had achieved "mission accomplished" with Blanco, so Blanco told Card personally that she would not sign a waiver. She also demanded that Card read her the statement Bush was going to deliver the next day at a press conference the White House had announced. Finally, Blanco threatened Card with the truth: If they didn't leave her alone, she was going to reveal to the public that the reason the administration had delayed supplying assistance was to gain control. "You're the most political White House in all of our history," Blanco said that night to Card.

"Madame, you know not what you speak," Card replied.

"Many prominent political people have originated out of Louisiana," Blanco said, "so don't worry about us recognizing politics. We can smell it."[21]

Card didn't have a response. The telephone call ended. Despite the repeated pressure, Blanco had refused to give Rove and the Bush administration what they wanted.

The next day in the Rose Garden, Bush announced the deployment of federal troops to Louisiana—without the benefit of Blanco signing a waiver. He also tried to backtrack to explain why his administration had botched the rescue effort so badly. "The magnitude," Bush said as Rove and Cheney stood nearby watching, "of responding to a crisis over a disaster area that is larger than the size of Great Britain has created tremendous problems that have strained state and local capabilities. The result is that many of our citizens simply are not getting the help they need, especially in New Orleans. And that is unacceptable."

Unfortunately for Rove, the national media was now refusing to buy his spin. "Faced with one of the worst political crises of his administration," the *New York Times* declared, "President Bush abruptly overhauled his September schedule on Saturday as the White House scrambled to gain control of a situation that Republicans said threatened to undermine Mr. Bush's second-term agenda and the party's long-term ambitions. In a sign of mounting anxiety at the White House, Mr. Bush made a rare Saturday appearance in the Rose Garden before live television cameras to announce that he was dispatching additional active-duty troops to the Gulf Coast."[22] He had affected a more solemn tone, observers noted, than he displayed on Friday when, on the tarmac at the airport in New Orleans, he remembered his getaways to the city while he lived in Houston as a young adult. In fact, this moment of reflection had seemed to indicate that Bush was not taking the disaster as seriously as he should have been. He had come to New Orleans to tour the disaster area, yet at the airport upon his departure instead of commenting on the horrors he had just witnessed, he was reminiscing about fun-filled vacations from his younger days.

It was clear on Saturday that Bush was still trying to blame the crisis in New Orleans on local government—that is to say, on Blanco. "I knew Rove was not going to let the president go down in flames over this without fighting back," Mann says. "Their MO is to destroy anyone who gets in their way. Kathleen Blanco was just someone else in their way and they needed to take her down. Their MO is not just to defend, but to destroy."[23] Indeed, in an effort coordinated by Rove, Bush administration officials—Donald Rumsfeld, Condoleezza Rice, and chairman of the Joint Chiefs of Staff Richard Myers—were heading to Louisiana, all to blame the poor response to the disaster on state officials. In addition, since his appearance at the Gulf on Friday was now seen as humiliating, Bush was returning to Louisiana and Mississippi on Monday, again under Rove's now more careful handling.

More excuses were suggested. It was said that part of the reason the administration had responded slowly to the crisis was because so many of its members had been on vacation. For instance, Rice had been in Greece for the wedding of White House communications director Nicolle Devenish. Rice didn't return to the United States until Thursday, three days after Katrina hit on Monday, and she ended up in New York. Rove did not seem to be prepared to explain why, if Rice was so concerned about what was happening in New Orleans, she had chosen to spend the night in New York where, in addition to a shopping spree to buy shoes (where a woman was said to have accosted her, shouting, "How dare you shop for shoes while thousands are dying and homeless!"), she took in a Broadway show.

As it happened, while Blanco and her aides watched the federal government do little, they completed the rescues of thousands of people stranded at the Convention Center and the Superdome on their own by commandeering buses from around the state and transporting people from downtown New Orleans to various surrounding cities—using only the National Guard under Blanco's command. When the federal troops finally *did* start arriving over the weekend, the refugees had been cleared out. The troops made a show for the media, but they were too late. The damage had been done. After one of the most agonizing weeks in American history, with Bush and his key department secretaries embarrassed on national television, the blame, despite Rove's efforts to the contrary, ended up being placed firmly on the federal government. The administration, not Blanco and the state of Louisiana, took the hit, especially Michael Brown, who became a poster boy for ineptitude and was forced to resign from his job. Following Katrina, Bush's approval rating began to slip even more. "In the middle of the worst disaster in American history," Adam Sharp, an aide to Mary Landrieu, says, "the president was nowhere to be found and was still clearing brush on the ranch, when the previous iconic image people had of him was standing in the still-smoldering rubble of the World Trade Center 24 hours after the attacks and saying, 'I can hear you.' People were asking, 'Where is that moment here?'"[24]

The fallout from Katrina for the administration was immense. "Well, if 9/11 is one bookend of the Bush administration," Thomas Friedman wrote in the *New York Times* on September 7, "Katrina may be the other. If 9/11 put the wind at President Bush's back, Katrina's put the wind in his face. If the Bush-Cheney team seemed to be the right guys to deal with Osama, they seem exactly the wrong guys to deal with Katrina—and all the rot and misplaced priorities it's exposed here at home."[25] Or as Jason Stanford, a longtime observer of Bush from Texas, puts it: "Katrina really gave people a context in which to understand the Bush presidency. They're really just that bad at government. It's all politics all the time and actually doing the job is never that important unless you're rewarding big campaign contributors."[26] Some singled out Rove. "After Rove tried the political trick on Blanco and failed, he never recovered as a political guru," says Douglas Brinkley, author of *The Great Deluge*. "It is the turning point for Rove. It was all of the Bush administration versus this one dog-faced politician. Rove couldn't use the whole power of the White House to bully a grandma in Louisiana."[27]

In all of the drama of Katrina, there is one lingering image that might come to define the Bush presidency, a let-them-eat-cake snapshot that did not seem devastating at the time but in retrospect could not appear more damaging. "Hurricane Katrina clearly changed the public perception of Bush's presidency," the *Atlantic Monthly* observed. "Less examined is the role Rove played in the defining moment of the administration's response: when Air Force One flew over Louisiana and Bush gazed down from on high at the wreckage without ordering his plane down. Bush advisers Matthew Dowd and Dan Bartlett wanted the president on the ground immediately . . . but were overruled by Rove for reasons that are still unclear: 'Karl did not want the plane to land in Louisiana.' Rove's political acumen seemed to be deserting him altogether."[28]

Despite the criticism that part of the reason Katrina became a national catastrophe was because the Bush administration was out of touch with the reality of the moment, there was little evidence in the days after Katrina that Bush and others in his inner circle had reached any more clarity on the subject. Just the opposite. In a public appearance on September 21, Bush went so far as to link, through a turn of phrase that can only be called profoundly—and sadly—disingenuous, the natural disaster to the topic of, once again, terrorism. Appearing at a luncheon for the Republican Jewish Coalition, Bush made the following observation: "We look at the destruction caused by Katrina, and our hearts break. [The terrorists are] the kind of people who look at Katrina and wish they had caused it. We're in a war against these people."[29]

A year and a half later, after he had resigned from the Bush administration and been out of government for a period of time, Michael Brown admitted to the scheme Rove had concocted to try to save Bush's image in the wake of his failure to handle the Katrina crisis. "Unbeknownst to me," Brown said, "certain people in the White House were thinking, 'We had to federalize Louisiana because [Blanco is] a white, female Democratic governor, and we have a chance to rub her nose in it. We can't do it to Haley [Barbour] because Haley's a white male Republican governor. And we can't do a thing to him. So we're just gonna federalize Louisiana.'"[30]

"I think it is evil to politicize a disaster," Kathleen Blanco says. "But, in the end, Katrina showed that the president had no clothes."[31]

⁂

Of all of the stories and subplots, there would be one that, in many ways, symbolized the whole of Katrina, what it revealed about the Bush administration, and how it would affect the lives of so many people. On Friday, Mary Landrieu had been with Bush and Blanco as they toured the 17th Street Canal, where, at last, major work had commenced to repair the damage that had been caused when the levee broke. "Then, on Saturday," Landrieu says, "George Stephanopoulos called and asked to do an interview with me, and I said, 'George, I'm tired of doing interviews. I have to work. And nothing you are airing is accurately showing what's going on down here.' He wanted to go to the Superdome, and I said, 'We still have people stranded on their roofs. If you want to tell the right story, I will help you tell the right story. You get a helicopter and I'll go up and I will show you what is actually happening. It's awful what's happening at the Superdome, but the reason the people can't understand the story is because the entire region is under 20 feet of water. People can't get into the Superdome to help. They can't get out. People are drowning in their homes.'

"So George and I went up in the helicopter and for three hours his jaw was dropping. Then I said, 'George, before we finish I have to show you one positive thing because I can't send you back to Washington to produce a story that shows nothing but devastation and disaster.' So I told the pilot to tack right so I can show George the 17th Street Canal and the work that was going on there. I swear as my name is Mary Landrieu I thought that what I saw with the president was still there— people working, trucks, sandbags, everything. Then I looked down and saw one little crane. It was like someone took a knife and stabbed me through my heart. I lost it." There, in the cabin of the helicopter, as they flew above the breached canal below them, Landrieu sat devastated.

"I could not believe that the president of the United States, staged by Karl Rove himself, had come down to the city of New Orleans and basically put up a stage prop. It was like you had gone to a studio in California and filmed a movie. They put the props up and the minute we were gone they took them down. All the dump trucks were gone. All the Coast Guard people were gone. It was an empty spot with one little crane. It was the saddest thing I have ever seen in my life. At that moment I knew what was going on and I've been a changed woman ever since. It truly changed my life."[32]

CHAPTER NINE

SCANDALS

Katrina may have been a turning point in how Karl Rove's career was viewed, but it was not the last dilemma he would have to deal with. Over the coming months, there would be a blur of investigations, scandals, and indictments, all of which somehow had Rove at the center of events. Indeed, the administration was still reeling from the fallout of its mishandling of Katrina when, on September 28, 2005, Congressman Tom DeLay of Texas, one of the most powerful Republicans in Congress in his role as majority leader in the House of Representatives—and a close ally of Rove's—saw his career abruptly ended by a grand jury indictment for conspiracy to violate election laws in Texas. The narrative that brought DeLay down had started in 2001, and it was put in motion by Rove himself. Early in Bush's first term, Rove concluded that in order to shore up support for Bush, he needed to control Congress. To ensure Republican control of the House, Rove decided to redistrict certain states to shift Republican-leaning districts still represented by Democrats over to the Republicans. There was no better place to start than Bush's home state of Texas.

"The White House in its political division was intimately involved in redistricting almost from the time they won the White House," says Mark Angle, a senior aide to former congressman Martin Frost, the head of the House Texas delegation. "The Republicans held all of the statewide offices in Texas but they couldn't shake the fact the Democrats held a majority in the congressional delegation and were winning five districts that otherwise should have gone to Republicans. That's what Rove was frustrated about."[1]

So, in 2001, as a first step, Rove approached the lieutenant governor of Texas, Bill Ratliff, to ask if he would waive a rule blocking redistricting. He said no and "ratted out Rove," according to Angle, "by disclosing that he had gotten the call from Rove."[2] Undeterred, Rove proceeded, focusing on electing a majority of Republicans in the state House who would then undertake redistricting. For help, Rove approached DeLay. "Karl told DeLay," says journalist James Moore, "'This is the way we need the map to look so we can maintain control of Texas and pick up seats.' The original plan for redistricting came from Rove."[3]

"Republicans won a majority in the state House in 2002 because," Angle says, "DeLay designed a plan to use his [political action committee], Texans for a Republican Majority. He used corporate money, which is illegal in Texas, and laundered it through the Republican National Committee." DeLay sent $190,000 in corporate money from his PAC to the RNC, and the RNC supplied checks totaling $190,000 to five candidates running in key state House races. "They were arrogant enough even to let the numbers add up," Angle says.[4] Since it was illegal to use corporate money to finance campaigns in Texas—lawmakers were worried about the undue influence corporations could have on candidates through large contributions—this was, in effect, money laundering.

The Republicans, now in control of the Texas legislature, pushed through a redistricting plan that in effect would cause a shift in five seats in the Texas congressional delegation. A new lieutenant governor, Republican David Dewhurst, was still reluctant to waive a rule blocking redistricting, but after Karen Hughes spent a day with him he reversed himself, allowing redistricting to move forward. Once the plan was drawn up, it was submitted to the United States Department of Justice, which had to approve the plan. Six Justice Department attorneys and two analysts reviewed the plan; all objected. However, a White House political appointee in the Justice Department, Hans A. von Spakovsky, overruled them and approved the plan. Not only that, the memo detailing the staff attorneys' objections was quarantined and an order was issued demanding that the attorneys not speak to one another about the case. The case represented a stunning violation of Justice Department procedure, since the actions of one man were able to overturn the opinions of six attorneys and two analysts, but that's how badly the administration wanted the plan to move forward.

The redistricting plan worked. In the 2004 election, six House seats shifted from Democrats to Republicans, the five seats that were targeted as well as the one represented by Frost. This now gave Republicans control of the Texas US congressional delegation. "Rove went to Texas," says journalist Marie Cocco, who has written about voting rights issues that have emerged during the Bush administration, "and in state elections figured you could manipulate the machinery of voting—not the machine, the machinery of voting—in a way that would affect the outcome."[5]

But DeLay's money-laundering scheme had not gone unnoticed. Two of his former aides were indicted in September 2004 on charges related to the scam. The first person to raise questions about wrongdoing was Chris Bell, a congressman from Houston whose seat was eliminated in the redistricting. In his final months as a lame duck, Bell filed a complaint with the House Ethics Committee, which unanimously censured DeLay.

"DeLay was one of the most powerful guys in Washington at the time," Bell says. "We kept the pressure on and in October 2004 he was unanimously admonished by the Ethics Committee. It woke people up to the fact that DeLay was not invincible."[6] A year later, with his air of invulnerability now shattered, DeLay was indicted by a grand jury in

Houston for money laundering—illegally sending corporate money to the RNC, which in turn supplied it to candidates in Texas. The person who was untouched by the takedown of the scheme he had started, one he had relentlessly pushed forward until it was successful, was Rove.

One of DeLay's strongest supporters was Bush. On December 14, 2005, Bush said in an interview that he believed DeLay was innocent and that he wanted the beleaguered Texan to return to his post as House majority leader as soon as possible. On the issue of his resuming his leadership position, Bush offered: "I hope that he will [return] because I like him," Bush said, "and plus, when he's over there we get our votes through the House." In the interview, the subject of Rove also came up. "We're still as close as we've ever been," Bush said, by way of defending Rove. "We've been through a lot."[7]

"DeLay did the heavy lifting but Rove was involved in the overall strategy," Bell says. "A lot of pressure on people in Texas came from Rove and the White House. Public sentiment was overwhelming against redistricting. To get politicians to sign on to something that's not going to make them more popular, you'll need a different source of motivation—and that came from DeLay and Rove."[8] Or, as Mark Angle describes their one-two approach, "DeLay was swinging the ax but Rove was sharpening the blade."[9]

While DeLay was dealing with his problems in Texas, another scandal was unfolding in Washington, this one involving the powerful, charismatic, black-fedora-wearing K Street lobbyist named Jack Abramoff. From 1981 until 1985, Abramoff had served as chairman of the College Republican National Committee—the same job Rove had held during the 1970s—and members of his staff had included Ralph Reed and Grover Norquist, both of whom would go on to have careers of their own in the

Republican Party. Abramoff came into real power in Washington in 1994, on the heels of the revolution ushered in by Newt Gingrich and his Contract with America. When the powerful, left-leaning, Democrat-friendly lobbying firm of Preston Gates and Ellis realized they didn't have access to the new Republicans in charge, they hired Abramoff for his extensive connections in the party, particularly among the Republicans who had just taken charge of Capitol Hill. One of the congressmen with whom Abramoff developed an especially close relationship was Tom DeLay.

It was during the high-flying 1990s that Abramoff had teamed up with Michael Scanlon, who had once been DeLay's press secretary, and the two of them developed a variety of business interests together. One scheme they concocted, later the subject of an extensive Senate investigation that led to the pair being discredited and a federal criminal investigation, was referred to as Gimme Five. Gimme Five was used to raise exorbitant sums of money in consulting fees from Indian tribes with gambling interests in Texas, Michigan, Louisiana, and Mississippi. In fact, the total amount of fees paid by the tribes was so high—as much as $85 million—it was considered criminal. The amount of money they made, and the way they made it, amounted to fraud. Among other practices, Abramoff and Scanlon pitted the interests of one tribe against another, taking fees from one tribe to get legislation passed to close down the casino of another tribe, then going to that second tribe, the one with the closed casino, to collect a fee to lobby to have their casino reopened. Both federal prosecutors and Senate investigators considered this to be an outrageous form of bilking. "It was a scam operation pure and simple," says a source familiar with the scheme. "Anyone remotely familiar with what they were doing would have recognized the scam too. A lot of people were looking the other way."[10]

On a more legitimate basis, Abramoff owned a trendy restaurant in Washington called Signatures, located in the Penn Quarter neighborhood.

Besides scamming Indian tribes, Abramoff and Scanlon illegally lobbied members of Congress, bribing them with free dinners at Signatures, free nights out in skyboxes at sporting events in Washington, and free trips abroad, such as golf outings to expensive courses in countries like Scotland. It would be a golfing trip to Scotland, paid for by Abramoff and misrepresented on government papers, that would call into question the actions of Congressman Bob Ney of Ohio. Abramoff was not selective about whom he attempted to bribe and coerce for his clients, either; he went after congressmen, federal department officials, even members of the White House staff. As the year 2005 passed and he increasingly became the target of various investigations, Abramoff began to cooperate with prosecutors in the hope of gaining leniency before one of the investigations could turn into indictments.

Finally, on January 3, 2006, he pleaded guilty to three felony counts related to defrauding Indian tribes and public officials. As he left the Washington courthouse that day, he was wearing his trademark trench coat and black fedora, after pleading guilty to conspiracy, fraud, and tax evasion—all related to his transactions with the Indian tribes and the government officials he had been dealing with on their behalf. The next day, he pleaded guilty to two more felony counts related to a casino in Florida. On March 29, he was sentenced to five years in prison and ordered to pay $21 million in restitution. "Not long ago," the *New York Times* reported in January 2006, "Mr. Abramoff was perhaps Washington's most aggressive—and, at $750 an hour, most highly compensated—deal maker, a flamboyant man who moved fluidly through the nexus of money and power. Now his decision to cooperate in a broadening corruption and bribery investigation has thrust him into the role of a corporate insider turning against the company that claimed just to be doing business as usual."[11]

Naturally, as the midterm election year of 2006 proceeded, the White

House wanted to do all it could to distance itself from the Abramoff scandal. This was not easy, because Abramoff had had extensive contact with the White House. Visitor logs would show that in March 2001, only weeks after the Bush administration had come into office, Abramoff had met with Rove about hiring two people for Interior Department jobs; Abramoff was a member of the transition committee for the Interior Department, a government agency he especially cared about since it often dealt with issues concerning Indian tribes. What's more, there had been a meeting in January 2004 at the White House where Abramoff had a conversation with a staffer about the chances of his buying the Old Post Office Building from the federal government. Charges would be brought against David F. Safavian, of the White House budget office, for lying about his relationship with Abramoff; Safavian would be convicted.

Then there was the problem with Susan Ralston. A former Abramoff aide, Ralston had gone to work for Rove in 2001.[12] Many observers believed that it was Ralston who was the conduit between Rove and Abramoff. With her in the middle, each man could deny it when they were asked if they had spoken to one another about various business and political matters. According to reports, there were hundreds of contacts between Abramoff and the White House, with Ralston as the point person. Ralston had been at the White House for some time but had been promoted following the 2004 election. Her title was special assistant to the president, which commanded a handsome salary of $122,000, well up from her previous salary of $64,700. When using Ralston as a go-between wasn't workable for some reason, Rove and Abramoff met outside the White House so that Abramoff's name would not appear in the White House log books. They often rendezvoused on street corners near 1600 Pennsylvania Avenue.[13]

Even with these attempts to conceal their involvement, in October

2006, the Government Reform Committee of the House of Representatives revealed that between January 2001, when Bush came into office, and March 2004—a period of some 40 months—Abramoff or someone from his office had had at least 485 contacts with White House officials. At least 10 meetings between Abramoff and Rove also were documented. In addition, the report noted that Abramoff and his staff had spent $25,000 entertaining White House officials.

So when the Bush administration attempted to portray its relationship with Abramoff as "casual," even going as far as to suggest there were no pictures of Bush and Abramoff together (which was untrue), they were being disingenuous at best. Billing records and e-mails from Abramoff's office proved that Ralston was in touch regularly with Abramoff on behalf of Rove to get seats for sporting events. If she wasn't acting as the message-passer for Rove, she was funneling information between Abramoff and Ken Mehlman, a political strategist at the White House who would go on to become the chairman of the Republican National Committee.[14]

⇌

On October 28, 2005, the Bush administration suffered another blow when I. Lewis "Scooter" Libby, chief of staff for Vice President Dick Cheney, was indicted by a federal grand jury on five counts of perjury and obstruction of justice, making him the highest-ranking White House official to be indicted in two decades.

The indictment grew out of a case involving Valerie Plame and her husband, Joseph C. Wilson IV. In 2002, in his State of the Union address, Bush, in building his justification for the United States to invade Iraq, claimed that Saddam Hussein was trying to purchase yellowcake uranium from Niger. Not long after, the CIA dispatched Wilson, a former ambassador, to Niger to investigate. Once the war began in March 2003, critics began to question Bush's justification for the invasion, especially when no weapons of mass destruction were found. On July 6, 2003, Wilson went public with his findings in an op-ed piece in the *New York Times*, revealing that on his trip to Niger he had found no evidence to support Bush's claim that Saddam had been trying to buy uranium.

It would later be revealed that Cheney saw Wilson's op-ed piece as an assault on the credibility of the president and the vice president on one of the most important issues at play in the Bush administration: the justification for the United States' going to war. The bottom line was that Cheney was furious with Wilson because he had dared to tell the truth about Saddam's activities related to weapons of mass destruction.

Wilson was one of the first vocal critics to argue that Bush had gone to war based on false premises. The White House—that is, Cheney, Libby, and Rove—responded by launching a campaign to destroy Wilson and his wife by revealing that Plame was a CIA agent. The only problem was that disclosing the identity of a CIA agent is a felony, if the agent is covert. Plame was covert.

The plan was thorough. Rove, Libby, and Richard Armitage, deputy secretary at the Department of State, leaked Plame's identity to seven different journalists, among them reporters who worked for *Time* and the *New York Times*. Robert Novak broke the story about Plame in his syndicated column on July 14, 2003. (The column focused on Wilson's trip to Africa, with Plame's name thrown in for good measure.) Armitage had leaked Plame's name to Novak, who confirmed it with Rove. After all, Rove had had a history of supplying Novak with information for his syndicated column.[15] Rove leaked Plame's name to Matthew Cooper of *Time*. "Rove, Cheney, and Libby were all involved in a concerted plan to retaliate against Joe Wilson by leaking Valerie Plame's name," says Melanie Sloan, an attorney for Plame and Wilson. "We know that Rove talked to Novak. He was the first to talk to

Cooper. Rove was definitely a part of getting this information out."[16]

Some believe Rove was more than just involved. "The plan was hatched by Rove," James Moore says. "Armitage is the perfect guy for this because he had separation from the White House and the vice president but he was close to Libby. He was the right guy to choreograph to leak it. At the same time he was doing it, Rove was leaking it to Matt Cooper. It was virtually the same day. This is the way Rove works. Karl or Libby found out about Plame—I'm still not convinced it wasn't Karl—and he puts the plan in action. Karl thinks, 'I'll get Libby doing this and maybe we'll get Armitage to leak it out so we'll have a few degrees of separation from the administration. And we'll confirm it off the record as senior unnamed administration officials.' That's consistently how Rove works. That's what he does. The whole idea of destroying your enemies and destroying the messenger to destroy the message—that is all Karl. Anyone who doesn't believe he sat down and read that op-ed piece and thought, 'How in the hell can I get this sonuvabitch?' doesn't know Karl."[17]

The scandal blew up so badly that the Department of Justice assigned a special prosecutor, Patrick Fitzgerald, to investigate. Fitzgerald interviewed almost 50 people, among them the president and the vice president, and amassed mounds of documents, phone logs, e-mails, and the like. During grand jury testimony, Libby lied about how he had learned of Plame's identity and whether he had leaked her name. This led to his indictment. Rove might have been indicted, too, based on his initial grand jury appearances, had he not returned on a subsequent occasion to qualify his earlier testimony. In all, Rove would appear before the grand jury, always without his attorney, as is the custom with a grand jury, on four occasions. It was when his attorney realized that Rove had not told the grand jury the truth that Rove, at the insistence of his attorney, who had found out about the discrepancies, made the appearance to correct the misinformation he had given.

"He did that largely because of Viveca Novak [no relation to Robert], my colleague at *Time*," Matthew Cooper says, "who told Rove's lawyer that I was his source, and then he went ahead and recalibrated his testimony. It took the prosecutor some time in deciding not to charge him."[18] A source adds, "With Libby, there were multiple witnesses. There is only one in the case of Rove. If you believe he was lying, his lie was much less baroque than Libby's. Libby made up a big story about Tim Russert having been the one to tell him Valerie Plame's identity, whereas Rove simply said, 'I forgot' [about talking to Matt Cooper], which is harder to disprove."[19] According to Wayne Slater, the journalist, "Karl was saying, by going back in to the grand jury, 'You can't indict me for perjury and obstruction of justice if I'm coming back to you and telling you I was wrong.' It was close."[20]

As the day of reckoning approached—would Fitzgerald indict Rove?— tension mounted. On the morning Fitzgerald was to announce his decision about Rove, journalists staked out Rove's house in upper northwest Washington. With three Secret Service agents to escort him to the White House, Rove emerged to acknowledge the press. When asked how he felt, Rove responded, "A very good mood today. I'm going to have a very good day." He had been just as happy the previous night, when he had stopped by a party for a former congressman and interior secretary, Manuel Luján Jr., being held at the law firm of Jones Day. That night, he appeared chipper and upbeat as he posed for pictures, fully knowing that the following morning, because the grand jury's term was due to expire, Fitzgerald would announce a decision on whether or not he would indict Rove.

Then the decision: Rove would not be indicted for now. He probably would not be indicted in the future, since doing so would require the convening of a new grand jury. "After months of uncertainty and four grand jury appearances," the *New York Times* reported on October 29, 2005, "Karl Rove escaped the worst possible outcome . . . and a collective sigh of relief swept the Bush administration and the Republican Party. Mr. Rove remained under a legal cloud: not indicted, but still at the center of the unfinished business in the C.I.A. leak case. He was absent from public view for most of the day, and conspicuously avoided giving any appearance that he had begun to celebrate."[21] Not quite a week later, Bush, attending the 34-nation Summit of the Americas, was asked four questions about Rove and the Plame affair; each time, he refused to answer.

Finally, Rove got his life back to normal, as reported by the *Times* on November 11: "Hunkered down for almost all of October while a grand jury considered his fate, Karl Rove has rebounded as a visible presence at the White House over the last two weeks. . . . He is running meetings and pursuing candidates for the 2006 elections—and, associates say, devising long-term political plans that suggest he does not believe he will face future legal trouble despite the C.I.A. leak investigation in which he has been involved."[22]

In the end, even though Rove was deeply involved in the scheme and may have been its ringleader, it would be Libby, not Rove, who was indicted. After a protracted legal battle, Libby was found guilty. "Libby," Jason Stanford says, "did everything possible to implicate Rove—he literally made a federal case out of it—and Rove still had his office."[23]

As of June 2006, Fitzgerald made it official. He would not bring charges against Rove; this decision came after months of negotiations between Fitzgerald and Rove's attorney, Robert D. Luskin. It was Luskin who had sent Rove back in to the grand jury one last time to correct his testimony. At first, Rove said he had not revealed Plame's name to Cooper, but when an e-mail he had sent to Stephen J. Hadley, deputy national security adviser, confirmed that he *had*, Luskin took the unusual step of advising Rove to return to the grand jury and plead bad memory. Rove told the grand jury he had forgotten that he had revealed Plame's name. In short, Rove had dodged a bullet.

It was at around this time that the cumulative effects of Rove's actions were beginning to catch up with him. He may have gotten Bush elected governor of Texas twice and president of the United States twice, but in order to achieve these four feats he had had to carry out some acts that were at times unethical, perhaps even illegal. What's more, Rove began to contemplate seriously his dream of a permanent Republican majority—a Republican dynasty that would last the rest of his life, if not longer. Some saw this vision as dangerous to democracy.

"Rove's legacy," James Moore says, "will be that he has found a way to jigger democracy so it looks like democracy when it really isn't. It's dangerous, but that's what he does very, very well."[24] Even some high-level Republicans had begun to view Rove as a threat. At a social gathering in Texas in the summer of 2006, not long before the midterm elections, a well-known Democratic operative was talking with James A. Baker III, one of George H. W. Bush's most reliable confidants, and his wife, Susan, when Susan Baker made a stunning pronouncement. "You know," she said to the two men, "Karl Rove has got to go or the country may not make it."[25]

CHAPTER TEN

BOTTOMING OUT

"If anything," veteran Republican strategist Ed Rollins says, "this administration clearly needed someone who could walk in there and say, 'Listen. You're in deep shit and here's why. You've got serious problems on the Hill. You've got serious problems with the Republican base. You've got Republicans across this country very unhappy. And you're not doing what's in the best interest of either building your own legacy or, equally as important, doing what's in the best interest of the country.'"[1] Or as Matt Towery puts it, "Bush needed Rove but the end result was a disaster. Bush was now being held responsible for what Rove had done, much of which was the result of Rove's style of politics. People began to look at Bush as someone who had a good heart but who had no business being president."[2]

That would be the assessment of many voters as the country headed into the midterm elections of 2006. Bush may have won the presidency in 2000 as well as control of both the House and the Senate (the latter of which he had lost when Senator James Jeffords became an Independent); Rove may have won back the Senate in 2002 and kept control of the House, in part by risking the prestige of the office of the presidency by having Bush campaign for congressional candidates as if he were campaigning for the presidency itself; Rove may have capped off his political career with an unexpected and impressive reelection victory for Bush in

2004 while Republicans built their majorities in both the House and the Senate; but all of that was in the past. As the midterm elections of 2006 approached, Rove was facing obstacles that looked as if they were going to be all but impossible to surmount. Critics began to question what Bush had done to end up with such anemic approval ratings in national opinion polls, what he had done to generate such dislike not just from the Democrats, but also from elements of his own party.

Since Bush's reelection, Rove had overseen the disaster of attempted Social Security reform. The administration had endured run-of-the-mill blunders, such as the nominations of Bernard Kerik and John Bolton, in addition to embarrassing missteps like the nomination of Harriet Miers, the president's personal attorney, who had no substantive experience in the judiciary, for a seat on the US Supreme Court. But even more debilitating was the humiliation caused by the way the administration had handled the aftermath of Hurricane Katrina. If ever an administration had failed to serve the best interests of the American people, it was then. Bush had managed to politicize one of the worst human tragedies ever to unfold in the homeland, with Rove leading the charge. The disgust many felt for the administration as a result of Katrina now appeared to have a long-term effect.

That had happened in part because, during the week after Katrina hit, the national media had no longer accepted at face value what the administration was telling them. Members of the media themselves—key reporters as well as the anchors for the network news programs—were present in New Orleans to witness not only the incompetent and inadequate manner in which the administration had responded to the disaster, but also the way that Karl Rove and his surrogates had attempted to manipulate the facts about the disaster in their favor. Their ability to spin had been overwhelmed by their mishandling of events on the ground. There were especially disturbing moments, such as when one news broadcaster confronted Michael Brown on live television about the number of refugees at the Convention Center. He said he hadn't even known they were there until *that day*, Friday, September 2. "I've heard you say during the course of a number of interviews that you found out about the Convention Center today," Ted Koppel said to Brown on *Nightline* that Friday—the fourth day after the storm hit. "Don't you guys watch television? Don't you guys listen to the radio?" When Brown tried to sidestep the question, Koppel slapped him with another: "Here we are essentially five days after the storm hit and you're talking about what's going to happen in the next couple of days. . . . You didn't make preparations for what was going to happen in the event that [a major hurricane hit]? Why didn't you?"

"Part of the Katrina story was the failure of the Bush image makers," says Adam Sharp, an aide to Louisiana senator Mary Landrieu. "Not only did the administration handle the response badly, they handled the public relations poorly. The administration was not prepared for television anchors from national news organizations to have such anger in their voices over the federal response. You started seeing new coverage we hadn't seen since Walter Cronkite came back from Vietnam. The administration wasn't prepared for that. Finally, they drastically underestimated the extent to which the Katrina disaster affected the psyche of the American people. The administration thought this was a story people would view as 'something happening to people I don't know' and by the weekend it would be over. It didn't happen that way."[3]

Armed with this new attitude toward the administration, the national media seemed to cover the ensuing scandals much differently going forward. A level of skepticism entered into the coverage that had not been there previously. Looking like a political gangster in his trench coat and black fedora, Jack Abramoff had been paraded across the front pages of papers across the country, and his connection to the various members of the Bush administration, Rove among them, was obvious. But there were more scandals, all reported by the media, and now in unvarnished terms. Abramoff's case led to the fall of Bob Ney, a Republican player, and if his money laundering in Texas had not brought down Tom DeLay, Abramoff would have spelled the end of him, too. On top of all this, Congressman Randy "Duke" Cunningham, a Vietnam veteran and a powerful Republican from California, had seen his career ended by a financial scandal that landed him in prison.

Everywhere Rove looked there was trouble, even in the White House. He might have dodged prosecution at the hands of Patrick Fitzgerald but Scooter Libby had not. To top it all off, before the November election rolled around, there would even be a pair of sex scandals, both with homosexual overtones. Mark Foley, a congressman from Florida, would be busted for sending sexually explicit e-mails to underage congressional pages, while Ted Haggard, a conservative Christian leader with such access to the Bush administration that he joined in on weekly conference calls with the White House, was exposed in Colorado for repeatedly hiring a male prostitute who supplied him not just with sex, but also with crystal methamphetamine. All of these scandals were covered extensively by a media no longer willing to dismiss a story because of some spin-control cover story issued by the White House.

Even these episodes paled in comparison to the larger issue of the war in Iraq. Now heading into its fourth year, the war had turned into a political quagmire for the Bush administration. There was simply no other way to present it to the American public: Bush had fabricated a set of reasons that the United States should invade Iraq and, once there, the American military had found itself caught in the middle of a civil war being waged among ethnic factions that had been at odds since the country's inception. As a result of the failure in Iraq, Rove watched as Bush's poll numbers plunged into the 30s. Only Richard Nixon at the peak of the Watergate scandal had so lost the support of the American public. Rove had been able to use Bush in the 2002 midterm elections to help Republicans win across the country, but the opposite would be true in 2006. Many Republicans in close races asked the president *not* to show up in their districts, or even their states, to campaign for them. Here was the troubling concern felt by many: The war was not going well, but Bush did not seem to be willing to make any fundamental changes in how it was being waged. "Bush and Rove are both incredibly egotistical and obstinate," Congressman Tom Tancredo says, "and I worry that we are doing what we are doing in Iraq because of that obstinacy. I pray men and women have not died in Iraq because of the president's arrogance. I don't know the answer to that."[4]

Earlier in 2006, as it was becoming apparent to some just how troubled the Bush administration had become, Josh Bolten, who had been named chief of staff at the White House, made a decisive move that he hoped might help sort out some of the administration's problems. In short, he demoted Rove. In April, saying the White House staff was undergoing restructuring, Bolten took away a number of the duties Rove had been handling daily since he had assumed the title of deputy chief of staff at the beginning of the second term. Specifically, Rove's responsibility for policy-making was removed. This is how *Vanity Fair* would describe the episode: "[T]he new White House chief of staff, Josh Bolten, stripped Rove of his formal responsibility for developing domestic policy . . . and Rove was relegated to a smaller, windowless office in the West Wing, a few steps farther away from the Oval Office. It is not clear how much the staff shake-up actually diminished Rove's status or duties. . . . But those who know him say that the changes had to be a blow to a man as proud and prickly as Rove."[5] It was said at the time Rove was unhappy with his new office, both its location and its lack of windows. The office had been an important element in the myth Rove had created about himself, and now, in the wake of a litany of scandals and errors of judgment, he was relegated to a space resembling a large closet—and had been sent there by a new chief of staff whom he did not consider to be his equal.

In the opinions of some in the Bush administration, the demotion was inevitable. "For purposes of comparison," the *Atlantic Monthly* reported, "a former Bush official cited the productiveness of the first two years of Bush's presidency, the period that generated not just No Child Left Behind but three tax cuts and the Medicare prescription-drug benefit. At the time, Bolten was deputy chief of staff for policy, and relations with Congress had not yet soured. . . . When Bolten left to run the Office of Management and Budget, in 2003, the balance shifted in Rove's favor, and then shifted further after the reelection."[6] With Bolten back, now as chief of staff, it had been only a matter of time before he realigned Rove's place in the Bush White House in an attempt to reinstate a more deliberative process in the administration's policy making.

Heading into the homestretch of the midterm elections, there were clear signs that the Bush administration was going to have problems. In late August, Dick DeVos, formerly an ardent backer of Bush's and now a candidate for governor in Michigan, stunned the administration in particular and the Republican Party in general by viciously attacking Bush for what DeVos said was his failure to meet with leaders from the American automobile industry. "We're being ignored here in Michigan by the White House, and it has got to stop," DeVos warned. DeVos's communications director, John Truscott, was clear about why the candidate had made his remarks when he did. He had timed his comments to coincide with Rove's appearance at a Michigan fund-raiser. When reporters asked if DeVos was worried that he might anger Rove with his comment, Truscott replied, "That never even crossed our mind."[7]

Even as Republican candidates for governor were insulting him, the Republican Party continued to defend Rove. He was a major fund-raiser for Republicans, the party noted, bringing in $10,357,486 at 75 events in

29 states.[8] He still was in charge of the early morning planning meetings held in the White House mess. He briefed the president on political issues every morning at 8:30. His duties might have been realigned, but he still had power.

Yet the reality of what was happening in the country seemed lost on Rove. On the Monday before the midterm elections, a day when the Republican candidate for governor of Florida, Charlie Crist, refused to make an appearance with Bush at a campaign event in the Panhandle, Rove appeared on a Boston-based radio talk show hosted by a right-leaning Republican. Obviously, the talk show host wanted to know how the Republicans were going to do in the midterm elections. Rove offered the following assessment: "Well, for the past six weeks or so, I've been looking at as many as 68 polls every week, for as many as 68 races for the House, the Senate and governorships. And so I see the national polls, like everybody else does, but I get a chance to look at the data all across the country, and I see in these individual races that candidates have been able to create it as a choice between them and their opponent. Not just on local issues, but on big national issues as well. And as a result, it gives me a sense of optimism that we'll have a Republican Senate and a Republican House."[9]

Even though Rove had said earlier in the campaign season that he would not make predictions, he just had, so why stop now? "I feel good about the Senate," he said, "and the House is a race by race, district by district battle, that when you add it up, I see us with a majority. And it's not going to be pretty, and it's required a lot of effort, but our candidates have been sterling, and the involvement of the national figures, the president, the vice president, the First Lady, Senator [John] McCain, Governor [Mitt] Romney, Mayor [Rudolph] Giuliani, has just been terrific in helping make certain that our candidates have the resources to fight the battle, and then air cover to help them explain the message."

In the end, on election day, the message of the Republican Party did not translate. Despite his obsession with polls, his insistence that he had the best view on the American electorate, his prognostication without making predictions, Rove could not have been more wrong. The Republicans lost 29 seats in the House and 6 in the Senate, relinquishing control of both chambers of Congress to the Democrats. If Rove had been the architect of Bush's reelection in 2004, he was also the architect of the Republicans' defeat in the Congress two years later.

To make matters worse, on the day after the defeat, Bush accepted the resignation of Donald Rumsfeld as secretary of defense, an implied admission that the Bush administration's failed policy on Iraq had been one of the contributing factors, if not the primary factor, in the defeat. At seven o'clock on the Wednesday morning after the midterm election, Bush had held a staff meeting in the Oval Office, attended by Rove, Josh Bolten, and Dan Bartlett, now counselor to the president, to discuss how they were going to deal with the new Democratic Congress. It is not clear what decisions were made. Then Bush walked through the photo op to do what he had been saying for some time he would never do: get rid of Rumsfeld. "Faced with the collapse of his Republican majority in Congress," the *New York Times* reported, "President Bush responded swiftly on Wednesday by announcing the departure of Defense Secretary Donald H. Rumsfeld and vowing to work with Democrats 'to find common ground' on the war in Iraq and domestic issues."[10] This came only days after Bush had said that Rumsfeld would remain defense secretary until the end of Bush's second term. But he and Rumsfeld had had what Bush called "a series of thoughtful conversations" and decided it was time for Rumsfeld to go.

Ten days later, the *Times* weighed in on Rove's role in the election debacle: "Karl Rove, the top White House political strategist, is coming off the worst election defeat of his career to face a daunting task: saving the president's agenda with a Congress not only controlled by Democrats, but also filled with Republican members resentful of the way he and the White House conducted the losing campaign."[11] The decision to announce the departure of Rumsfeld one day after the loss was considered to be a major political blunder by most observers, especially Republicans who believed that they could have held at least the Senate had Rumsfeld left office before the election. At the White House it was Rove who had argued most strongly that Rumsfeld should stay on until after the election. But a bigger blunder seems to have been Rove's unwillingness to listen to Republicans who were warning that the president's position on the war in Iraq was potentially lethal for them—a feeling that was ultimately justified by the election's outcome. Had Rumsfeld resigned before the election, a move Rove could have lobbied for but didn't, the election results could have been much different.

While Bush's reelection had been the pinnacle of Rove's career, the loss of Congress was the nadir. That fact was not lost on Republican Party players. "At the end of the day," Ed Rollins says, "there were a lot of people who knew that the 2006 elections were going bad, and Rove was the cheerleader. 'No, no, no, it's not true, not true. My polls indicate we're gonna pick up 10 seats, or 15 seats, or whatever.' People lost confidence in him before the election. Anybody who could read the numbers, it wasn't out there. People knew things were turning bad. Every private pollster who was doing it for Republicans knew we were in deep trouble. I don't know what his format is, because I've never been privileged to see it, but it certainly wasn't accurate. The 2004 election was much closer than he anticipated it being, and, certainly, 2006 was a disaster. So, as the guy that's supposed to be the guru, I think he fell on his face. I think people in the business weren't in fear of him anymore. There was a period where you had to do it his way or else you paid a very heavy price. After 2006, there were a lot of people who were going to do their own thing and didn't think of him as the great guru anymore."[12]

CHAPTER ELEVEN

BLIND JUSTICE

1.

Just when it appeared matters could not get much worse for Karl Rove, they did. He had been demoted at the White House. He had lost the 2006 midterm elections. Now, not long after that defeat, a scandal would emerge from the Bush administration from which he would ultimately be unable to extricate himself. It began when the White House fired eight United States attorneys. In all, nationwide there are 93 US attorneys who are appointed by the president. It is their responsibility to oversee federal investigations that, when warranted, can lead to prosecution. Even though US attorneys serve at the pleasure of the president and are considered political appointees, traditionally the attorneys have gone out of their way to remain nonpartisan. Moreover, a president has almost never selectively fired US attorneys, and certainly not for political reasons. Under normal circumstances, if a president wants to make a change in the US attorney system, as Bill Clinton did after he was reelected in 1996, he will fire all 93 attorneys so he can replace them as a group and avoid any appearance of partiality. Therefore, when it became clear that Bush was going to fire seven US attorneys—an eighth had been replaced earlier in 2006—questions began to be asked.

The attorneys, all of whom had been appointed by Bush, worked in eight different states. They were David C. Iglesias of Albuquerque, New Mexico; Daniel G. Bogden of Las Vegas; Paul K. Charlton of Phoenix;

H. E. "Bud" Cummins of Little Rock, Arkansas; Carol S. Lam of San Diego; John McKay of Seattle; Margaret Chiara of Grand Rapids, Michigan; and Kevin V. Ryan of San Francisco. A plan coordinated by the White House and the Department of Justice was put in motion to remove the seven attorneys. On December 7, 2006, calls went out from the Justice Department asking for their resignations. The eighth, Cummins, had been removed in the summer to make room for Timothy Griffin, a former Rove aide who had been in charge of opposition research in the 2004 presidential election.

The troubling aspect of the firings was the belief held by many that the attorneys had been replaced not because of poor job performance, but because they would not kowtow to the political pressure the administration was exerting on them. Critics of the Justice Department's actions contended that the attorneys either had not prosecuted enough Democrats or, even worse, they had dared to prosecute—and in some cases been able to convict—Republicans, as had Lam, who prosecuted and convicted Randy "Duke" Cunningham. On the other hand, some of the attorneys— all were devoted Republicans—had not pursued Democrats to the degree desired by the administration. There were stories about Iglesias being reluctant to charge Democrats he was still investigating when doing so more quickly would have been politically advantageous to the Republicans in his state. Forget that, historically, US attorneys had never answered to the White House about prosecutions; this was the Bush administration, and political matters were handled differently.

"Presidents sweep the board clean when they come into office," Cummins says, "they appoint their own, and then it has been the practice that the attorneys were left alone until they committed some real malfeasance. There was a hands-off attitude until there was another change at the White House. This was the first time a select group was replaced that was appointed by that president. I don't think any president has gone out and said, 'I want to do something different' with his own appoint-ments."[1]

Behind everything political in the Bush White House, of course, was Karl Rove. "Rove," James Moore says, "blows out Carol Lam in San Diego. Paul Charlton in Phoenix was on the verge of issuing indict-ments. Bud Cummins was chased away because he was investigating a Republican governor. Rove was guilty of hubris. I think the genius might have turned into an idiot in this particular case—to think that you could get away with firing US attorneys. But that's Rove's style: 'We'll do whatever the hell we want and we'll deny it and we'll stonewall investigations and eventually the public will get sick of it all and we'll have won.'"[2] As Garry Mauro, the former Texas land commissioner, says: "Rove is dangerous. He used the US attorney office when he wasn't *in* the White House. I don't see how you'd expect him not to use the US attorney office when he *was* in the White House. If you look at the US attorneys, it's exactly what he did in Texas."[3]

The Justice Department, including Attorney General Alberto Gonzales, claimed that the attorneys were being replaced for perfor-mance reasons, but that didn't seem believable. "Internal Justice Department performance reports," the *New York Times* revealed on February 25, 2007, "for six of the eight United States attorneys who have been dismissed in recent months rated them 'well regarded,' 'capable' or 'very competent.' . . . The reviews, each of them 6 to 12 pages long, were carried out by Justice Department officials from 2003 to 2006. Each report was based on extensive interviews, conducted over several days with judges, other federal law enforcement agencies and staff mem-bers."[4] Cummins's evaluation had been especially good. Even so, he was replaced on a temporary basis by Griffin, who would later withdraw his name from consideration. The report stated, "United States Attorney Cummins was very competent and highly regarded by the federal, judiciary, law enforcement and civil client agencies." His office's antiterrorism program was "well-managed," and its counternarcotics efforts were "very successful."[5] As for Lam, she was "an effective manager and respected leader in the district."[6]

Because the attorneys had received such excellent evaluations, they were especially vocal in March when they appeared before Congress to testify about the reasons they believed they had been fired. Iglesias recounted a telephone call he had received from Senator Pete Domenici of New Mexico in late October, just before the midterm elections. Iglesias said he had felt sick when he got off the phone with Domenici, who had called him at home. "Are these going to be filed before November?" Iglesias said Domenici asked him, referring to indictments in a corruption case involving Democrats. "I don't think so," Iglesias recalled saying. "I'm very sorry to hear that," Domenici said. "And then the line went dead," Iglesias told the senators on the Judiciary Committee. "I felt leaned on," he added. "I felt pressured to get these matters moving."[7]

In retrospect, it would become clear that the attorneys were replaced not because of concerns about their performance but because they were not deemed loyal enough. They were not "Bushies." "Apparently," Cummins says, "I made a disloyalty list that was made up by the guys who wanted to put Tim Griffin into the job." Of the other seven, he says, "They didn't treat them the same way. When they fired them, they told them less and really didn't give them an explanation and pretty quickly Congress reacted to that. It appears they already had people in mind to replace all these people, arguably Tim Griffin types—insiders, friends, that kind of thing. But they backed off the plan when they saw they tapped a nerve. I think this was part of an overall plan. I've been an eyewitness to the whole deal and I think I know as much about it as anybody and I am completely convinced that their decisions were not made on performance issues."[8]

Other evidence suggested that was true. In May, a study reported by Donald Shields of the University of Missouri at St. Louis and John Cragan of Illinois State University determined that the Bush Justice Department had investigated four times as many Democrats, either in office or running for office, as they had Republicans. This would represent what would come to be known as selective prosecution. Under pressure from the White House and the Department of Justice, US attorneys would launch investigations that could only be seen to have political motivations behind them.

"It is clear that part of what was going on at the Justice Department was they were doing two things," says Marie Cocco, the journalist. "They had taken the criminal part of the Justice Department—the US attorneys—and the voting rights section and turned them into an operation for throwing elections for Republicans. Obviously, some of the US attorneys who were fired were fired because they didn't indict Democrats, didn't indict Democrats fast enough, or didn't lay off Republicans. That's the criminal part. They were using the criminal justice system to affect the outcome of elections.

"Simultaneously, there were several things they were doing at the voting rights level that were having the same effect. There was the issue of the ID law in Georgia [requiring voters to show photo identification]. Republicans went around screaming, 'Fraud, fraud, fraud, fraud.' They trumped up all these charges that there were armies of illegal voters, specifically immigrants, who were illegally voting. In every single case of fraud or phantom voters or houses that didn't exist, all were not true. Interestingly, these cases for the most part always seemed to come about in closely contested swing states."[9]

At first, the White House claimed Rove had had nothing to do with the US attorney firings. Then internal memos surfaced proving he had been involved with the scheme from the beginning. "Rove's plan for a permanent majority was to muck up the voting mechanism," Cocco says. "How do you do that? You have [secretary of state] Ken Blackwell of Ohio say there has to be a certain kind of paper for the ballot. You claim there is fraud everywhere on the eve of an election, which makes some minority voters afraid to go to the polls and it makes Democrats divert their resources to answer your allegations. It's the constant kicking of sand in the gears."[10]

To an extent, Rove got what he wanted: a White House that would allow him to use the Justice Department to affect the political system of the country. Along the way, many people would be harmed, some severely. In the end it might have been the unfolding of what the press and the political establishment called the US attorney scandal that brought down Rove. Before it did, he was able to do much damage, not just to the concept of democracy as American citizens had come to know it, but to some of those individual citizens themselves.

2.

Not long after George W. Bush was inaugurated for his second term on a cold Washington day in January 2005, Steven M. Biskupic, the United States attorney in Milwaukee, found himself in a predicament not unlike those affecting a number of other US attorneys, as it turned out. Even though Biskupic had been appointed by Bush in 2002 and had, from all indications, performed his job admirably, his name was on a list circulating in the White House of US attorneys who were candidates for firing. The list with Biskupic's name on it had been compiled at the Department of Justice sometime before March 2005.

According to reports, Rick Wiley, the executive director of the Republican Party of Wisconsin, had ordered his office to produce a report on election abuse. The 30-page *Fraud in Wisconsin 2004: A Timeline/ Summary* ended up at the White House and the Justice Department. "The report was prepared for Karl Rove," a source later told the *Milwaukee Journal Sentinel*. "Rick wanted it so he could give it to Rove."[11]

At the same time the report was making the rounds in Washington, Biskupic announced that an investigation conducted by his office could not identify widespread election fraud in Wisconsin in 2004. This came in the wake of claims made by the White House, sources of which were never revealed, that as of the summer of 2004 voter fraud cases in Wisconsin that had supposedly been reported to the Bush administration were not being prosecuted aggressively enough. It is not clear if Biskupic's apparent unwillingness to comply with his political bosses, who were close to Rove, put him on the tentative to-be-fired list, but there his name was.

Other evidence suggests that Biskupic's reluctance to fall into line had put him in Rove's crosshairs. On a computer printout of an article from the *Milwaukee Journal Sentinel* dated February 2, 2005, detailing voter irregularities in Milwaukee, a copy of which had somehow made its way to the White House, the name "Rove_K" appeared at the bottom of each of the two pages. One of the annotated pages contained a hand-written reminder, "discuss w/ Harriet," presumably meaning Harriet Miers, who was counsel to the president. Clearly, the issue of voter fraud was on Rove's mind, and he intended to advance the issue with Miers.

Rove was sending signals that Biskupic was not doing his job and bringing forward enough voter fraud cases. "Because Biskupic is a straight shooter," Joe Wineke, chairman of the Democratic Party of Wisconsin, says, "he was supposedly above trying to mollify the Bush administration. I think that's just hogwash. The US attorneys talk to each other all the time. They go to these little conferences. They go out and have their cocktails or whatever. You can't tell me Biskupic didn't know that they were not happy with him and that he better do something to protect his job. After all, retribution is the price you pay if you don't do what they want."[12]

According to a report, at a gathering of US attorneys from around the country in Washington, Biskupic *had* said to David Iglesias that "they are pounding away on me pretty good" on the issue of voter fraud, but were "still not happy with me."[13] Biskupic had filed 14 cases altogether—and he did so only after being pressured—but no doubt Rove wanted to see hundreds of cases filed. Wisconsin was an excellent state to file such charges in, because there, unlike in many states, it was illegal for a felon on probation to vote. What's more, in 2004, the state's results in the presidential race had been extremely close. Aggressively prosecuting voter fraud, which might intimidate Democrats into not voting in the future, could only help the Republican Party.

As the year 2005 unfolded, it could not have been in Biskupic's best interests to remain out of step with Rove and his superiors at the Department of Justice, which is more than likely the reason that he ended up on the proposed to-be-fired list. Biskupic may have been doing the job he had been appointed by Bush to do, but if he was a "loyal Bushie," he would not have insisted on breaking ranks over voter fraud, a topic dear to Rove's heart. So Biskupic, who wanted to keep his job, had a problem—what to do?

Enter Georgia Thompson. Hardworking, conscientious, intensely private, Thompson was a veteran of the travel industry who had been hired in July 2001 at an annual salary of $75, 824 to work for the state of Wisconsin when Scott McCallum, a Republican, was governor.[14] In 2002, when Jim Doyle, a Democrat, defeated McCallum, Thompson had voted for McCallum, most probably because, being virtually apolitical and having no interest in partisan politics, she considered McCallum her boss, so she voted for him. A change of political parties in the statehouse had no discernable effect on Thompson's duties as a purchasing supervisor in the Department of Administration, so she went about her job as usual. In 2005, as part of that job, she sat on a seven-person panel charged with awarding to an outside company a travel contract worth $750,000 over three years.

The complicated process for selecting the winner of the contract was defined by established state guidelines. Companies were asked to submit a written proposal followed by a dog-and-pony-show-style in-person pitch complete with a PowerPoint presentation. A state-approved grading system was used to evaluate each company, with scores being determined by considering the overall bids as well as both the written and in-person presentations. At the end of this lengthy process, of the 10 companies considered, Adelman Travel scored 1,026.6 and Omega World Travel came in at 1,027.3, out of a possible 1,200 points. That Adelman was a Wisconsin-based company and Omega was not was a consideration, but not a final determining factor. The bidding was essentially a dead heat.

So, again following state guidelines, Thompson called for a best-and-final offer. Adelman submitted the lowest bid, and the panel awarded that company the contract. To any objective observer, the process of awarding the contract would have appeared routine and uneventful, the kind of normal, by-the-rules procedure that takes place every day in any state government in the country. Not to Steven Biskupic. In late 2005 and early 2006, under pressure to keep his job by being more sensitive to Rove's concerns about voter fraud, Biskupic looked at the orderly process by which the travel contract had been awarded and decided to charge someone with fraud. That person was a modest, well-intentioned woman who had never had any criminal run-ins in her life—Georgia Thompson.

To Biskupic, the source of the fraud was simple. Over the better part of a year, Craig Adelman, the owner of Adelman Travel, had contributed $10,000 to Jim Doyle's reelection campaign. Other employees at the company had given an additional $10,000, bringing the total to $20,000. According to Biskupic, Thompson—and he singled her out as the only one on the panel who was guilty of fraud—had pushed to award

Adelman Travel the state contract not because Adelman's best-and-final offer had been the lowest, but because Craig Adelman and his employees had given contributions totaling $20,000 to the Doyle campaign—contributions that were completely legal and disclosed to the public in compliance with campaign finance laws.

What's more, to bring charges against Thompson, Biskupic had to overlook a number of inconvenient facts, among them that Thompson had not acted alone in awarding the contract, but as part of a state committee; that Thompson did not profit personally from the alleged fraud; that Thompson had never met Craig Adelman and had no knowledge that he and his employees had contributed money to Doyle's campaign; that neither Doyle nor anyone on his behalf had pressured Thompson during the awarding of the contract; that neither Adelman nor anyone on his behalf had bribed her; that she had actually voted against Doyle in the last election; and finally—and this was most disturbing—that she had never met Doyle himself before or after he was elected governor.

All of the evidence to the contrary, Biskupic handed down an indictment against Thompson for felony fraud charges on January 24, 2006. (The state cancelled the Adelman contract as soon as the indictment was issued.) "Georgia Thompson, 55, a purchasing division supervisor with the state Department of Administration," one paper reported, "has been charged with two federal felonies: causing misapplication of funds and participating in a scheme to defraud the state of Wisconsin of the right to honest services."[15] Thompson "intentionally inflated her scores for Adelman," according to the indictment, "and suggested that other committee members do the same." She took these actions, the indictment said, "to cause political advantage for her supervisors" and—now the indictment *did* try to bring in a personal element—to guarantee herself job security. That she had been working in the travel industry for more than 25 years, had performed well as an employee of the state, and did not anticipate losing her job did not seem relevant to Biskupic. Again, he was willing to disregard overwhelming evidence to the contrary to hand down an indictment. He was back in the good graces of the powers above him. That very month, Biskupic's name was removed from the list of US attorneys who were under consideration for firing.

If Adelman and Doyle were supposed to have profited from the alleged fraud, they should have been indicted instead of Thompson, who did not benefit in any way from the awarding of the contract. This led observers to speculate that Thompson was being set up by Biskupic to make her testify against the governor. Later, Stephen Hurley, Thompson's attorney, would say the prosecution had indeed made gestures designed to put the squeeze on Thompson. "The government said more than once that [Thompson] might be able to avoid prosecution if she gave information about those higher up," Hurley said. On May 29 and 30, just before the trial was set to begin, the state had offered Thompson a plea bargain: cop to two misdemeanors, which carried no prison time, in exchange for testimony about those above her, such as Doyle.

If the plan was to get Thompson to rat on her bosses, it didn't work. Then again, Thompson could not have provided information that did not exist. Undeterred, Biskupic took the case to trial in the summer. During the trial, testimony revealed that Doyle and Marc Marotta, one of the governor's aides, had had meetings and telephone conversations with Adelman's company during the period when Thompson's panel was considering the bids, but no testimony linked Doyle or anyone on his staff to Thompson. There also was no evidence of a "pay to play" deal, so Biskupic underscored the notion that Thompson was acting on her own to curry favor with her bosses and achieve job security that might result in a raise. It did not seem to occur to Biskupic that any employee working under any boss in any job in the country carries out actions with precisely those motivations. What employee *doesn't* want to please his or her boss? And the raise Thompson got after the contract was awarded, though not *because* of the contract, was a mere $1,000. Rarely in the American legal system had a merit raise—and a modest one at that—been perceived by the prosecution as a bribe that constituted fraud. That didn't stop Biskupic from viciously attacking Thompson during his closing arguments. "She lied; we know she lied," Biskupic railed. "It couldn't have worked better [for Adelman] if they had had one of their own employees on that committee."[16]

Then, in June, amazingly, the federal jury found Thompson guilty on both charges. Following the conviction, jurors' statements to the press indicated that they felt they had convicted Doyle and his top aide, not Thompson. They felt the governor was corrupt. "The jury foreman," Joe Wineke says, "was quoted in the press after the conviction saying, 'While the evidence wasn't that strong, we knew the governor was involved and the governor was telling her to do it and she was trying to please him.' The governor didn't even know who she was. But the jury convicted the governor. They assumed the governor was behind this. They couldn't get the governor, so they got Georgia Thompson. It was a failure of the jury system. They went in with the preconceived notion that she was guilty."[17] Doyle had a history of extremely aggressive fund-raising; in addition, he was not above rewarding key contributors with favors. All of his actions had been completely aboveboard and legal, but because as attorney general he had been critical of Tommy Thompson, the former Republican governor, for the same sort of aggressive fund-raising, Doyle had set himself up to be attacked for being hypocritical. But Doyle was not before the jury; Thompson was. She became collateral damage.

Damage, indeed. From the time she was indicted until the end of the trial, Thompson lost everything. She resigned from her job before she could be fired, because the state of Wisconsin—and in particular Doyle—offered her little to no support in her defense. "It is clear that

Georgia Thompson acted on her own," Doyle said about the conviction, "and that no other state employee was involved. As I have stated before, I have zero tolerance for ethical lapses in government. When public servants abuse the public's trust, they forfeit their rights to continue in the state's employ."[18] It never became apparent exactly what "ethical lapses" Thompson was guilty of, let alone what precisely she had been trying to achieve on her own.

Besides resigning from her job, Thompson spent all of her life savings and pension on legal bills; she was also forced to sell her home. In all, her case cost her more than $300,000. Now, with a guilty verdict having been handed down, she had lost her freedom. With prison looming, the prosecutors again tried to put the squeeze on Thompson, offering her a plea bargain in exchange for testimony against her higher-ups. In three separate phone calls in September the prosecutors offered Hurley a deal; Biskupic himself even joined the last conference call. Hurley insisted that Thompson's answer had not changed: She would cut no deal because she was innocent. Finally, Biskupic got the hint—and dropped the offer.

At the sentencing hearing in late September, after Judge Rudolph T. Randa ordered her to serve 18 months in prison, the prosecution convinced him to incarcerate her as she awaited her appeal. Even though Thompson was not a flight risk and could have remained free on bail pending appeal, Biskupic got what he wanted and Randa ordered her to prison. On the brink of the November election, the newspaper headlines blared that a "Doyle aide," which the media were calling Thompson even though she had never met the governor, was heading to prison. Rove couldn't have planned the timing better himself. The race for governor pitted Doyle, who was trying to win reelection, against Mark Green, a Republican.

Indeed, as if it had been taken right out of the Rove playbook, the Thompson case provided the Green campaign with the ammunition it needed to pound away at Doyle in the press and in its advertising campaign. In the time leading up to the election, the Republicans spent $4 million on advertising trying to tie Doyle to Thompson. Most of the money was spent after Thompson was convicted, sentenced, and ordered off to prison. One television ad even featured her name on the screen as prison cell doors shut. In the end, despite the considerable efforts of the Republicans, Doyle was reelected by an eight-point margin. The Thompson case played a vital role in Green and the Republicans' effort to defeat Doyle, but because the unpopular war in Iraq remained a central issue in Wisconsin, it was not enough.

Then something peculiar happened. On April 5, 2007, after Thompson had served almost 4 months in her 18-month sentence at a federal prison in Pekin, Illinois, the US Court of Appeals for the Seventh Circuit, located in Chicago, heard oral arguments for Thompson's appeal. The three-judge panel listened for just 26 minutes before making a stunning decision. The judges wanted to know the obvious: If the exchange of money involved Doyle and Adelman, why were they not indicted along with, or perhaps even instead of, Thompson? "Am I missing something?" one judge asked the assistant US attorney arguing the case.[19]

Judge Diane Wood summed up the feeling of the court when she said to the prosecution, "I have to say it strikes me that your evidence is beyond thin. I'm not sure what your actual theory in this case is."[20] Finally, the appeals court not only reversed the decision of the lower court, it ordered the case be sent back to the district in Milwaukee and the judgment changed to an acquittal, bypassing any notion of a retrial. Then the appellate court demanded that Thompson be set free that very day, before the court could bother to issue its mandatory written decision. The Wisconsin media were so stunned that the *Milwaukee Journal Sentinel* ran an editorial finally vocalizing what many who had followed the case believed Thompson had become—an "unwitting political prisoner."[21]

When the Seventh Circuit court issued its written opinion on April 20, Chief Judge Frank Easterbrook, a Reagan appointee, called Biskupic's case against Thompson "preposterous." The state of Wisconsin agreed, reinstating Thompson at her old salary (though in a different job) and granting her $67,161 in back pay. But no remuneration could compensate for the real damage the US attorney had done to her life. The heartache, the systematic destruction of her reputation, the four months she had wrongly spent in prison—none of that could be given back to Georgia Thompson.

"Everybody knows Rove is the architect of all this do-whatever-you-have-to-do-to-win politics," Joe Wineke says. "With Georgia Thompson, this was a witch hunt and all of the fingers point to Karl Rove. There was no way this was coming from the people in the Republican Party in Wisconsin. This was about reapportionment in 2012. This was all about the future. The last time Wisconsin went Republican was for Reagan in 1984, and each election has been determined by a small margin. Rove wanted to permanently realign the state. He was looking at who was going to be governor in 2010 and beyond, so they could realign the state. That's why they wanted to take out the governor at that time. This was not that related to Doyle per se except he happened to be a Democrat."[22]

3.

Steven Biskupic then took additional steps concerning widespread voter fraud in Wisconsin. As White House officials later acknowledged, Rove himself had taken to both Bush and the Justice Department complaints he said originated with the Republican Party in Wisconsin about voter irregularities in the state. Because of this, Justice Department officials, undoubtedly aware of Rove's feelings about the subject, attempted to redefine what constituted a prosecutable crime. In the past, voter fraud cases were prosecuted only if they involved a conspiracy to commit voter fraud. Individual cases were not prosecuted, especially if the questionable vote occurred as a result of the normal political campaign process or a mistake on the part of the voter. All of that changed after 2000, when the state fell in the Electoral College column for Al Gore in yet another close election.

"Since 2002," said a memorandum generated by a Justice Department official in the Public Integrity Section, "the department has brought more cases against alien voters, felon voters, and double voters than ever before. Previously, cases were only brought against conspiracies to corrupt the process rather than individual offenders acting alone. For deterrence purposes, the Attorney General decided to add the pursuit of individuals who vote when not eligible to vote (non-citizens, felons) or who vote more than once. The department is currently undertaking three pilot projects to determine what works in developing the cases and obtaining convictions and what works with juries in such matters to gain convictions." One pilot project, the memorandum said, concerned felon voting in Milwaukee—the district covered by US attorney Steven Biskupic.

As of mid-June 2007, of the 14 voter fraud cases brought in Milwaukee, six had been dismissed, one had concluded in a hung jury, and two had ended in acquittal. Only five had resulted in a conviction. Among the five, one conviction was in a case in which the person in question realized she had made a mistake and called City Hall to rescind her vote. In the upside-down world of the Bush Justice Department, fueled by Rove's efforts to ramp up prosecution of voter fraud cases—a classic method of suppressing voter turnout—it's a crime even if it's an accident and the so-called criminal tries to correct what she has done.

In October 2004, at a Democratic rally held in Milwaukee by Reverend Al Sharpton, Kimberly Prude, a 40-year-old African American grandmother working as a volunteer at the rally, was so swept up in the emotion that she joined hundreds of others who had come to hear

Sharpton speak as they marched en masse to City Hall to vote. She stood in line with the others, registered, and cast an absentee ballot for John Kerry. It was the first time in her life that she had voted. It was only later, Prude eventually contended, that she realized she had committed a crime, when her probation officer explained her blunder to her. Prude was four years into a period of probation she had been ordered to serve by a judge for once having tried to cash a counterfeit government check in the amount of $1,254.

When she had been arrested for attempting to cash the check, she had pleaded guilty. Her sentence was suspended and she was instead placed on probation for six years. She was still on probation—and a convicted felon—when she cast her vote for Kerry, which was illegal because Wisconsin forbids felons who are on probation from voting. As soon as Prude realized her mistake, she called City Hall and told an official what happened. "I voted," she said. "I wasn't supposed to, so what do I do with my vote?" To which the official said, "Oh, don't worry about it, honey. It happens all the time." So Prude did what she was told: She didn't worry about it. She went on with her life.

But the next thing she knew, police officers showed up at her home and charged her with voter fraud. Although she didn't know it, hers was one of the test cases being pursued by the Justice Department to redefine a law that applied only to conspiracies so it could be used against individuals. Biskupic did as he was expected to; the US attorney's office pressed charges against Prude, claiming a probation officer had told her *before* the rally that she was not supposed to vote. That she had tried to rescind her vote was beside the point to Biskupic, whose office went forward with its prosecution.

Eventually, in September 2005, following a three-day trial, Prude was found guilty. She had been taken to jail immediately upon her arrest, since she had violated the terms of her probation by committing the crime of voting, so as soon as the trial was over and the judge sentenced her to two years in prison, she was escorted from the courtroom and back to jail. Ultimately, she was not moved to a federal prison, but instead remained in jail in Milwaukee pending an appeal that saw the higher court fail to overturn the ruling. "She was at the wrong place at the wrong time," says Purvi Patel, Prude's appellate attorney. "All of them at the Sharpton rally were encouraged to go register and vote, so they did."[23] Or as Prude herself said on the stand during the trial, "I made a big mistake, like I said, and I truly apologize for it."[24] Some political observers are more cynical. "With Kimberly Prude," Joe Wineke says, "Biskupic had to make it look as if he'd go after black people."[25]

Later, in May 2007, from the Robert E. Ellsworth Correctional Center in Racine County, Wisconsin, Prude told the *Milwaukee Journal Sentinel*: "At this point, I'm not interested in voting."[26] Who could blame her? But her words, spoken from a prison she was in because of a Rove-inspired program to reinterpret voter fraud laws, is the very definition of voter suppression.

It was in this atmosphere of paranoia and winning at all costs that the case against Don Siegelman of Alabama would be brought forward. Rarely if ever in the United States has a former governor been tried, convicted, and sent to prison for an act that happens every day in the American political system. But that's what happened to Siegelman as a result of a prosecution orchestrated by Rove. "If I could speak to Karl Rove," Don Siegelman says, "I would tell him, 'You stole democracy from America. Your actions to use the Justice Department to control elections have subverted the Constitution of the United States and eroded the basic freedoms of our citizens. By placing personal power and political gain ahead of what is right, fair, and just, you have committed a high crime against America."[27]

CHAPTER TWELVE

THE UNITED STATES
VERSUS DON SIEGELMAN

1.

On Monday, November 18, 2002, almost two full weeks after election day, a conference call was placed concerning the race for governor of Alabama, which was still undecided. That year the race was between Don Siegelman, a Democrat and incumbent running for reelection, and Bob Riley, a Republican. The election had been marred by controversy. Late on election day, with all of the 1.3 million votes seemingly counted and the election final, it had looked as if Siegelman had won by a little more than 3,000 votes. Then, well after midnight, the tally mysteriously shifted, giving Riley the win by almost exactly the same margin. Siegelman had already made his acceptance speech, so the next day, when the shift was reported, he refused to concede.

As both sides maneuvered over the coming days, partisans for the respective candidates continued to take action. One Siegelman supporter, an attorney in northeastern Alabama's Jackson County, decided to help his candidate by engaging in some freelance dirty tricks. The Ku Klux Klan was holding a rally in Jackson County on Saturday, November 16, and the attorney—without the knowledge of the Siegelman campaign—showed up early to place Riley signs at the site. He hoped that photographs of the rally, with the Riley signs in the background, would be posted on the Internet and give the impression that the Klan was holding the rally to support Riley.

What the Siegelman supporter did not know was that *he* had been photographed putting up the signs by a volunteer campaign worker for Riley named Dana Jill Simpson, who had snapped pictures of him with a disposable camera. On the Monday after the Klan rally, according to her sworn affidavit, Simpson encountered the Siegelman supporter showing his pictures to other attorneys at the county courthouse in Scottboro. When Simpson asked to see the pictures, he gladly showed them to her, gave her shots to take with her, and told her where to find the pictures on the Internet. Simpson immediately called Rob Riley, the candidate's son, and told him about the Siegelman supporter's pictures *and* her own photos of him putting up the signs at the Klan rally site. Riley told Simpson the campaign had been receiving phone calls about the pictures on the Internet; now he understood how the pictures had gotten there. Riley suggested he set up a conference call so Simpson could share her information with other Riley staffers. As a group, they would decide what to do.

On the conference call were Simpson and Rob Riley as well as William "Bill" Canary, a political consultant, and Terry Butts, an attorney. During the call, Riley expressed anger over the Riley signs at the Klan rally site and their placement there by a Siegelman supporter. When he said he wanted to go to the press with the story, Butts countered, saying he felt he could use Simpson's pictures as a bargaining chip to make Siegelman concede the election at once, maybe even before the 10 o'clock news that night. It was agreed that Butts would confront Siegelman with the pictures, just to see what he would do. Butts said he would tell Siegelman he would be spared the humiliation of the pictures being released if he conceded.

Then Riley suggested that if they *did* release the pictures without confronting Siegelman, he would not be a problem in the future. The

Rileys did not want to win just the current race, they never wanted to run against Siegelman again.

"Let's just get this election behind us," Canary said. "Anyway, don't worry about Don Siegelman. My girls are going to get him. They will take care of him."

"Your girls," Simpson said. "Who are your girls?"

Canary responded that his "girls" were his wife, Leura Canary, the US attorney in the Middle District of Alabama, and Alice Martin, the US attorney in the Northern District. When Simpson asked Canary how he was connected to Martin, Canary said he had once worked on one of her campaigns.

"Are you sure the girls can take care of Siegelman?" Riley wanted to know, pressing the issue. He still wanted to release the pictures to the press.

"Don't worry," Canary said. "I've already gotten it worked out with Karl. Karl has spoken with the Justice Department and they are already pursuing Siegelman." When pressed, Canary made it clear it was his understanding that Rove had visited the Justice Department in person to make sure they were doing what he wanted them to. This seemed to satisfy Riley once and for all.[1]

Arrangements were made for Simpson to give the Riley campaign both sets of pictures—those the Siegelman supporter had given her as well as the pictures she had taken of him putting up the signs—and the conference call ended. Later that afternoon, Butts confronted Siegelman. Later, it would be revealed that Butts assured Siegelman the pictures would not be released.[2] He also promised Siegelman that the Justice Department would not prosecute him in the future—*if* he conceded the election.[3] As Butts had predicted, Siegelman conceded that night, making Bob Riley the next governor of Alabama. In the end Butts kept his first promise to Siegelman, though not the second.

This relatively brief phone exchange contained vital information about a questionable election and a politically motivated prosecution. Before it was all over, Don Siegelman would find himself in prison serving an 88-month sentence for an act he, his attorneys, and many observers believe was not a crime. His attorneys filed appeals on his behalf, and after a protracted battle he was released from prison pending his appeals. At the center of the story that landed him in prison in the first place was Karl Rove.

2.

To appreciate what happened to Don Siegelman, it's necessary to understand the place Alabama holds in the political career of Karl Rove. In 1992, as President George H. W. Bush was running for reelection, Robert A. Mosbacher Jr., the son of Bush's close friend and former secretary of commerce Robert A. Mosbacher Sr., was heading up his reelection committee, Victory '92, in Texas. When Rove leaked a piece of misinformation about Mosbacher Jr. to syndicated columnist Robert Novak, Mosbacher fired him as the fund-raising mail servicer for the state campaign, which reduced Rove's firm to handing only the campaign of the Republican candidate for railroad commissioner in Texas, Barry Williamson. The highlight of that campaign came when Rove tipped off the press that the Democratic candidate, Lena Guerrero, a Mexican American who was a rising star in the party in Texas, had lied about her college record. She said she had completed her bachelor's degree when she had not. This pivotal detail was more than slightly ironic, considering that Rove had not finished his college degree either, although he never seems to have lied about it.

Then, in 1994, Rove finally got the opportunity to make a name for himself not only in Texas, where he was running the gubernatorial campaign of George W. Bush against incumbent Ann Richards, but also in

Alabama. In many ways Rove fit right in in Alabama, since, as far as conservative politics was concerned, Alabama was similar to Texas. Like most Texans, the vast majority of Alabamans embraced religion and lived according to what are often termed traditional "family values." To get elected in Alabama a candidate had to be, among other things, pro-life, pro–tort reform, against gay marriage, against gambling.

Also like Texas, for generations after the administration of Franklin D. Roosevelt, Alabama had been solidly Democratic. The term "yellow dog Democrat" described the attitude in the state, meaning they would vote for a yellow dog before they'd vote for a Republican. But the solidly Democratic South started to break up after President Lyndon B. Johnson signed the Civil Rights Act of 1964. Democratic support wavered in the 1970s, with a majority of Alabamans voting for Richard Nixon in 1972, but then going for Jimmy Carter in 1976. Then, in the 1980s, Alabama went for Ronald Reagan, and in the process, candidates in races down the ballot from the presidency began to see Republicans winning. In the early 1990s, the state was a prime target for the Republican Party. Even though the nation elected Bill Clinton in 1992, George H. W. Bush carried Alabama.

In 1994, the Alabama state Republican Party wanted to make further inroads, so it targeted the state's judicial races. For decades, the Democratic Party had so dominated Alabama judgeships that in many elections the Republican Party did not bother to put up a complete slate of candidates. They wanted to change that, and party leaders brought in Rove to accomplish the task. Rove had been struggling for two decades to make it into big-league politics and was just beginning to achieve that goal as pilot of the Bush campaign for governor, but he saw the assignment in Alabama as a way to further his plans for Bush on a national level, so he signed on.

Specifically, the Business Council of Alabama—an organization supportive of but not directly affiliated with the Republican Party— approached Rove about working with Republican candidates running for the state Supreme Court. It would not necessarily be a walk-in-the-park job for Rove since no Republican had been elected to the Alabama state Supreme Court in the 20th century. But, since Rove had reversed the political makeup of the Texas Supreme Court during his time in that state, he was certain he could make a difference in Alabama.

The key race was for the chief justice position, which saw Perry O. Hooper, a longtime member of the Republican Party in Alabama, challenging the incumbent, Democrat Ernest "Sonny" Hornsby. In Alabama, campaigns for judgeships traditionally had been relatively gentlemanly for politcs, but Rove didn't play by those rules. He directed Hooper and three other Republican candidates whose bids for associate judgeships he was handling to hit the campaign trail and attack the Democratic candidates for being in the back pocket of trial lawyers—"ambulance chasers" who, they charged, were throwing the American legal system out of balance by winning enormous verdicts in order to collect grotesquely large legal fees. Medical costs, health insurance, automobile insurance—all had risen because of the verdicts, they said, some of which ran into the multiple millions. Here was one example of how the judicial system was out of whack. The plaintiff's attorneys and therefore the Democrats were to blame—or so went the rhetoric. What's more, they said, the problem wasn't entirely with the trial lawyers, it was also with the bench, whose "activist" judges were taking it upon themselves to make the laws, not merely interpret them. This message appealed to voters in a deeply populist state like Alabama.

As his candidates barnstormed the state over the summer, Rove began executing his strategy. In one associate justice race, Rove began a whisper campaign about Mark Kennedy, four-term Alabama governor George Wallace's son-in-law. Kennedy's area of special interest was children's rights, and he had been a juvenile- and family-court judge for years and helped to found the Children's Trust Fund of Alabama.

Taking a candidate's perceived strength and somehow turning it on its head was a Rove trademark. In this case, the whisper campaign suggested erroneously that Kennedy was a pedophile.

In the chief justice race, Rove ran a negative ad against Hornsby implying—based on no evidence at all—that he was calling lawyers to ask for contributions. The ad reduced Hornsby to the level of a shakedown artist. "I saw an article in the paper about lawyers complaining about judges calling them for campaign contributions," Perry O. Hooper says. "So a guy working with Karl took that article and turned it into what I think is a classic television ad. It showed a man talking on the phone, saying, 'You want $500 from each lawyer in the firm?' The man had a southern accent. It was humorous and it seemed to work. We put together that ad right in the library of my house."[4] The ad took a general practice—judges asking lawyers for campaign contributions—and made it look as if it applied only to Hornsby, which was misleading, to say the least.

On election day, November 8, it was clear Rove's tactics had made the race for chief justice a surprisingly competitive one, although Hornsby appeared to be winning by 304 votes. Rove called for a recount; as it turned out, it would be among the most protracted recounts in the state's history. By November 21, as the ballots were counted and recounted, a mere nine votes separated the two candidates. In one recount, Hooper pulled ahead. Finally, the battle came down to whether 2,000 late-arriving absentee ballots that were not notarized (and were presumed to be primarily for Hornsby) would be counted. The battle wound its way through the legal system in Alabama and, finally, all the way to the US Supreme Court, which ruled against Hornsby and named Hooper the winner. The Alabama secretary of state declared Hooper victorious by 262 votes. With Rove carefully watching and directing Hooper's interests at each step in the recount process, the ordeal took almost a year.

But he had done it. Perry Hooper became the first Republican chief justice voted onto the Alabama Supreme Court. "A Republican had never been elected to the Supreme Court in the history of Alabama, not in an open primary," Hooper says. "I was the first—and the only Republican elected in 1994. Karl Rove showed up one day and he did a great job. He was serious. He believed in winning. The people who worked with him were brilliant. He was just a smart guy. Anybody who could get me elected had to be pretty smart."[5] Hooper—one could even argue Rove—had broken the ice for Republicans in Alabama. It would not be long before the composition of the state's Supreme Court shifted from being entirely Democratic to being entirely Republican.

Helping Rove achieve this historic transformation was a political operative from the administration of George H. W. Bush. It was William "Bill" Canary who had insisted that the Business Council of Alabama hire Rove in the first place. Canary had his own pedigree. As chief of staff for the Republican National Committee and national field director for the 1992 Bush campaign, Canary was so effective that Rich Bond, Republican National Committee chairman in 1992 and 1993, would tell *Time* that Canary was a "political paratrooper" who could "get things fixed."[6] The magazine itself called Canary a "legend in Republican circles."[7] In Canary, Rove found a kindred spirit.

In 1996, Rove ran Harold See's campaign for an Alabama judgeship—and again he was successful in a race that became known for its negative tone and dirty tricks. Then, in 1998, once the team of Rove and Canary had been successful with Hooper's Supreme Court race, they worked together on William Pryor's race for attorney general. After being appointed in 1996 to finish the term that Jeff Sessions left early when he was elected to the United States Senate, Pryor was running for reelection. He won. But the race that was noteworthy in 1998 was not the fight for attorney general; it was the contest for governor. Running against Governor Forrest Hood "Fob" James was the aggressive, ambitious, politically savvy lieutenant governor, Don Siegelman, who would win with an impressive 58 percent of the vote, making Siegelman the only politician in Alabama history who would be elected to all four of the state's top offices—secretary of state, attorney general, lieutenant governor, and now governor.

⇶

Siegelman won despite efforts to defeat him mounted by lobbyist Jack Abramoff, who would later team up with associate Michael Scanlon and political operative and former Christian Coalition executive director Ralph Reed. Abramoff pumped massive sums of money from the Mississippi Band of Choctaw Indians into James's campaign. A central issue in Siegelman's campaign was establishing a lottery to fund free tuition to state colleges and universities for high school graduates with a B or better grade point average as well as a prekindergarten program in the public schools. But Siegelman's plan, designed to raise Alabama from near the bottom of the national rankings for education, was viewed by the Choctaw Indians as competition for their lucrative casinos in neighboring Mississippi. They wanted Siegelman defeated before he could even propose the lottery officially. "Probably Abramoff's most valued Tribal client was the Choctaw," the final report of the US Senate Committee on Indian Affairs would state. "Since 1995, when the Choctaw first hired Abramoff, a history of dramatic victories emerged, with Abramoff successfully advocating the Tribe's sovereignty and anti-tax interests before Congress. In many instances, Abramoff had the Tribe use conduits to conceal its grassroots activities from the world—activities often conducted by former Christian Coalition Executive Director Ralph Reed."[8]

The anti-Siegelman forces took their defeat hard. "We lost Fob in Alabama," Reed wrote in an e-mail to Abramoff. But Abramoff and Reed saw this as an opportunity to drain money from the Choctaw in the name of protecting the tribe from future competition. "Abramoff discussed various legislative proposals in Mississippi and elsewhere that threatened the market share of the Choctaw's casino operations, and which the Tribe wanted to somehow counter," the Senate report stated. "It just so happened that . . . Ralph Reed . . . had reached out to Abramoff: 'Hey, now that I'm done with electoral politics, I need to start humping in corporate accounts! I'm counting on you to help me with some contacts.'" Reed had been successful as a political consultant following his years heading the Christian Coalition; now he hoped to move on to corporate clients. "Abramoff," the Senate report said, "saw an opportunity: he suggested a grassroots effort and recommended the Choctaw hire Reed to orchestrate an anti-gaming effort." The scheme that had failed in the 1998 election in Alabama would be turned into an ongoing "effort" that in the end might prove more effective.

Meanwhile, Siegelman's enemies decided to get even with him as soon as he got into office. To do so, they used the method Rove had all but perfected in his career: discrediting him by having a government agency or individual make him the subject of an investigation. Even though he had occupied three other major state offices and had never before been investigated, just three months into his term as governor Siegelman became the target of an investigation by Alabama attorney general William Pryor. Specifically, Pryor was looking into the dealings between Siegelman and a contributor to his campaign, Phillip Bobo, MD. Pryor— whose election Rove had orchestrated—initiated the investigation just as Siegelman became the first governor in the nation to endorse Al Gore for president and joined Gore on a campaign swing through Florida.

Later in 1999, Americans for Tax Reform, headed by Grover Norquist, a close associate of Abramoff's, used Reed to make a $300,000 donation to Citizens Against Legalized Lottery of Birmingham, Alabama. Norquist had based his career on fighting government growth, famously saying, "I don't want to abolish government. I simply want to reduce it to the size where I can drag it into the bathroom and drown it in the bathtub." Because he had shown no interest in religious matters before, it was surprising that he would get involved in an issue that was taking on a religious theme, with church leaders across the state urging congregants to vote against the lottery proposal in a referendum. Eventually, Norquist's organization made three more donations totaling $850,000 to the Christian Coalition of Alabama—the state chapter of the group for which Reed had been executive director—to fight the lottery. In time, it would be revealed that these monies came from the Mississippi Choctaw Indian tribe. Congressman Bob Riley even introduced a bill in the United States Congress that would have forbidden the construction of a casino in Wetumpka, Alabama, a town about an hour by car from the Choctaw casino in Mississippi.

Major forces were opposed to a lottery in Alabama, although Siegelman continued to hope establishing one could generate money to improve the state's educational system. The funds being used to oppose the lottery supposedly were donated by religious organizations such as the Christian Coalition, but in reality money was coming from the gambling interests of the Mississippi Band of Choctaw Indians. Abramoff, Scanlon, Reed, and Norquist were the middlemen channeling these funds, and all four were taking fees for their efforts,[9] some of them so large that Abramoff and Scanlon would be indicted for them. As for the lottery itself, Alabamans killed the proposal in the statewide referendum held in October 1999.

In 2001, Siegelman announced his intention to run for reelection. From early on, it was clear that one of his opponents would be Bob Riley. That Scanlon had once served as Congressman Riley's press secretary suggests how close Riley was to Abramoff. As these events were unfolding in Alabama, President Bush announced that his new US attorney for the Middle District of Alabama would be Leura Canary, wife of Bill Canary. Almost immediately, she joined Pryor's investigation of Siegelman, making it a joint state–federal investigation. It was a potentially disturbing joining of forces. Pryor, a Rove client, had teamed up with Leura Canary, the wife of one of Rove's best friends and his close colleague, to investigate Siegelman, whose proposed state lottery had threatened the business interests of a client of Abramoff's, and Abramoff was a vital Rove ally. To top matters off, Bill Canary again signed on to manage Pryor's campaign for attorney general—for a fee of $40,000—when Canary's wife was investigating Siegelman in tandem with Pryor. Rarely in politics had one scenario contained so many layers of conflicts of interest. The interconnections were blatant and bold, signaling the parties' apparent disregard for the appearance of impropriety. But all of the players had one factor in common: All were working with Karl Rove to focus their combined energies on defeating a man who had become, almost by happenstance, their common opponent—Don Siegelman.

⚏

As the year 2002 unfolded, Leura Canary and Pryor continued to investigate Siegelman. It appeared that information gleaned directly from the investigation was being used routinely in attacks on Siegelman by Steve Windom, a Republican candidate for governor whose primary campaign was being run by Bill Canary for a fee of $38,000. When Riley eventually defeated Windom in the Republican primary, Bill Canary joined the Riley campaign, where he continued to orchestrate attacks against Siegelman. In one week in late October, as election day approached, large sums of money were given to the Riley campaign. One donation of $600,000 from the Republican Governors Association and the Republican National State Election Committee included $500,000 from Michael Scanlon; later, that money was believed to have come from the Mississippi Choctaw Indians.[10] An additional $600,000 was given to the state Republican Party in Alabama.[11]

The massive influx of money paid off. The race was a squeaker. But by late evening, it appeared that Siegelman had won by just more than 3,000 votes. It was close, but it was a win; Siegelman made his acceptance speech. Then, after midnight, once all of the poll workers had left, a glitch was discovered on a computer at a single polling place in Baldwin County, one of the most heavily Republican counties in the state. In the county's original count, Siegelman had received 19,070 votes to Riley's 31,052. After the computer glitch was discovered, Siegelman had 12,736 votes and Riley's total remained unchanged. The glitch subtracted a little more than 6,000 votes from Siegelman's total, giving Riley the election by about 3,000 votes. Of the 28 races on the ballot in Baldwin County, the glitch affected only the governor's race. Not a single vote in any other race on the ballot was affected by the glitch. Statistically, the odds of a glitch as large as this one affecting only one race in a predominantly Republican county are next to impossible.

"There should be no way to produce two different results with the computerized vote tabulation," observed James H. Gundlach, an expert on electronic voting. "That is, the system should not allow access to computer code or procedures that can produce different results. . . . Someone is controlling the computer to produce the different results. Once any computer produces different election results, any results produced by the same equipment operated by the same people should be considered too suspect to certify without an independent supervised recount."[12]

The Elections Board, all Republicans, declared Riley the winner after the glitch was resolved, so Siegelman challenged the results and demanded a statewide recount. But Pryor—the state attorney general and a Rove client—announced that he would prosecute anyone who attempted a hand recount of ballots.[13] Any plans Siegelman might have had to continue to fight for a recount, even if he had to pursue it through the courts, ended with the telephone call from Butts about Simpson's pictures of the Riley signs being planted at the Klan rally site. In the wake of Riley's victory, Abramoff e-mailed Scanlon that he had already informed the Choctaw tribe in Mississippi that "without [Scanlon's] efforts in Alabama, [the casinos] would have had to spend millions over the next four years." On April 9, 2003, only three months after Riley was sworn in as governor, Bush nominated Pryor for a seat on the 11th US Circuit Court of Appeals.

3.

As the election year of 2002 was playing out, Leura Canary continued her inquiries into the Siegelman matter. At one point, Siegelman's lawyers, claiming the obvious—that Leura Canary had a conflict of interest since her husband had direct political and business connections with opponents of Siegelman's—filed papers demanding that Canary recuse herself from the case. Canary responded that the Department of Justice had determined that no conflict of interest existed. Still, Canary had decided to recuse herself, claiming to have done so on her own. The recusal, though, ended up being in name only, as the Siegelman case remained under the jurisdiction of her office in the Middle District, only now being handled by her subordinates. In fact, the subordinate Canary first appointed to take over the case was Julia Weller, whose husband, Christopher William Weller, had been chairman of Pryor's 1998 campaign for attorney general—a campaign managed by Bill Canary and Karl Rove. In the end Weller, a member of the same country-club set as the Canarys, was replaced by another assistant US attorney, Louis Franklin.

Not to worry—for Siegelman's enemies, in any case. A second US attorney in Alabama, Alice Martin in the Northern District, had also launched an investigation of Siegelman. Her inquiry had been proceeding simultaneously with that being performed by Canary's office. Then, in November 2003, a poll showed that if a rematch of the 2002 race were to be held, Siegelman would defeat Riley. Soon after, Martin indicted Siegelman for Medicaid fraud.

Canary's Middle District investigation cooled down as Martin's Northern District case heated up. Then, in May and June of 2004, Martin's case began to run into trouble as judges were forced to recuse themselves because of various conflicts of interest. Finally, US District Judge U. W. Clemon took the case and in pretrial hearings grilled the prosecution about the merits of the case. The allegations in the case were simple: Phillip Bobo, a physician practicing in Tuscaloosa and a Siegelman supporter, and members of the Siegelman administration had rigged state Medicare contracts to benefit Bobo, presumably as repayment for his support.

When it looked as if Clemon might dismiss the Northern District case, Canary's Middle District office reconvened its grand jury, which had not been in session for 14 months. It indicted Siegelman in May, holding the indictment under seal. After a hearing in which the Northern District prosecutors were unable to show probable cause for the Medicare fraud case, Judge Clemon dismissed all charges against Siegelman, "with prejudice," in October 2004. Clemon's ruling ended any potential legal action against Siegelman in the Northern District.

It was now that Rove made another trip to the Justice Department, this time to get assurances from the top brass in the Public Integrity Section that, with the case in the Northern District dismissed, Leura Canary's office would be allowed to pursue its case against Siegelman in the Middle District.[14] It would. Canary's Middle District updated its indictment in October, then again in December. As if to blur the lines between the cases, two of the investigators working on the case in Martin's district began investigating Siegelman for Canary's district.

As the Siegelman case waited to go to trial in the Middle District, Alice Martin in the Northern District brought a 36-count indictment against Richard Scrushy, CEO of HealthSouth, one of the largest chains of medical rehabilitation servicers in the country, with facilities outside the United States as well. At trial, Martin lost on all 36 counts, a defeat so humiliating that, combined with the headline-grabbing pretrial dismissal of the Siegelman case, critics began to demand her removal. Instead, despite her apparent misjudgments as a US attorney, US Attorney General Alberto Gonzalez held a press conference in Birmingham to restate his unwavering support for Martin.

So it came as some surprise in May 2005, when Canary's Middle District went public with its indictment of Siegelman, that many of the charges against him centered on his dealings with Scrushy, who was also indicted. Siegelman had made it known that he intended to run for governor again. After indicting Siegelman and Scrushy in May 2005, a year passed before the trial began—one month before the Democratic primary for governor. In September 2005, Siegelman had been up in some polls by as much as 30 points; early on, he was considered to be the best Democratic candidate to run against Riley. By the time of the Democratic primary in June 2006, Siegelman had been so damaged by the endless reporting on the investigations and trial that he lost to the state's lieutenant governor, Lucy Baxley, by 60 points.

Some people knew what was going to happen to Siegelman, whether he did or not. In late January or early February 2005, Jill Simpson, who had helped the Riley campaign force Siegelman to concede the contested election of 2002, was in Rob Riley's office in Birmingham when he told her in no uncertain terms that Siegelman would be indicted in Montgomery. Only a few months later, Canary's office handed down the indictment.

Then there was the trial itself. Overseeing the proceedings was US district judge Mark E. Fuller, who had his own conflicts of interest—conflicts he refused to acknowledge and for which he would not recuse himself. His long-standing ties to the Republican Party were well known; he had worked on several Republican campaigns and sat on the Executive Committee of the state Republican Party. Republican governor Fob James had appointed Fuller district attorney in the 12th Judicial Circuit, where he had served from 1997 until 2002. Then, at the urging of Alabama's two Republican senators, Jeff Sessions and Richard Shelby, Bush nominated him for a federal judgeship in the Middle District, and, in November 2002, he—unlike many of Bush's nominees—was confirmed without incident by the US Senate.

Fuller's business relationships were also problematic. Specifically, his conflicts of interest involved money: While Fuller was a sitting federal judge, he was also a major player in companies that received huge government contracts, notably from the military. Referring to himself as "the undersigned" in a ruling he issued on the subject of his recusal in the Siegelman case, Fuller wrote: "[T]he undersigned is currently, and has been for several years, a shareholder in several privately held companies which derive income from customers which include, but are not limited to, various agencies of the United States Government. . . . [But] the undersigned is [not] currently an officer, director, or fiduciary to such companies. In fact, since taking the federal bench in 2002, the undersigned has only been a shareholder in the companies."[15]

Indeed, in 2002, Fuller had been the president of a Colorado Springs, Colorado–based company, Doss Aviation, that had various subsidiaries, and Fuller's official mailing address as president of Doss was the courthouse at One Church Street in Montgomery. At the time of the Siegelman trial, according to company records, Fuller controlled 43.75 percent in the corporation, meaning that his ownership position in Doss—he was the controlling shareholder—was worth between $1 million and $5 million and his annual income from the company totaled somewhere between $100,000 and $1 million—much more than he made as a federal judge.[16] In 2005, Fuller may have been the company's former president, but he was still a major stockholder who derived significant income from the company. Doss received much of its income from federal contracts, which over time totaled more than $258 million.[17] What's more, Fuller benefited significantly when, as the Siegelman trial was pending, Doss received a $178 million federal contract said to have been guided through the procurement process by Senator Jeff Sessions, who was succeeded as Alabama attorney general by William Pryor—the first person to launch an investigation of Siegelman, and a Rove client.[18]

Next came the charges. A hodgepodge of counts was brought against Siegelman and Scrushy, ranging from bribery to fraud to depriving Alabama citizens of honest services. Among the charges was the claim that Scrushy had contributed $500,000 to a nonprofit organization established to relieve the debt amassed by a political group in Alabama that had supported Siegelman's education lottery but was not affiliated with Siegelman or his campaign. According to the prosecution, Scrushy donated the money in order to win a seat on a state hospital regulatory board called the Alabama Certificate of Need Board. To arrive at an indictment, the prosecution had to dismiss relevant facts. Because Scrushy already had served on the board three times—in appointments made by both Democratic and Republican governors—he did not want to serve on the board a fourth time, but Siegelman convinced him to do so. In addition, Scrushy was also a Republican—he had contributed $350,000 to a previous Fob James campaign—who had supported Siegelman's opponent.

Strangely, the government never contended that Siegelman benefited personally from the contribution, which did not even go to his campaign. And not only did Siegelman not profit, Scrushy didn't either, since at that time HealthSouth had no business pending before the board. The transactions were what they were. Siegelman had coerced a well-respected Alabama businessman to serve again on a board he did not want to serve on and then he had talked him into donating money to a pro-lottery group. No laws were broken, no crimes committed. Transactions such as these, and some much more nefarious and yet still legal, take place every day in the American political system. But to the Middle District US Attorney's Office and the US Department of Justice, they were the basis for bringing to trial the CEO of a major corporation and, more important, a former governor—a former *Democratic* governor who still harbored hopes of having a political career.

Finally, there were the trial proceedings themselves. "In all there were four defendants," a source close to Siegelman says, "Siegelman and Scrushy as well as two staffers who would be acquitted. Each defendant had different charges brought against him. But the judge would not allow the trials to be separated even though all of the charges did not apply to all of the defendants and each defendant had a completely different set of charges. So there were four defendants and four sets of attorneys. When a lawyer stood to speak, he had to stand behind his client and say, 'Okay, what I'm about to say deals with my client and not the others.' It was a circus. It was confusing to those involved in the cases, much less the jurors."[19] In addition, besides refusing to recuse himself, Fuller almost exclusively rejected defense objections, while supporting legal moves made by the prosecution. Moreover, Fuller disallowed Siegelman his best defense: that the prosecution was politically motivated. On April 16, 2006, Louis Franklin filed a motion seeking to prevent Siegelman from using selective prosecution as one of his defenses. "[The government] respectfully moves this Court for an Order precluding the defendants, counsel for the defendants, and defendants' witnesses from mentioning, referencing, introducing, offering, or attempting to introduce or offer any evidence, testimony, or argument that politics was a motivating factor in the government's decision to prosecute the defendants." Fuller granted the motion.[20]

On June 26, 2006, after being defeated in his bid for governor, Siegelman was acquitted on 26 of the 32 counts against him. The acquittals included more than 100 acts that had supposedly constituted a Racketeer Influenced and Corrupt Organizations (RICO) Act indictment. But the jury could not make a decision on the other counts. Twice the jury told the judge they could not reach a decision; twice the judge instructed them to return a verdict. Finally, on June 29, the jury found Siegelman and Scrushy guilty on federal bribery charges. Siegelman was found guilty of obstruction of justice for the method in which he had paid for a motorcycle, although he was acquitted of receiving the motorcycle illegally.

Then, in the wake of the verdict, it became known that two of the jurors had been e-mailing each other during the trial—a violation of juror conduct. The e-mails that surfaced indicated that the jurors had been attempting to find ways to convince other jurors that Siegelman and Scrushy were guilty. During deliberations, one juror sent the following two e-mails. One read, " . . . judge really helping w/jurors. . . . still having difficulties with #30 . . . any ideas? keep pushing on ur side. . . . did not understand ur thoughts on statute but received links." A second e-mail from the same juror read, "I can't see anything we miss'd. u? articles usent outstanding! gov & pastor up shit creek. [Scrushy is an ordained minister.] good thing no one likes them anyway. all public officials r scum; especially this 1. pastor is reall a piece of work. . . . they missed before, but we won't. . . . also, keepworking on 30. . . . will update u on other meeting."

When the irregularity came to Fuller's attention, he did not question the jurors about their actions and failed to secure their computers to prevent a loss of evidence. He would not even ask the jurors if they had written the e-mails. In a hearing, Fuller relented that "it is indeed apparent that juror misconduct occurred," yet he did not order a new trial. The conviction stood.

A year passed as legal wrangling unfolded. On June 28, 2007, Fuller sentenced Scrushy to almost seven years in prison and 500 hours of community service to follow his prison time; he also ordered him to pay $150,000 in fines and $267,000 to the United Way of Central Alabama. As for Siegelman, Fuller sentenced him to 88 months in federal prison and imposed $181,325 in fines. Fuller denied Siegelman's request to post bond so that he could be free pending an appeal, as well as his plea for a 45-day period to get his affairs in order before reporting to prison—a request routinely granted to white-color criminals who do not pose a risk to society. Fuller ordered Siegelman to be escorted from the courtroom in handcuffs and leg shackles, after which he was taken directly to a federal prison in Atlanta. (Later, he would be moved to Louisiana.) "While it is true the good exceeds the bad," Fuller said as he sentenced Siegelman, "I must impose a fair punishment to reassure all that come before this court that justice is blind."[21]

There was never any doubt that the target of the prosecution was Siegelman. "One of the most astonishing things I have learned in studying this case," Scott Horton wrote in *Harper's,* "is that federal prosecutors offered Scrushy a plea bargain deal in which he would walk out of court a free man, provided that he give false testimony to help convict Siegelman. Hearing that helped persuade me that law enforcement was never the agenda of the prosecutors in this case. Indeed, it was just the opposite." Horton also declared: "I accuse the court of allowing farcical charges to proceed before it, of doing manifest injustice and colluding in the conviction of an innocent man. The pursuit of justice must now be unrelenting. Without it we surrender to the forces of tyranny which are now descending upon our country."[22] Or, as an editorial in the *New*

York Times would state: "Putting political opponents in jail is the sort of thing that happens in third-world dictatorships. In the United States, prosecutions are supposed to be scrupulously nonpartisan. This principle appears to have broken down in Alberto Gonzalez's Justice Department—where lawyers were improperly hired for nonpolitical jobs based on party membership, and United States attorneys were apparently fired for political reasons."[23]

On June 26, 2007, as he emerged from the courthouse in Montgomery on his way to prison, Don Siegelman identified for the crowd that had gathered who he believed was behind his prosecution and ultimate conviction. "The origins of this case are political," Siegelman told reporters in the crush of people before law enforcement officers could whisk him away. "There's no question that Karl Rove's fingerprints are all over this case, from the inception."[24]

♊

"Most people aren't aware that after Texas, Karl Rove made his name in Alabama," Don Siegelman says. "He came to Alabama in the mid-1990s and led a movement to take over the appellate courts for the GOP. His partner in this effort was Bill Canary, the husband of the US attorney whose office prosecuted me. Canary was one of Rove's closest allies. Another was Bill Pryor, the attorney general who began the investigation of me 12 weeks after I took office. A client of Rove's, Pryor had intervened to stop a recount in the controversial 2002 governor's race in which I had won before a middle-of-the-night recount. So all roads lead to Karl Rove, who wanted me out of the way because I was a threat not only in Alabama but also on the national level. I was the first Democratic governor to endorse Al Gore. Heading toward 2004, I had spoken out at a Democratic Governors Association meeting against Bush's policy in Iraq and his education and economic programs, and I was ready to take that message to key primary states.

"So, without a doubt, this prosecution of me was not a righteous prosecution. It was a political prosecution. Every major development in the investigation of me coincided with developments in my campaigns. Whenever polls showed me heading toward victory, the US attorney moved my case forward. During the periods in which there was no political activity on my part, the case went quiet. A simple analysis of the timeline proves this point. They were so focused on destroying me politically they didn't do a very good job of hiding what they were doing.

"I know of no example where any candidate has ever been prosecuted for appointing a contributor to a nonpaying board. In my case, the contributor had even served on the nonpaying board under three other governors. I will say this: America is not immune to losing its freedom. We must insure that we have an independent Justice Department. The Justice Department cannot be used to influence the outcomes of elections in America. In campaigns, Rove was accustomed to performing dirty tricks, going back to when he was in the Young Republicans. He perfected the art of political destruction in Texas and executed those same policies in the White House using the Justice Department.

"They were trying to set up a Republican dynasty and Rove was using any means necessary to win elections, including stealing elections as they did in Florida and Alabama, and indicting and prosecuting their political opponents. These are crimes. This is criminal activity. The men and women responsible should be held fully accountable by the United States Congress."[25]

CHAPTER THIRTEEN

GOOD-BYE

"Turn over a scandal in Washington these days and the chances are you'll find Karl Rove," the *New York Times* wrote on April 1, 2007, in an editorial entitled "The Rovian Era." "His tracks are everywhere: whether it's helping to purge United States attorneys, coaching bureaucrats on how to spend taxpayers' money to promote Republican candidates, hijacking the White House Office of Faith-Based and Community Initiatives for partisan politics, or helping to organize a hit on the character of one of the first people to publicly reveal the twisting of intelligence reports on Iraq." The perpetual spin cycle of the Clinton years now seemed harmless compared to the Bush administration's apparent willingness to blur the lines between government and party politics.

According to the *Times*, it was Rove who had orchestrated the removal of Bud Cummins as the Little Rock US attorney so he could be replaced with Rove's former aide, Timothy Griffin; Rove who had been involved in David Iglesias's firing; and Rove who had been behind "the wildly inappropriate and perhaps illegal" staff meeting held at the General Services Administration to discuss how government contracts could be handed out to help Republican candidates for Congress in 2008. For that meeting, an obvious violation of the Hatch Act, Rove had provided a PowerPoint slide show indicating what House and Senate seats the Republicans might be able to pick up. And the list went on. It was clear from the editorial, just as it was obvious to some in the Bush administration, that Rove had been involved in a number of practices that would result in public ridicule and perhaps legal action.

Still, the general feeling within political circles was that in the administration, Rove remained untouchable. Since so many of the pundits had bought into the idea that Rove was "Bush's brain," the media could not imagine a Bush White House without Rove, despite the fact that since Bush's reelection, his administration had gone through one debacle after another and Rove was at least in part if not entirely responsible for many of them. Indeed, about the only political dilemma Rove was not being held accountable for was the now profoundly unpopular war in Iraq. For that, the blame still fell squarely on Bush and Cheney. Regardless, few observers imagined Rove could be a target for removal from the Bush administration.

Only a handful of insiders who had known the Bushes for years felt otherwise. "Servants can always be fired," Roger Stone says. "It's a class thing. Karl was still a servant. He was not a Bush. Servants are expendable."[1] Still, Rove held a special place in the Bush world. "Karl had one foot in the political world and one foot in the government world," Stone adds. "The only other person to do that with the Bushes was James A. Baker III. The Bushes don't mix government service and politics because they really don't understand how good government can be the best politics. They have a tin ear with politics, which is how you can win the war in Iraq and have a 90 percent approval rating, as the first President Bush did, and lose the next presidential election. The old man had a tin ear and he couldn't communicate with people below his class. As for the second President Bush, if he had actually been a compassionate conservative he could have been a successful president. The people wanted a healer. They wanted a high moral tone. Bush didn't do that. He gave them Enron and Halliburton. That is not conservatism. That is crony capitalism." Now, Bush had given the country a seemingly never-ending series of political gaffes and scandals, and for those Rove was more than slightly to blame.

Of the major initiatives Rove had embraced, Bush could not point to one that was successful enough to be part of his legacy. Social Security reform had failed. Bush's attempt at immigration reform, which he had championed in the second term, had failed. Bush's effort to reform the health care system by creating medical savings accounts had failed. Bush's concept of faith-based initiatives had failed. Bush's tax cuts, which had been carefully targeted for the upper one half of 1 percent of the population, had left the country with a historically massive debt, which meant that, while Wall Street might have boomed during the Bush years, the overall economy, and especially the mortgage industry, would be seen as a failure. The one substantive piece of government reform, his education policy called No Child Left Behind, had become so unpopular, with its emphasis on testing instead of educating, that many observers believed Congress would refuse to renew it, thereby causing that program to end in failure. All in all, with his domestic agenda in a shambles, Bush was going to be known as the president who had taken the nation into a preemptive war based on fabricated justifications, and he would have no domestic policy successes to offset that criticism. Memories of his lauded leadership in the days after September 11 were now just that—memories. Bush was looking at a legacy defined by untruths and failures. But along the way, the upper one half of 1 percent of the population had seen an accumulation of wealth like none ever witnessed. So perhaps Bush had been successful after all, at least in the eyes of the constituency he actually cared about.

Rove had helped him win four elections. He had helped him govern. But now Bush's time in government was growing short, and Rove looked to be the target of more criticism, and perhaps even of legal actions by prosecutors or actions with legal consequences originating in the Congress. The Senate Judiciary Committee, headed by Vermont's Patrick Leahy, had already subpoenaed Rove. The White House was going to argue that Rove would not have to cooperate due to executive privilege, but it was going to be a fight—there was no doubt about it. Even the wizard behind the curtain can become a liability—and a big one. As of the summer of 2007, the Democrats had been saying for two months that members of the Senate Judiciary Committee "think they've got Karl," according to one well-placed Republican operative. They had the paper trail they were going to use to destroy him slowly.[2]

⚏

On a Sunday in midsummer, George W. Bush accompanied Karl Rove to the Episcopalian Church Rove sometimes attended. Though he did not consider himself a believer, Rove still went to church on occasion, at least for appearance's sake. On the other hand, Bush enjoyed attending church and had since he had joined the Methodist Church years before at his wife's urging. So, on this Sunday, Rove thought he was doing what he often did: spending time with the man for whom he had worked, almost exclusively, for nearly a decade and a half. The two men entered the church along with their wives. They made their way to the front of the congregation. Then, during their time in the church, Bush gave Rove some stunning news.

"Karl," Bush said, "there's too much heat on you. It's time for you to go."[3]

In the calm solitude of the church, these were no doubt the last words Rove expected to hear. But Bush had said them. They were now a reality. As anyone who serves at the pleasure of the president knows, Rove had to do as he was told.

"Yes, sir, Mr. President. I understand."

He did, too. After that Sunday, what Rove had to do was invent a story he could tell the world—literally the world, since news of his departure from the White House would be splashed on the front pages of newspapers around the globe—that would claim he was leaving of his own accord when in fact he was not. So, in the coming days, Rove was absolutely silent about what his plans were. In meeting after meeting at the White House, he did not give even a hint about what he was going to do. But he had worked out the cover story, one presumably approved by Bush, that he would announce at the right moment.

Rove had been thinking about leaving the White House for some time, the cover story went. Josh Bolten, the White House chief of staff, had told key White House officials, such as Rove, that if they didn't resign before Labor Day of 2007 they had to stay—though the reason for this rule was never explained effectively—until Bush left office in January 2009. Rove had run his last political campaign, the midterm election of 2006, so he was no longer needed, not for political reasons anyway. The administration didn't need him for policy making, since Bolten had taken his policy portfolio away from him. So the cover story had to have level after level of reasonable-sounding excuses for Rove's doing what some political observers had thought he would never do—leave the White House before Bush—even if the departure were logical. But Rove had worked out all of the kinks in his cover story. Now he needed a reporter to tell it to. He chose Paul A. Gigot of the *Wall Street Journal*, a paper that had always been friendly to Bush and Rove.

On Saturday, August 11, Rove arranged for a visit from Gigot in the "book-lined living room of his townhome," where "a relaxed, cheerful and typically rambunctious Mr. Rove hands over two sheets of paper on which he has tapped out a pair of outlines," Gigot later wrote. One listed what Rove considered to be his accomplishments; the other documented what he felt was going to happen in the future. Giving Gigot these documents was Rove's way of saying, "Here is what I've done and here is what I will have made happen," but as for Rove being there to see it all through, he told Gigot, he would not be: As of August 31, he was resigning his position at the White House.

"I just think it's time," Rove told Gigot. "There's always something that can keep you here, and as much as I'd like to be here, I've got to do this for the sake of my family." The reason was peculiar. He *had* no family at home except for his wife, since his son was in college, and his wife had long since gotten used to the schedule Rove had now kept throughout their marriage. But when Gigot wrote up his interview for publication, he made no mention of that incongruity.

Gigot did ask Rove if he felt any pressure from Congress, perhaps because of the subpoena the Senate Judiciary Committee had issued to him regarding the investigation of the leaking of CIA operative Valerie Plame's identity. "I know they'll say that," Rove offered. "But I'm not going to stay or leave based on whether it pleases the mob."

"I'm a myth," Rove told Gigot, apparently unaware of how crass the remark would sound. "There's the Mark of Rove. I read about some of the things I'm supposed to have done, and I have to try not to laugh."

Maybe, but others wouldn't. Not John McCain or Max Cleland or Jim Hightower or Ann Richards or Sonny Hornsby or Mike Moeller or John Kerry or John Edwards or Al Gore—and the list would go on.

⇌

When the announcement of his resignation ran in the *Wall Street Journal*, the political world was shocked. "Dubya Loses His 'Brain,'" the *New York Daily News* declared. "Rove Will Resign as Bush Adviser at End of Month," the *New York Times* announced on its front page above a sub-headline that said "Served Longest as Aide—A Bare-Knuckle Style of Politics." And this appeared in the *Washington Post*: "Karl Rove, Counselor to President Bush, to Resign."

But the headlines did not reflect the emotions at the press conference staged for Rove. As Bush stood beside Rove at a podium on the White House grounds, with Marine One, the presidential helicopter, in the background, Bush was warm and embracing as he said good-bye to the man whom earlier he had told he had to leave. Rove was devastated by the moment. "In an unusually emotional appearance with President Bush on the South Lawn of the White House," one report noted, "Mr. Rove cited a desire to 'start thinking about the next chapter in our family's life. . . . It always seemed there was a better time to leave out there in the future, but now is the time.'"[4]

Bush barely spoke. In the impromptu photo op that followed, when the president tried to get Laura Bush to pose with him and Rove for the press corps, it appeared that the First Lady was doing everything in her power not to be photographed with the pair. In the end, though, she was, briefly and awkwardly, and they all headed for Marine One for the ride to Air Force One and Rove's final trip to Texas aboard the airplane with the president. They had come so far together; now the journey had come to an end. Surely Rove had expected more, but in the final analysis Bush really was the one in charge, despite what the Myth of Rove might have represented to the public.

The Sunday after the announcement of his resignation, Rove continued the mythmaking as he appeared on three of the morning news programs. On *Fox News Sunday*, as he was talking to host Chris Wallace, he was at it again. "I mean," he said, "I'm a myth, and they're . . ." He stopped. "You know, I'm Grendel. . . ." (In the Anglo-Saxon poem *Beowulf*, Grendel is feared by everyone, except Beowulf.) "They're after me."

Rove was talking about his enemies, of course, but it was Bush, not his enemies, who had finally forced him to leave the political stage he did not want to depart, not at least until Bush left, too.

Several days later, a political consultant was flying on a private jet in Texas. Because of the circumstances of the day, he was in the company of one of Bush's counselors who had been friends with the consultant for years, and for some reason that was unclear to the consultant, Bush's counselor wanted to talk about Karl Rove and why the president had had to tell him to resign.

"There were four main reasons," the counselor said. First, problems might still arise in Texas as a result of information Jack Abramoff may not have yet given regarding the DeLay investigation. Second, government documents had been altered by Rove's former assistant Susan Ralston when she had changed Rove's calendar, at his instruction, to cover up meetings he had had with Abramoff. Third, potential violations of the Hatch Act had occurred when Rove's PowerPoint presentation was used in lecturing government workers about how to help Republicans get elected. Fourth, the Senate Judiciary Committee had the e-mails that proved Rove was involved in the US attorney scandal. With all of this, Bush had no choice but to let Rove go.

Now it was over. On August 31, Rove completed his last day at the White House. He returned to Texas, settling in Ingram, where he and his wife owned a bed-and-breakfast.

⬥

Over the next weeks, Rove stayed out of the limelight for the most part. It was said he was spending most of his time holed up in the relative quiet of his home in rural Texas. When he was spotted flying back to Washington, it was on a commercial flight. It was said he had had little communication with Bush. That too would have been a drastic change in his life, since for well over a decade he had begun almost every day with some form of conversation with Bush, formal or otherwise, when Bush was president, governor, or candidate. But while Rove reportedly had little or no contact with Bush after his departure from the White House, he would never be able to sever his identity from that of Bush and his two administrations, first as governor and then as president. The decisions made by Bush, especially those reached in pivotal moments as president, would be impossible for Rove to escape as well. This would be borne out in public appearances such as the one he made at Regent University, the institution of higher learning founded by evangelist Pat Robertson, in Virginia Beach, Virginia.

Rove appeared at the university on October 26, 2007, as part of an annual debate series entitled Clash of the Titans. On this occasion, Rove, along with Jeb Bush, the president's brother and the former governor of Florida, debated the question "Should America Bring Democracy to the World?" with Barry McCaffrey, the retired US Army general, and Max Cleland, the former senator from Georgia who blamed Rove for his defeat. Television journalist Charlie Rose moderated.

Cleland had waited for years to confront Rove, and this marked the first occasion the two men had been on a stage together. Rove and Bush sat at one end of the stage; they took the position that it was the responsibility of the United States to advance democracy in the rest of the world. "It is in [the interests of] our national security to aid in the spread of democracy," Rove said at one point. "Democracies with rare exception don't attack their neighbors, democracies don't encourage terrorism, harbor training camps, encourage the spread of hatred and intolerance." To this, Bush added, "If not the United States, who? And what would the world look like without the United States' leadership in this area?"[5]

Sitting at the other end of the stage with Cleland and taking a view different from that of Rove and Bush, McCaffrey warned against nation building. "We should articulate that we are a liberal democracy, but we should not forget the disaster of intervening in very different cultures, histories, and legal systems." Cleland was more direct in his argument against nation building. "I do believe that we ought to lead as a nation and as individuals by example," he said. "We really can't force Christianity on anybody or democracy on anybody."

For much of the debate, Cleland had to work hard to control his anger with Rove. Later, he would say he could feel the hairs rising on the back of his neck, he was so ready to snap and go after Rove, but he maintained his composure out of respect for the dignity of the occasion. Finally, Cleland had had all he could take. When given the chance to pose a question to Rove, he made his move.

"Why didn't the Bush White House go after Osama bin Laden?" Cleland demanded of Rove. "Why are we wasting time in Iraq? Invading Iraq after September 11 was like invading Mexico after Pearl Harbor."

It was the best shot Cleland had; it was also a question to which he truly wanted an answer. That one answer could give some insight into the very heart of the Bush administration. The question asked, Rove now had to answer. To respond, Rove relied on a tactic that had worked for him for years now, perhaps all the way back to his debating days in Utah. He answered the attack with an attack.

"Senator, with all due respect," Rove said to Cleland, "the US military and US intelligence agencies made every effort possible to get Osama bin Laden, and frankly I don't think it reflects well on our military and intelligence services to suggest that they didn't."

In fact, Cleland had not suggested that the military and intelligence services of the United States had failed; his question had been posed about decisions made by President Bush and his administration, which, of course, included Rove. But instead of answering the question and giving the audience some kind of window onto the thinking of the Bush administration on these two important historical developments—the pursuit of bin Laden and the invasion of Iraq—Rove simply went on the attack and, not surprisingly, blamed other people. It had been the military and intelligence services of the United States that had failed in the pursuit of Osama bin Laden, not anyone within the Bush administration. What's more, Cleland was now suspect because *he* was attacking the military and intelligence communities by asking Rove a question that would make them look bad. The artful dodger as always, Rove sidestepped the question, refusing to give any information, and attacked Cleland in the process. It was a typical Rovian strategy. He had based his entire career on the approach.

That, finally, to Cleland, was what was saddest. "Rove has such a clean mind," Cleland says. "In his career he knew exactly what he was doing. He knew the tools of American politics like few people. The sad part about it is, he is a highly skilled and highly trained political assassin. Bush used him to cover up Bush's weaknesses. He used him to go out and destroy the Democrats in the Senate and the House. With his tremendous skill, Rove could have been a powerful force for good in American politics. But that didn't happen. When you look at someone whose only goal is to destroy his opponent and win, someone whose ruthlessness borders on being evil, his name is Karl Rove. In many ways George W. Bush and Karl Rove have brought the United States to a place more and more people are seeing: a disaster abroad, another Vietnam created which the American people cannot get out of with dignity and honor, and a legacy of failed domestic policies, including an economic disaster that has left the country beholden to China and Japan for years to come. It's an American tragedy."[6]

ACKNOWLEDGMENTS

I would like to thank John Aaron, Joe Abate, Stephanie Allen, Matt Angle, Detective Al Barrios, Lieutenant Don Batchelder, Chris Bell, Daniel Bice, Earle Black, Governor Kathleen Blanco, Liz Carpenter, Erika Fortgang Casriel, Marie Centanni, Senator Max Cleland, Marie Cocco, David Cogswell, Matthew Cooper, Craig Crawford, Monica Crowley, H. E. "Bud" Cummins III, Richard Curtis, Will Dana, Steven Duble, Vic Feazell, Buddy Floyd, Glenn Grieves, Gordon Hamel, Mickey Herskowitz, Sander Hicks, Chip Hill, Judge Perry O. Hooper, Scott Horton (for his reporting in *Harper's*), T. Q. Houlton, Detective John Hubbard, Stephen P. Hurley, Senator James Jeffords, Arthur Klebanoff, Ott Knight, Joe Koons, Senator Mary Landieu, Bob Mann, Garry Mauro, Arnold Mazer, Cindy McCain, Senator John McCain, Craig McDonald, Bill Miller, Mike Moeller, Alan Moore, James Moore, Georgette Mosbacher, Dr. Barbara Mowder, Rob O'Hare, Purvi G. Patel, Tom Pauken, Scott Reed, Peter and Cindy Rinfret, Ed Rollins, Bonnie Rowan, Mark Sanders, Charles Schultz (of the Bill Clements Papers, Cushing Library, Texas A&M University), Adam Sharp, Richard Shepard, George Shipley, Governor Don Siegelman, L. B. Siegelman, Wayne Slater, Melanie Sloan, Glenn Smith, Erik Smulson, Jason Stanford, Roger Stone, Rachel Strauch-Nelson, Kandy Straud, William Sullivan, Orson Swindle, Congressman Tom Tancredo, Matt Towery, Nanette Varian, Deborah Wheeler (of the George H. W. Bush Presidential Library), Daniel White, Angie Williams, Mary Williams, Ambassador Joseph Wilson, Joe Wineke.

At International Creative Management, I would like to thank Tina Wexler and Lisa Bankoff. At Modern Times, I would like to thank Nancy Bailey, Beth Davey, Meredith Quinn, Shannon Welch, and Leigh Haber. For his help with research and his friendship, I would like to thank Matt Everett.

ENDNOTES

CHAPTER ONE

1 Ed Rollins. Interview by the author, June 2007.
2 Dan Balz. "A Campaign Trail Leading to Austin: As Support Arrives in Droves, Gov. Bush Prepares to Launch Formal Effort." *Washington Post,* March 7, 1999.
3 Roger Stone. Interview by the author, June 2007.
4 David Von Drehle. "Republicans Admire Bill . . . McKinley, That Is." *Washington Post,* July 24, 1999.
5 Tom Pauken. Interview by the author, June 2007.
6 Matt Towery. Interview by the author, December 2007.
7 Tom Tancredo. Interview by the author, July 2007.
8 Ed Rollins. Interview by the author, June 2007.

CHAPTER TWO

1 David M. Shribman. "George W. Bush's Main Man." *Boston Globe,* July 23, 2000.
2 Matt Canham and Thomas Burr. "Rove: Ex-Utahn in Crisis; Unethical Revenge Would Not Surprise His U. Poli-Sci Prof; Rove Known as a Fierce Competitor." *Salt Lake Tribune,* November 6, 2005.
3 Melinda Henneberger. "Driving W." *New York Times Magazine*, May 14, 2000.
4 Ibid.
5 Ibid.
6 Matt Canham and Thomas Burr. "Rove: Ex-Utahn in Crisis; Unethical Revenge Would Not Surprise His U. Poli-Sci Prof; Rove Known as a Fierce Competitor." *Salt Lake Tribune,* November 6, 2005.
7 Melinda Henneberger. "Driving W." *New York Times Magazine*, May 14, 2000.
8 David M. Shribman. "George W. Bush's Main Man." *Boston Globe,* July 23, 2000.
9 Louis Dubose. "Bush's Hit Man." *The Nation*, March 5, 2001.
10 Joe Abate. Interview by the author, June 2007; other information in this paragraph also comes from that interview.
11 Rebecca Walsh. "Did Karl Rove Dodge the Draft?" *Salt Lake Tribune*, September 18, 2004.
12 Melinda Henneberger. "Driving W." *New York Times Magazine*, May 14, 2000.
13 Roger Stone. Interview by the author, May 2007.
14 Joe Abate. Interview by the author, June 2007.
15 Roger Stone. Interview by the author, May 2007.

16 Sheryl Gay Stolberg. "Rove Strategy Paper Found in Nixon Archive." *New York Times*, July 14, 2007.

17 Roger Stone. Interview by the author, May 2007.

18 Joe Abate. Interview by the author, June 2007.

19 John Saar. "GOP Probes Official as Teacher of 'Tricks.'" *Washington Post*, August 10, 1973.

20 Joe Abate. Interview by the author, June 2007.

21 Ibid.; other information in this paragraph also comes from that interview.

22 Nicholas Lemann. "The Controller." *New Yorker*, May 12, 2003.

23 Ibid.

CHAPTER THREE

1 Todd S. Purdum. "Karl Rove's Split Personality." *Vanity Fair*, December 2006.

2 Vic Feazell. Interview by the author, August 2007.

3 Ibid.

4 Ibid.

5 Garry Mauro. Interview by the author, June 2007.

6 Scott Horton. "It Started in Texas: Karl Rove's Political Prosecutions." *Harper's*, July 19, 2007.

7 Ed Rollins. Interview by the author, June 2007.

8 Matt Towery. Interview by the author, December 2007.

9 Interview with an unnamed source by the author, June 2007; other information and quotes in the preceding two paragraphs also come from that interview.

10 James C. Moore and Wayne Slater. *Bush's Brain: How Karl Rove Made George W. Bush Presidential*. New York: Wiley, 2003. p. 46.

11 David Maraniss. "Texas Campaign Office Bugged; Aide to GOP Challenger Accuses Governor's Camp of Eavesdropping." *Washington Post*, October 7, 1986.

12 "White, Clements Staffers Cleared in Bugging Incident." United Press International, October 28, 1986.

13 Melinda Henneberger. "Driving W." *New York Times*, May 14, 2000.

14 Bill Miller. Interview by the author, June 2007.

15 Garry Mauro. Interview by the author, June 2007.

16 Tom Pauken. Interview by the author, June 2007.

17 Alison Mitchell. "The 2000 Campaign: The Populist Appeal; The Inside Outsiders Behind John McCain." *New York Times*, February 6, 2000.

18 Interview with an unnamed Victory '88 staffer by the author, June 2007.

19 Ibid.

20 Louis Debose. "Bush's Hit Man." *The Nation*, March 5, 2001.

21 The source for the Rove smear of Weaver is a highly placed staff member of Victory '88. The smear is also referenced in "Karl Rove in a Corner" by Joshua Green, *Atlantic Monthly*, November 2004. Green writes: "Rove spread a rumor

that Weaver made a pass at a young man at a state Republican function. Weaver won't reply to the smear, but those close to him told me of their outrage at the nearly two-decades-old lie."

22 Interview with an unnamed Victory '88 staffer by the author, June 2007.

23 Interview with an unnamed source by the author, June 2007.

24 Interview with an unnamed Victory '88 staffer by the author, June 2007.

25 Tom Pauken. Interview by the author, June 2007.

26 Mike Moeller. Interview by the author, June 2007.

27 Rove supplied the questionnaire to the Senate Foreign Relations Committee. It was later acquired by subpoena.

28 S. C. Gwynne. "Genius." *Texas Monthly*, March 2003.

29 James C. Moore. "Don't Expect the Truth from Karl Rove." *Los Angeles Times*, March 23, 2007.

30 Mike Moeller. Interview by the author, June 2007.

31 Ibid.

32 Ibid.

33 Ibid.

34 Mark Sanders. Interview by the author, June 2007.

35 Elisabeth Bumiller. "Rove and Novak, a 20-Year Friendship Born in Texas." *New York Times*, August 6, 2005.

36 Tom Pauken. Interview by the author, June 2007.

37 Paul Alexander. "All Hat, No Cattle." *Rolling Stone*, July 1999.

38 James Ridgeway. "Grime Pays." *Village Voice*, July 19, 2005.

39 S. C. Gwynne. "Genius." *Texas Monthly*, March 2003.

40 Interview with an unnamed Richards staffer by the author, July 2007.

41 Interview with an unnamed former GOP Senate staffer by the author, July 2007.

42 Garry Mauro. Interview by the author, June 2007.

43 Mickey Herskowitz. Interview by the author, August 2007.

44 Tom Pauken. Interview by the author, June 2007.

45 Scott Reed. Interview by the author, August 2007.

46 Tom Pauken. Interview by the author, June 2007.

47 Paul Alexander. "All Hat, No Cattle." *Rolling Stone*, July 1999.

CHAPTER FOUR

1 Dan Balz. "A Campaign Trail Leading to Austin: As Support Arrives in Droves, Gov. Bush Prepares to Launch Formal Effort." *Washington Post*, March 7, 1999.

2 Ibid.

3 Richard L. Berke. "Gov. Bush to Set Up Panel to Explore Presidential Bid." *New York Times*, February 26, 1999.

4 George Shipley. Interview by the author, July 2007.

5 Interview with an unnamed major Republican fundraiser by the author, June 2007.

6 Craig McDonald. Interview by the author, summer 2003.

7 Ed Rollins. Interview by the author, June 2007.

8 Adam Nagourney. "Bush Iowa Trip Signals Real Start of 2000 Race for the Presidency." *New York Times*, June 13, 1999.

9 All of the quotes from Bush come from the announcement speech, copies of which were handed out to reporters in advance of delivery.

10 The numbers were confirmed by a source close to Herskowitz.

11 Mickey Herskowitz. Interview by the author, July 2007.

12 Ibid.

13 Tucker Carlson. "Devil May Care." *Talk*, September 1999.

14 Frank Bruni. "The New Administration: Settling In; New White House Staff Faces a Few Mysteries." *New York Times*, January 24, 2001.

15 James Hatfield. *Fortunate Son: George W. Bush and the Making of an American President*. New York: Soft Skull, 2001.

16 Ibid.

17 Dan Balz. "Bush Goes Further on Drug Question." *Washington Post*, August 20, 1999.

18 James Hatfield. *Fortunate Son: George W. Bush and the Making of an American President*. New York: Soft Skull, 2001.

19 Daryl Lindsey. "Publisher Halts George W. Bush Bio." *Salon*, October 21, 1999.

20 The exchange comes from Leslie Stahl's interview with James Hatfield broadcast on *60 Minutes* on CBS, February 13, 2000.

21 Craig Crawford. Interview by the author, July 2007.

22 Dan Balz. "Bush's Campaign Strategy Sets the Pace for 2000." *Washington Post*, July 4, 1999.

23 Dan Balz. "Absent Bush, GOP Rivals Seem to Stand Out at NH Forum." *Washington Post*, October 29, 1999.

24 Richard L. Berke. "Allies of Bush Say Missteps Cost Him in New Hampshire." *New York Times*, December 19, 1999.

25 Dan Balz. "Bush Concedes McCain's Surge." *Washington Post*, December 10, 1999.

26 Michael Kranish and Curtis Wilkie. "Bush, Gore Wrap Up Iowa." *Boston Globe*, January 25, 2000.

27 Dan Balz. "McCain Trounces Bush By 18; Gore Deals Bradley His Second Defeat." *Washington Post*, February 2, 2000.

28 Mark McKinnon. Interview in "Karl Rove: The Architect." *Frontline*, PBS, April 12, 2005.

29 Frank Bruni with Mark Lacey. "The 2000 Campaign: The Strategies: Put on the Defense, Bush Talks Tough as McCain Rides High on His Victory." *New York Times*, February 4. 2000.

30 Tim Grieve. "Bush's War over Gay Marriage." *Salon*, February 26, 2004.

31 Melinda Henneberger. "Driving W." *New York Times*, May 14, 2000.

32 David M. Shribman. "George W. Bush's Main Man." *Boston Globe*, July 23, 2000.

33 David Talbot. "Creepier Than Nixon." *Salon,* March 31, 2004.

34 Michael Abramowitz. "Book Tells of Dissent in Bush's Inner Circle." *Washington Post,* September 3, 2007.

35 Richard L. Berke. "The 2000 Campaign: The Image: Tested and Occasionally Tripped, Bush May Yet Rue a Mirror Crack'd." *New York Times*, September 18, 2000.

36 Richard L. Berke. "The 2000 Campaign: The Strategies; No Room for Error in the Final Weeks Before the Vote." *New York Times,* October 15, 2000.

37 Richard L. Berke. "Counting the Votes: Political memo; GOP Questioning Bush's Campaign." *New York Times,* November 13, 2000.

38 Nicholas Lemann. "The Controller." *New Yorker,* May 12, 2003.

39 Roger Stone. Interview by the author, June 2007.

40 Frank Bruni. "Man in the News; Fierce Ambition; Karl Rove." *New York Times,* January 5, 2001.

41 Tom Pauken. Interview by the author, June 2007.

42 Nicholas Lemann. "The Controller." *New Yorker,* May 12, 2003.

43 Mark Sanders. Interview by the author, June 2007.

44 Joshua Green. "The Rove Presidency." *Atlantic Monthly,* September 2007.

45 Todd S. Purdum. "Karl Rove's Split Personality." *Vanity Fair,* December 2006.

46 George Shipley. Interview by the author, July 2007.

47 Matt Towery. Interview by the author, December 2007.

CHAPTER FIVE

1 Gordon Hamel. Interviews by the author, summer 2007.

2 Interview with an unnamed source by the author, June 2007.

3 David Talbot. "Creepier Than Nixon." *Salon,* March 31, 2004.

4 Bill Miller. Interview by the author, June 2007.

5 Roger Stone. Interview by the author, June 2007.

6 Ed Rollins. Interview by the author, June 2007.

7 This account comes from a document provided to the author by the source.

8 Paul Alexander. "The Reluctant Revolutionary." *Rolling Stone,* July 2001.

9 Ed Rollins. Interview by the author, June 2007.

10 Richard L. Berke and Frank Bruni. "Crew of Listing Bush Ship Draws Republican Scowls." *New York Times,* July 2, 2001.

11 Ibid.

12 James Carney and John F. Dickerson. "W. and the 'Boy Genius.'" *Time,* November 18, 2002.

13 David E. Sanger and Don Van Natta Jr. "After the Attacks: The Events; In Four Days, a National Crisis Changes Bush's Presidency." *New York Times,* September 16, 2001.

14 Ibid.

15 R. W. Apple Jr. "After the Attacks: The Trip Back; Aides Say Bush Was One Target of Hijacked Jet." *New York Times,* September 13, 2001.

16 Maureen Dowd. "Liberties; Autumn of Fears." *New York Times*, September 23, 2001.

17 Nora Boustany. "At Luncheon Briefing, White House Insider Keeps Them Hungry." *Washington Post*, October 19, 2001.

18 Ibid.

19 Editorial Board. "Bush's 'Open Door' Slammed; Tancredo Calls His 'Altruistic Views' a Threat to Security." *Washington Times*, April 19, 2002.

20 Quotes and information in this and the preceding paragraph come from documents acquired by the author.

21 James Carney and John F. Dickerson. "W. and the 'Boy Genius.'" *Time*, November 18, 2002.

22 Max Cleland. Interview by the author, December 2007.

23 Elisabeth Bumiller and David E. Sanger. "The 2002 Elections: The Strategist; Republicans Say Rove Was Mastermind of Big Victory." *New York Times*, November 7, 2002.

24 James Carney and John F. Dickerson. "W. and the 'Boy Genius.'" *Time*, November 18, 2002.

25 Evan Thomas. "How Bush Did It." *Newsweek*, November 15, 2004.

26 Michael Janofsky. "Rove Declares Nation Is Tilting to Republicans." *New York Times*, November 14, 2002.

27 Matt Towery. Interview by the author, December 2007.

28 Tom Tancredo. Interview by the author, July 2007.

CHAPTER SIX

1 Tom Tancredo. Interview by the author, July 2007.

2 David D. Kirkpatrick. "Conservatives Using Issue of Gay Unions as a Rallying Tool." *New York Times*, February 8, 2004.

3 Boris Kachka. "Are You There, God? It's Me, Hitchens." *New York*, April 26, 2007.

4 Joe Koons. Interview by the author, December 2007.

5 The offer was made to me by a longtime *Boston Globe* reporter as I was working on "Ready for His Close-Up," the first presidential profile of John Kerry, which appeared in *Rolling Stone*, April 11, 2002.

6 Interview with an unnamed source by the author, May 2007.

7 Interviews with unnamed sources by the author, summer 2004.

8 Jodi Wilgoren. "Kerry Attacks Bush Officials Who Received Draft Deferrals." *New York Times*, April 17, 2004.

9 Adam Nagourney and Robin Toner. "The 2004 Campaign: Republican Plans; Bush Planning August Attack Against Kerry." *New York Times*, August 1, 2004.

10 Kate Zernike and Jim Rutenberg, "The 2004 Campaign: Advertising; Friendly Fire: The Birth of an Attack on Kerry." *New York Times*, August 20, 2004.

11 Jim Rutenberg and Kate Zernike. "The 2004 Campaign: Advertising; Veterans' Group Had G.O.P. Lawyer." *New York Times*, August 25, 2004.

12 Mark Leibovich. "Loss Leader." *Washington Post*, September 10, 2004.

13 The information about Shrum and his views on the swift-boat controversy and its coverage in the media was conveyed to the author by David Wade in interviews conducted in the summer of 2004.

14 Roger Stone. Interview by the author, June 2007.

15 George Lardner Jr. and Lois Romano. "At Height of Vietnam, Bush Picks Guard." *Washington Post*, July 28, 1999.

16 Ibid.

17 Interview with an unnamed longtime Texas political strategist by the author, July 2007.

18 Maureen Balleza and Kate Zernike. "The 2004 Campaign: National Guard; Memos on Bush Are Fake but Accurate, Typist Says." *New York Times,* September 15, 2004.

19 William Safire. "First, Find the Forger." *New York Times*, September 22, 2004.

20 Dan Rather. "Dan Rather Statement on Memos." CBS News, September 20, 2004. http://www.cbsnews.com/stories/2004/09/20/politics/main644546.shtml.

21 Alessandra Stanley. "The 2004 Campaign: The TV Watch; Even Humbled, Dan Rather Has His Thorns." *New York Times*, September 21, 2004.

22 Interview with an unnamed source by the author, July 2007.

23 Noelle Straub. "CBS: Guard Memos Are Authentic; Dems Rip Bush's Service." *Boston Herald*, September 11, 2004.

24 Elisabeth Bumiller. "The Mystery of the Bulge in the Jacket." *New York Times*, October 9, 2004.

25 Mickey Herskowitz. Interview by the author, July 2007.

26 Elisabeth Bumiller. "Entering the Homestretch with a Smile." *New York Times*, November 1, 2004.

27 Daron R. Shaw. "Door-to-door with the GOP." *Hoover Digest*, Number 4, 2004 .

28 David Wade. Interview by the author, October 2004.

29 Richard W. Stevenson. "After a Tense Night, Bush Spends the Day Basking in Victory." *New York Times*, November 3, 2004.

30 Ibid.

31 Monica Crowley. Interview by the author, July 2007.

32 Todd S. Purdum and David D. Kirkpatrick. "Campaign Strategist Is in Position to Consolidate Republican Majority." *New York Times*, November 5, 2004.

33 Adam Nagourney. "'Moral Values' Carried Bush, Rove Says." *New York Times,* November 10, 2004.

34 One of many references comparing Rove and Hanna occurred in an editorial entitled "Billionaires for Bush" published in the July 21, 2003, issue of *The Nation*.

35 Todd S. Purdum. "Karl Rove's Split Personality." *Vanity Fair*, December 2006.

CHAPTER SEVEN

1 Brendan Murray and Heidi Przybyla. "Rove Uses Campaign Playbook to Mastermind Social Security Fight." Bloomberg News, March 2, 2005.

2 Ed Rollins. Interview by the author, June 2007.

3 Richard W. Stevenson. "Top Bush Strategist Adds Another Big Hat." *New York Times,* February 9, 2005.

4 David D. Kirkpatrick. "Bush Moved Conservatism Past Reactionary, Rove Says." *New York Times,* February 18, 2005.

5 Glenn Smith. Interview by the author, March 2007.

6 Ed Rollins. Interview by the author, June 2007.

7 Edmund L. Andrews. "Treasury Takes Social Security to Airwaves." *New York Times,* April 7, 2005.

8 Ibid.

9 David E. Sanger. "Bush Takes Social Security Campaign to Ohio." *New York Times,* April 16, 2005.

10 Ed Rollins. Interview by the author, June 2007.

11 Glenn Smith. Interview by the author, March 2007.

12 Jim VandeHei and Dan Balz. "Fall Elections Are Rove's Next Test: Reputation as Architect of Victory at Stake." *Washington Post,* June 17, 2006.

13 Ed Rollins. Interview by the author, June 2007.

14 Patrick D. Healy. "Rove Criticizes Liberals on 9/11." *New York Times,* June 23, 2005.

15 Juan Cole. "The Poisonous Rhetorical Legacy of Karl Rove." *Salon,* August 20, 2007.

16 Joe Conason. "Karl Rove Is a Liar." *Salon,* June 24, 2005.

CHAPTER EIGHT

1 Bob Mann. Interview by the author, March 2007.

2 Kathleen Blanco. Interview by the author, January 2008.

3 Mary Landrieu. Interview by the author, December 2007.

4 Ibid.

5 Adam Sharp. Interview by the author, December 2007.

6 Mary Landrieu. Interview by the author, December 2007.

7 Spencer S. Hsu, Joby Warrick, and Rob Stein. "Documents Highlight Bush-Blanco Standoff." *Washington Post,* December 5, 2005.

8 Bob Mann. Interview by the author, March 2007.

9 Mary Landrieu. Interview by the author, December 2007.

10 Kathleen Blanco. Interview by the author, January 2008.

11 Mary Landrieu. Interview by the author, December 2007.

12 Bob Mann. Interview by the author, March 2007.

13 Kathleen Blanco. Interview by the author, January 2008.

14 Ibid.

15 Adam Sharp. Interview by the author, December 2007.

16 Elisabeth Bumiller. "Casualty of Firestorm: Outrage, Bush and FEMA Chief." *New York Times,* September 10, 2005.

17 Kathleen Blanco. Interview by author, January 2008.

18 Mary Landrieu. Interview by the author, December 2007.

19 Kathleen Blanco. Interview by the author, January 2008.

20 Bob Mann. Interview by the author, March 2007.

21 Kathleen Blanco. Interview by the author, January 2008.

22 Elisabeth Bumiller and Adam Nagourney. "Storm and Crisis: Political Memo; As Anxiety Over Storm Increases, Bush Tries to Quell Political Crisis." *New York Times*, September 4, 2005.

23 Bob Mann. Interview by the author, March 2007.

24 Adam Sharp. Interview by the author, December 2007.

25 Thomas L. Friedman. "Osama and Katrina." *New York Times*, September 7, 2005.

26 Jason Stanford. Interview by the author, March 2007.

27 Douglas Brinkley. Interview by the author, March 2007.

28 Joshua Green. "The Rove Presidency." *Atlantic Monthly*, September 2007.

29 David E. Sanger. "Bush Compares Responses to Hurricane and Terrorism." *New York Times*, September 22, 2005.

30 Nahal Toosi. "Former FEMA Head in NYC: Party Politics Played Role in Katrina Response." Associated Press, January 20, 2007.

31 Kathleen Blanco. Interview by the author, January 2008.

32 Mary Landrieu. Interview by the author, December 2007.

CHAPTER NINE

1 Mark Angle. Interview by the author, March 2007.

2 Ibid.

3 James Moore. Interview by the author, March 2007.

4 Mark Angle. Interview by the author, March 2007.

5 Marie Cocco. Interview by the author, August 2007.

6 Chris Bell. Interview by the author, March 2007.

7 Richard W. Stevenson. "Bush Expresses a Belief in DeLay's Innocence." *New York Times*, December 15, 2005.

8 Chris Bell. Interview by the author, March 2007.

9 Mark Angle. Interview by the author, March 2007.

10 Interview with an unnamed source by the author, July 2007.

11 Sheryl Gay Stolberg. "Tremors Across Washington as Lobbyist Turns Star Witness." *New York Times*, January 4, 2006.

12 Peter H. Stone. "K Street Stumble." *National Journal*, March 27, 2004.

13 James Moore and Wayne Slater. *The Architect: Karl Rove and the Master Plan for Absolute Power*, New York: Crown, 2006. p. 8.

14 Philip Shenon. "Abramoff and Rove Had 82 Contacts, Report Says." *New York Times,* September 29, 2006. The article states: "[Susan] Ralston . . . was lobbied scores of times by Mr. Abramoff and his partners, the [congressional] report found, and was instrumental in passing messages between Mr. Abramoff and senior officials at the White House, including Mr. Rove and Ken Mehlman."

15 Rove's leak to Novak concerning a story, ultimately proven false, about Robert Mosbacher, Jr. during the 1992 George H. W. Bush presidential campaign was well documented.

16 Melanie Sloan. Interview by the author, March 2007.

17 James Moore. Interview by the author, March 2007.

18 Matthew Cooper. Interview by the author, March 2007.

19 Interview with an unnamed source by the author, March 2007.

20 Wayne Slater. Interview by the author, March 2007.

21 Anne E. Kornblut. "At Milestone in Inquiry, Rove, and the GOP, Breathe a Bit Easier." *New York Times*, October 29, 2005.

22 Anne E. Kornblut. "Rove Is More His Old Self at the White House." *New York Times*, November 11, 2005.

23 Jason Stanford. Interview by the author, March 2007.

24 James Moore. Interview by the author, March 2007.

25 Interview with an unnamed longtime Texas political journalist by the author, March 2007.

CHAPTER TEN

1 Ed Rollins. Interview by the author, June 2007.

2 Matt Towery. Interview by the author, December 2007.

3 Adam Sharp. Interview by the author, December 2007.

4 Tom Tancredo. Interview by the author, July 2007.

5 Todd S. Purdum. "Karl Rove's Split Personality." *Vanity Fair*, December 2006.

6 Joshua Green. "The Rove Presidency." *Atlantic Monthly*, September 2007.

7 Adam Nagourney and Jim Rutenberg. "Rove's Word Is No Longer G.O.P. Gospel." *New York Times*, September 3, 2006.

8 Ibid.

9 Hugh Hewitt. "Karl Rove on Election Eve." November 6, 2006. http://www.townhall.com/columnists/HughHewitt/2006/11/06/karl=rove=on=election=eve.

10 Sheryl Gay Stolberg and Jim Rutenberg. "Rumsfeld Resigns; Bush Vows to 'Find Common Ground.'" *New York Times*, November 9, 2006.

11 Jim Rutenberg and Adam Nagourney. "A Tough Road Ahead for the President's Closest Adviser." *New York Times*, November 19, 2006.

12 Ed Rollins. Interview by the author, June 2007.

CHAPTER ELEVEN

1 H. E. "Bud" Cummins. Interview by the author, March 2007.

2 James Moore. Interview by the author, March 2007.

3 Garry Mauro. Interview by the author, August 2007.

4 David Johnson. "Dismissed U.S. Attorneys Praised in Evaluations." *New York Times*, February 25, 2007.

5 Ibid.

6 Ibid.

7   Christopher Drew and Eric Lipton. "G.O.P. Anger in Swing State Eased Attorney's Exit." *New York Times*, March 18, 2007.

8   H. E. "Bud" Cummins. Interview by the author, March 2007.

9   Marie Cocco. Interview by the author, August 2007.

10 Ibid.

11 Daniel Bice. "State GOP Official Pushed Vote Fraud Issue." *Milwaukee Journal Sentinel*, April 7, 2007.

12 Joe Wineke. Interview by the author, August 2007.

13 Daniel Bice. Interview by the author, June 2007.

14 Gina Barton, Stacy Forster, and Steven Walters. "State Official Indicted in Travel Contract Case." *Milwaukee Journal Sentinel*, January 24, 2006.

15 Ibid.

16 Steve Schultze. "Official Convicted in Travel Deal." *Milwaukee Journal Sentinel*, June 12, 2006.

17 Joe Wineke. Interview by the author, August 2007.

18 Steve Schultze. "Official Convicted in Travel Deal." *Milwaukee Journal Sentinel*, June 12, 2006.

19 Steven Walters and John Diedrich. "Ex-State Official Freed: Judge Calls Evidence She Steered Travel Contract 'Beyond Thin.'" *Milwaukee Journal Sentinel*, April 5, 2007.

20 Ibid.

21 Gregory Stanford. "Biskupic Has Some Explaining to Do." *Milwaukee Journal Sentinel*, April 7, 2007.

22 Joe Wineke. Interview by the author, August 2007.

23 Purvi Patel. Interview by the author, August 2007.

24 Eric Lipton and Ian Urbina. "In 5-Year Effort, Scant Evidence of Voter Fraud." *New York Times*, April 12, 2007.

25 Joe Wineke. Interview by the author, August 2007.

26 Bill Glauber. "Her First Vote Put Her in Prison: Woman Is One of Five from City Convicted of Voter Fraud." *Milwaukee Journal Sentinel*, May 21, 2007.

27 Don Siegelman. Interview by the author, December 2007.

CHAPTER TWELVE

1   Affidavit of Jill Simpson. Filed in the State of Georgia, County of Dade, on May 21, 2007.

2   Ibid.

3   Ibid.

4   Perry O. Hooper. Interview by the author, July 2007.

5   Ibid.

6   Michael Kramer. "For Pete's Sake." *Time*, March 27, 1995.

7   Ibid.

8   *"Gimme Five."—Investigation of Tribal Lobbying Matters.* Final Report before the Committee on Indian Affairs, 109th Congress, 2nd Session. June 22, 2006.

9 Ibid.

10 Ibid.

11 Ibid.

12 James H. Gundlach. "A Statistical Analysis of Possible Electronic Ballot Box Stuffing, The Case of Baldwin County Alabama Governor's Race in 2002." A paper presented at the Annual Meeting of the Alabama Political Science Association in Troy, Alabama, on April 11, 2003. Copy supplied to the author.

13 Chip Hill. Interview by the author, June 2007.

14 Ibid.

15 From court papers supplied to the author.

16 Scott Horton. "The Pork Barrel World of Judge Mark Fuller." *Harper's*, August 6, 2007.

17 Ibid.

18 Ibid.

19 Chip Hill. Interview by the author, June 2007.

20 From court papers supplied to the author.

21 "Siegelman, Scrushy Get Prison Terms." Associated Press, June 28, 2007.

22 Scott Horton. "Delivering a Verdict on a Corrupt Prosecution." *Harper's*, June 20, 2007.

23 Editorial Board. "Selective Prosecution." *New York Times*, August 6, 2007.

24 Dan Froomkin. "A Rovian Plot?" Washingtonpost.com, June 27, 2007.

25 Don Siegelman. Interview by the author, December 2007.

CHAPTER THIRTEEN

1 Roger Stone. Interview by the author, June 2007.

2 Interview with an unnamed source by the author, August 2007.

3 The description of the scene comes from a source close to a key adviser to the president.

4 Jim Rutenberg and Steven Lee Myers. "Karl Rove, Top Strategist, Is Leaving the White House." *New York Times*, August 13, 2007.

5 From portions of the debate that were posted on CBN.com.

6 Max Cleland. Interview by the author, December 2007.

INDEX

Crawford, Craig, 93
Crist, Charlie, 220
Crow, Harlan, 156
Crowley, Monica, 171
Cummins, H.E. "Bud," 224, 225, 226, 264
Cunningham, Randy "Duke," 217, 224
Cuomo, Mario, 69
Curtis, Richard, 83, 86, 91, 92

D

Daley, Bill, 107
Danforth, John, 103
Dangerfield, Mark, 19
Daschle, Tom, 137
Davis, Rick, 100
Dawes, Charles G., 172
Dean, Howard, 150–51
Dean, John, 101–2, 117
Deaver, Michael, 7
Defense of Marriage Act, 146
DeLay, Tom, 114, 201, 202, 203–4, 205, 217, 271
Democratic Party
  in Alabama, 245, 248
  George W. Bush and, 67, 68
  as majority party under Roosevelt, 108, 109, 110
  represented in Congress, 122, 137, 140, 221
  Rove's plan to weaken, 110
  in Texas, 37, 49, 202, 203
Department of Homeland Security, 137, 138
Devenish, Nicolle, 197
DeVos, Dick, 219
Dewhurst, David, 202
Dirksen, Everett, 20
Dixon, Alan J., 21
Dobson, James D., 148
Dolan, John T. "Terry," 23, 24
Dole, Robert, 43, 63, 64
Domenici, Pete, 226
Dowd, Matthew, 198
Dowd, Maureen, 127–28
Doyle, Jim, 230, 231, 232, 233, 234–35, 236, 237
Dream and the Nightmare, The, 13, 67
Dukakis, Michael, 44, 46, 156
Durham, Frank, 3–4

E

Easterbrook, Frank, 237
Ederer, Ron, 50
Edgeworth, Robert, 23, 24
Edsall, Thomas, 33
Edwards, John, 150, 151, 152, 169, 170, 269
Eisenhower, Dwight D., 6–7, 137
Energy policy, 118–19
Estes, Ashley, 170
Evans, Don, 172
Eversberg, Helen, 41

F

Feazell, Vic, 34, 35–37, 43
FEMA, Hurricane Katrina and, 183, 185, 186, 188, 190
Fitzgerald, Patrick, 210, 211, 212, 217
Florida vote recount, 14, 107, 157
Foley, Mark, 217
Forbes, Steve, 94, 96
Ford, Gerald, 175
Fortunate Son, 86, 87, 89, 90, 91, 92
Franklin, Louis, 254, 259–60
Franks, Tommy, 144
Fraud in Wisconsin 2004, 228–29
Friedman, Thomas, 198
"Front porch" campaign, 11, 12, 68
Frost, Martin, 201, 202
Fuller, Mark E., 256–58, 259, 260–61
Fund for Limited Government, 29, 30–31

G

Gauger, Tim, 3
Gephardt, Richard, 150, 152
Gigot, Paul A., 268, 269
Gingrich, Newt, 14, 38, 205
Ginsberg, Benjamin, 157–58
Giuliani, Rudolph, 220
Goldwater, Barry, 14, 19, 59, 63
Gonzales, Alberto, 225, 256, 262
Goodner, David, 2
Gore, Al, 49, 66, 99, 101, 102, 103, 104–5, 106, 107, 168, 238, 250, 262, 269
Gramm, Phil, 32, 50, 57
Grant, Maggie, 193
Great Deluge, The, 198
Great Moments in History, 117
Green, Mark, 235, 236

Griffin, Timothy, 224, 225, 226, 264
Guerrero, Lena, 244
Gundlach, James H., 253
Gutierrez, Carlos, 178

H

Hadley, Stephen J., 212
Hagel, Chuck, 103
Hagen, Joe, 192
Haggard, Ted, 217
Haldeman, H.R., 7
Hamel, Gordon, 112, 113–14
Hance, Kent, 49
Hanna, Mark, 11, 13, 70, 117, 172
Hatch Act, 115, 264, 271
Hatfield, J.H., 83–87, 88, 89–92
Henry Lee Lucas Task Force, 34, 35
Herskowitz, Mickey, 63, 73–81, 82,
    166–67
Hicks, Sander, 91, 92
Hickson, Darby Tara, 42
Hightower, Jim, 32, 49–50, 51, 52, 53,
    54, 55, 269
Hitchens, Christopher, 148
Hoffmann, Roy F., 155, 156
Homeland Security. *See* Department of
    Homeland Security; Office of
    Homeland Security
Honore, Russel, 189–90, 192, 193
Hooper, Perry O., 246, 247–48
Hoover, Herbert, 172
Hornsby, Ernest "Sonny," 246, 247, 269
Horton, Scott, 261
Horton, Willie, 46
Hughes, Karen, 58, 59, 73, 76, 79, 80,
    88, 103, 113, 135, 170, 202
Hurley, Stephen, 233, 235
Hurricane Katrina, 15, 183–200, 215–16
Hussein, Saddam, 76, 138, 139, 141,
    143, 144, 166, 208, 209

I

Iglesias, David C., 223, 224, 226, 230,
    264
Immigration, illegal, 132, 133
Iowa caucus, 1, 96
Iraq invasion, 166, 167, 217, 273, 274
Iraq war, 143–46, 147, 154, 209, 217,
    218, 221, 222, 265
Iron Triangle, 58, 135

J

Jackson, Alfonso, 113
Jackson, Jesse, 50, 53
James, Forrest Hood "Fob," 248, 249,
    257, 258
Jeffords, James, 121, 122, 123, 137,
    214
Johnson, Lady Bird, 66
Johnson, Lyndon, 30, 65, 130, 245
Jordan, Hamilton, 7

K

Keating, Frank, 71
Kennedy, John F., 7, 18, 125
Kennedy, Mark, 246–47
Kennedy, Robert, 7
Kercheval, Hoppy, 178
Kerik, Bernard, 182, 215
Kerry, John, 150, 151–54, 155–56,
    158–60, 164, 167, 169, 170, 173,
    180, 239, 269
Kerry, Teresa Heinz, 170
Killian, Jerry, 162, 163
Knox, Marian Carr, 163
Koons, Joe, 149
Koontz, Russell, 51, 53, 54
Koppel, Ted, 216
Kyoto Treaty, 119

L

Lam, Carol S., 224, 225, 226
Land, Richard, 149
Landrieu, Mary, 184–85, 186–87, 188,
    189, 191, 194, 199–200, 216
Langston, Robert E., 134
Leahy, Patrick, 267
Lias, Tom, 25
Libby, I. Lewis "Scooter," 208, 209, 210,
    211, 212, 217
Liddy, G. Gordon, 178
Lieberman, Joe, 138
Lonsdale, Adrian L., 155, 156
Lucas, Henry Lee, 34–35
Luján, Manuel, Jr., 211
Luskin, Robert D., 212

M

MacDougald, Harry W., 163
Machiavelli, Nicolò, 13, 145
Magnet, Myron, 13, 67

Reed, Scott, 64
Reiter, Amy, 87
Reno, Janet, 2
Republican Party
    in Alabama, 245, 246, 248, 253
    Jeffords' departure from, 122, 123
    McKinley era domination of, 11, 110
    as permanent majority, 14, 15–16,
        108–11, 140, 141, 142, 171, 174,
        213
    political consultants running, 59
    redistricting and, 201, 202, 203
    Rove's effect on, 14–15
    Rove's fund-raising for, 219
    2006 losses for, 221, 222
    war on terrorism and, 130–31
Rice, Condoleezza, 124, 126, 184, 196,
    197
Richards, Ann, 10, 32, 50, 58, 59, 60,
    61, 62, 71, 111, 160, 244, 269
Ridge, Tom, 128, 138, 182
Riley, Bob (father), 191, 241–42, 243,
    251, 252, 253, 254, 255, 256
Riley, Rob (son), 242, 256
Robertson, Pat, 272
Robinson, Bernie, 26, 27
Rollins, Ed, 7, 15, 38, 71, 118, 122, 174,
    177, 179, 180, 214, 222
Romney, Mitt, 220
Roosevelt, Franklin, 108, 109, 125, 140,
    245
Rose, Charlie, 272
Rove, Alma (sister), 17
Rove, Andrew (son), 42
Rove, Eric (brother), 17
Rove, Karl
    in Alabama politics, 245–46, 247,
        248, 262
    appointments of, 31–32, 51
    arrogance of, 104, 105
    birth of, 17
    books favored by, 13, 14, 145
    Bush autobiography and, 75, 76, 77,
        78, 80
    Cheney and, 103, 128, 148
    collaboration with Greg Rampton,
        33–34, 37–38, 50, 51
    in College Republicans, 21, 22, 23,
        24, 25, 26, 27, 28–29, 30
    demotion of, 218–19

as deputy chief of staff for policy,
    174–75, 180, 182, 218, 219–20
direct mail work of, 8, 22, 29, 31, 42,
    59
dirty tricks of, 9, 10, 15, 16, 21, 26–27,
    29, 39–41, 46–47, 49, 50, 52,
    56–57, 58, 59, 60–61, 65, 103,
    263 (see also Rove, Karl, smear
    campaigns of)
divorce of, 31, 32
Don Siegelman and, 243, 244, 252,
    255, 262, 263
early interest in politics, 18–19
education of, 17–18, 19, 20–21, 22,
    23, 24
family problems affecting, 19–20,
    32–33
firings of, 9, 57, 59, 62–63, 244, 267,
    270–71
first meeting with George W. Bush,
    28, 47, 48
grooming Bush for president, 67–68
Hatch Act violation and, 264, 271
Hurricane Katrina and, 186–87, 188,
    189, 191, 192, 193, 194, 195, 196,
    197, 198, 199, 200, 201, 215
idol of, 172
Iraq and, 3–5, 145–46
Jack Abramoff and, 207, 208
legacy of, 14, 15–16, 108, 213
as liability, 213, 266–67
on liberal reaction to September 11,
    181–82
on mandate for Bush, 173
marriages of, 31, 42
media control by, 2, 4, 58, 59, 68–69
military service avoided by, 22–24,
    139, 154
moves to Texas, 30, 31
myth of, 9, 10, 13, 14, 19, 21, 24, 48,
    116, 117, 218, 269, 270
nicknames of, 2, 13, 14, 171
permanent Republican majority as
    goal of, 14, 15–16, 108–11, 140,
    141, 142, 171, 174, 213, 227
as policy maker, 117–18, 123, 136
as political strategist
    for Bill Clements, 32, 33, 38–41
    for George W. Bush, 1, 7, 10–11,
        12, 31, 58, 59–60, 62, 65, 66, 68,